ORPHANS OF THE EAS

ORPHANS OF THE EAST

*Postwar Eastern European Cinema
and the Revolutionary Subject*

Constantin Parvulescu

Indiana University Press

Bloomington & Indianapolis

This book is a publication of

Indiana University Press
Office of Scholarly Publishing
Herman B Wells Library 350
1320 East 10th Street
Bloomington, Indiana 47405 USA

iupress.indiana.edu

⊖ The paper used in this publication meets the minimum requirements
of the American National Standard for Information Sciences—
Permanence of Paper for Printed Library Materials, ANSI Z39.48–1992.

Manufactured in the United States of America

Library of Congress Cataloging-in-Publication Data

Parvulescu, Constantin.
  Orphans of the East : postwar Eastern European cinema
and the revolutionary subject / Constantin Parvulescu.
    pages cm
  Includes bibliographical references and index.
  ISBN 978-0-253-01673-7 (cloth : alk. paper) — ISBN 978-0-253-01685-0
(pbk. : alk. paper) — ISBN 978-0-253-01765-9 (ebook) 1. Orphans in
motion pictures. 2. Abandoned children in motion pictures. 3. Motion
pictures—Europe, Eastern—History—20th century. I. Title.
  PN1995.9.O76P37 2015
  791.43'6526945—dc23

2014045514

1 2 3 4 5   20 19 18 17 16 15

Contents

Introduction: The Socialist Experience and Beyond *1*

1 Creatures of the Event:
Subject Production in the Reconstruction Era *17*

2 Producing Revolutionary Consciousness
in the Times of Radical Socialism *44*

3 The Testifying Orphan: Rethinking Modernity's Optimism *70*

4 Children of the Revolution:
The Rebirth of the Subject in Revisionist Discourse *92*

5 The Family of Victims: Stalinism Revisited in the 1980s *118*

Epilogue: The Abandoned Offspring of Late Socialism *138*

Notes *159*
Works Cited *177*
Index *183*

ORPHANS OF THE EAST

Introduction

The Socialist Experience and Beyond

Thus will orphan children have a second birth. After their first birth we spoke of their nurture and education, and after their second birth, when they have lost their parents, we ought to take measures that the misfortune of orphanhood may be as little sad to them as possible. In the first place, we say that the guardians of the law are lawgivers and fathers to them, not inferior to their natural fathers. Moreover, they shall take charge of them year by year as of their own kindred.

—Plato, *The Laws*

Our new man, in our new society, is to be molded by socialist organizations ... where intelligent educators will make him a communist ...

—Alexandra Kollontai, *Communism and the Family*

SINCE THE BOLSHEVIK REVOLUTION of 1917, communism became more than an oppositional discourse against capitalism. It developed into a political order that started to spread globally. One such expansion took place in Europe in the aftermath of World War II. With the aid of the Soviet occupation administration, Marxist-Leninist governments seized power in the region. One by one, Bulgaria, Romania, Hungary, Poland, East Germany, and Czechoslovakia began putting into practice socialist aspirations and started Eastern Europe on its path to communism.[1] On a national level, paths to communism did not unfold similarly. They engaged with different economic and social contexts, were articulated more or less in dependence on Moscow, and even ended—were denounced and memorialized, up to the present day—differently. Yet this book claims there was a certain unity in this diversity, which can be called the "Eastern European experience of socialism." This unity is defined by more than just the shared (communist) ideological basis, the imposition of a Soviet model of governance, and the

1

economic, political, and at times military control exercised by the Soviet Union over these states.[2]

Communist theory did not envision socialism as a political system; it was conceived of as process, a temporary and dynamic arrangement intended to secure the transition from capitalism (at various stages of its development) to communism. Its goal was as much to build a new order as to take apart the previous one, with its alienating political, economic, and social bonds. The main promise of socialism was not necessarily economic prosperity, individual fulfillment, and blissful personal relations, but gradual liberation from oppressive structures and preparation for life in a superior political order. Consequently, the Eastern European experience was an encounter of individual and collective subjects with an ideologically radical and procedurally accelerated development program, which left deep marks—not all negative—upon this part of Europe. Its success and failure must be judged accordingly, to the extent that it managed to transform visions of happiness and human fulfillment and bring hope and relief to the lives of the oppressed.

Leading these transformations was the Communist Party. The party had the visionary skills to implement radical change. From its enlightened inner circles, true revolutionary consciousness would spread towards the margins and alter the way in which the political subject perceived, understood, valuated, and acted in and upon the world. The two main means to achieve this goal were, one, political and economic transformation and, two, education and propaganda. Both were designed as temporary top-down measures, meant to be utilized until the revolutionary process could sustain itself. When enough transformation had been achieved, the role of political protagonist would be taken over by the working multitude. After its transformation, the once-guided community of workers would become the principal social and political force within the state, taking over this function from the higher echelons of the party. The latter would not be rendered irrelevant, but its normative input would shrink. It would become itself the object of transformation, absorbing ever-developing revolutionary energies and visions from the emancipated multitude in action.

This transfer of leadership reveals why subject production played such an important role in the political imaginary of communist discourse. It linked the initially centralized socialist governance to democratic political practices. But this process of transfer of revolutionary vision from the center to the margins did not materialize in any of the socialist countries. It was intensely referred to in discourse, but, in reality, a privileged red aristocracy—or in some cases, like Romania, a single person—accumulated almost all power. The multitude of workers was never trusted with a leading position, and this failure to enlighten and to trust them left behind several unanswered questions for leftist thought. The most important is this: At what moment in time did subject production propaganda transform from a means of persuasion and enlightenment into one of oppression and of legitimizing socialist power elites? In other words, when did socialism turn from a movement into a system, swapping liberation for oppression?

The purpose of this book is to address this and similar questions by analyzing particular moments in socialism's real or pretended effort to build the communist "new man."[3] Each chapter of this book focuses on an instant and a circumstance that affected the discourse on subject production, and more generally socialist modernization. And since socialist governments relied heavily on popular culture to spread their enlightening message to the masses, this book analyzes how subject production was presented and debated in cinemas. Film, the darling medium of the workers, with its capacity to show and enact for millions, narrated the biographies of these new humans referred to in Kollontai's epigraph. It mapped their psyche, chronicled their intellectual development, displayed their bodies, contemplated their demeanor, and documented their lifestyles. It showed how these new creatures worked, loved, and socialized; it highlighted their achievements and celebrated their struggle against reactionary forces.

This is why this book employs feature films as primary sources—films made in Eastern Europe about Eastern Europe: patriotic films, propaganda films, entertainment, and art-house cinema engaging in intellectual consideration of subject production. Each chapter scrutinizes one such film, made at a different date, by a different national cinema, but with one important thing in common: all have an orphan or abandoned child as their protagonist. This choice is motivated by the fact that the figure of the orphan is a key to understanding socialism's investment in human political capital. Representations of the lives of orphans, subjects who were in the direct custody of the institutions of the state, offered a handy narrative pretext for exploring the relationship between state power and the individual, the way in which the state aimed to change the person, and how the person reacted to being disciplined by the state. The figure of the orphan was also instrumental in advertising and investigating alternative and superior social bonds (superior to those of the traditional family), but also in approaching individual trauma, loss, memory, and rebellion. The orphan enabled films to explore the role of family ties and both individual and social alienation.

The figure of the orphan is also critical for understanding the post–World War II historical context. By the end of 1945, parentless children were ubiquitous in the cities of Eastern Europe. The numbers speak for themselves. As the historian Tony Judt documents, in devastated Berlin alone there were 53,000 parentless children, and tens of thousands more roamed the country. In liberated Czechoslovakia, there were 49,000; in Poland, 200,000; and in Yugoslavia about 300,000. And only a few hundred of them were Jewish (Judt 2005, 21). They could be seen anywhere, begging, stealing, looking for relatives, dying. Their presence turned into a powerful reminder of the grim deeds the generation of their parents had committed. They became a symbolic figure that gestured at the same time toward the traumatic experience of the war, the guilt of participating in it, and the hope of rebuilding civilization. They embodied a continent in search of new forms of political parenthood, promising itself not to repeat the mistakes of the past.

The postwar cinematic orphan differed from the prewar one, and its Eastern European version was also at variance with its Western one. In the emerging socialist states, the figure of the orphan was much more politicized. Both in prewar and in capitalism-informed commercial (and popular) narrative arts (cinema and fiction within and without the region), orphans were presented mainly as protagonists of sentimental and apolitical adoption chronicles. They awakened society's spirit of charity and its commitment to paternal care for the needy. Orphans functioned as social or individual pets and often embodied the perfect starting point of a rags-to-riches story, as exemplified by one of the most popular American comic strips, *Little Orphan Annie*, which was launched in 1924. (The strip inspired the well-known Broadway musical *Annie* and its 1984 and 1995 Hollywood adaptations.)

Annie is worth considering because, unlike the socialist stories depicting orphans, it was a typical political status quo narrative, symptomatic not only of the social tensions that developed before and during the Great Depression, but also of the way in which the American order, competing with socialism, envisioned dealing with it. *Annie* presents the adventures of a girl from an orphanage, the disenfranchised child with a pretty face, a quick mind, and a great heart, who ends up entering the family of a multimillionaire and benefiting from royal care. Her lottery-ticket adoption compensates for the fact that the structural inequalities of the system she lives in will not suffer major alterations. Her adoption thus mediates a mere truce between social classes. The rich will be more attentive to the condition of the poor and give up their mandarin lifestyle, as proven by the adoption of one who is not of their own breed, offering her a family, protection, and material affluence. In exchange, the poor will play along according to the existing political and economic rules, hoping for better times ahead but without revolting. The adoptee will bring jollity (love and entertainment), optimism, and spirituality into the lives of her adopters, and more importantly will become an embodiment of respect and gratitude. In exchange, the rich will use her to reach out to the needy, employing charity to preserve class privilege.

The figure of the adopted child was also a medium of presenting the disenfranchised as politically immature. Two other extremely popular cinematic products of the prewar and capitalist times, the Shirley Temple movies of the 1930s and Charlie Chaplin's *The Kid* (1921), served this interest and also stopped short of asking the more discomforting questions of their times. Like the popular American fiction of the turn of the twentieth century and later decades, they emphasized not only the usefulness of orphans in creating social (and family) reconciliation, but also suggested that adoption implied accepting the status quo. Even if sentimental in representation, the literary texts that inspired such films as the ones mentioned above portrayed orphans as members of the third or fourth class, as Friedrich Engels put it in his seminal study of the origins of exploitation in the family ([1884] 1993, 52, 63). The orphans' adoption was tantamount not only to access to a better life, but also to their reintegration into an economic system of exploitation—in this case, the domestic one. "These books [about orphans] were bestsellers of their day in part because they appealed to adults and told traditional stories about the ways children could be useful to [them]" (Sanders 2008, 42).[4]

In contrast, in the political films of socialist Eastern Europe, orphans less often played the role of community pacifiers as they rarely interacted with their adopters solely within the private sphere. What makes the orphans of Eastern European political film stand out from today's perspective is their second birth referred to by Plato in the epigraph above—that is, their becoming political subjects—and the fact that their predicament blurs the distinction between private and public, personal and political, nature and culture, given and chosen identities. The figure of the orphan in Eastern European film shows how socialist modernity conceives of the subject in a particular light. On the one hand, and very differently from *Annie*, it portrays the subject as a battleground of various competing political discourses. On the other hand, biopolitically, the orphan is regarded as displaced, denaturalized, and alienated from traditional socializing institutions such as the family. He or she comes through as a child of the state, produced, nurtured, socialized, and, in critical films, even exploited by it. Power seeks control over them by disciplining the most private aspects of their lives (what Michel Foucault called "the care of the self").[5]

With the mediating interface of the family and other informal networks removed, the orphan reveals the (dialectical-)materialist approach to the subject production of socialism, for which, as Boris Groys emphasizes, the human body and consciousness were only a product of the environment and discourse, "their thought and 'inner world' in general merely part of the material that needs to be ordered" (1992, 3). Moreover, the envisioning of the subject as orphan brings to the fore the interest of power to keep the subject in an uprooted predicament, which, of course, opens the door to discussion of key concepts in Eastern European studies such as totalitarianism (Hannah Arendt) or, more generally, governance in modernity (Foucault's technologies of the self); the production of bare life (Giorgio Agamben), with the latter's emphasis on the orphans' inclusion or exclusion from rights and the shelter of the law; and finally a certain way of envisioning political immunization (Roberto Esposito), emphasizing not individual immunity, as Western liberal democracy would have it, but articulating a discourse of the vulnerable individual, who can achieve immunity only by being part of a tight social organism.

Since many orphan stories are also adoption stories (of upbringing, reeducation, enlightenment), they often compare lost parents with adopters, communities of origin with those of destination. The comparison reveals the extent to which one or the other is able to render itself hospitable to difference and refrain from abusing the vulnerability and malleability of the parentless child. In the same way that Julia Kristeva and Jacques Derrida envision aliens, foreigners, and visitors as agents of estrangement,[6] the figure of the orphan functions as a cinematic and intellectual trope that shows not only how efficiently a political community can discipline or integrate otherness, but also how much it is willing to listen, learn, and let itself be transformed by its interaction with strangers—a question with complex implications for socialist governance and its realization of dialectical materialism. Moreover, as children of the state (or of the community), orphans ask a question that is symptomatic of modernity, the question regarding the future: Where are we going? Or, as an adoptee, in the passive voice, where are you taking me? They speak in the name of those who have lost or abandoned a certain political environment and have agreed to play along with the rules of a new one and its promise of revolution.

* * *

Each chapter of this book provides a detailed analysis of a film with an orphan or abandoned child as protagonist. Chapter 1, "Creatures of the Event," focuses on Géza Radványi and Béla Balázs's 1948 Hungarian film *Somewhere in Europe*. It depicts the end of the war and postwar disorder, and envisions a context of subject production that harks back to the origins of European polity. The survivors of the conflagration are presented as orphans existing in a generic territory referred to as "Europe" that has the historic chance to reconstruct itself from scratch. The film traces the way in which the immediate postwar political subject is produced, or, more precisely, produces itself in this context, alongside the rebuilding of civilization on the devastated continent. The film articulates an alternative leftist-Marxist vision of the future of post–World War II Europe as the only possible and legitimate post-fascist form of democratic order. Produced before the rise to power of the Hungarian pro-Soviet government, *Somewhere in Europe* presents a homegrown vision of socialism that does not hesitate to challenge some aspects of the Soviet-style subject production that was soon to become hegemonic in the region. It imagines its orphans as creating a vital and redemptive form of community that, imprinted by the violence of the war, can organize itself spontaneously into a vigorous and dynamic democracy without needing the paternalistic control of organized political apparatuses such as the Communist Party.

Chapter 2, "Producing Revolutionary Consciousness in the Times of Radical Socialism," shows how a socialist-realist film of the 1950s envisions the radical transformation of the subject in the new socialist order established in postwar Eastern Europe. The propagandistic message of *Story of a Young Couple* (Kurt Maetzig, GDR, 1953) claims that the *Bildung* of the socialist subject no longer parallels the production of the revolutionized political space, which was one of the main assumptions of *Somewhere in Europe*. The transformation of the subject takes place in an established ideological framework and a certain predetermined political structure. The orphans are envisioned as a malleable biopolitical substance to be molded by the discourses and social practices of the New Order. Socialism demands openness to change, dedicated and uncritical participation in its project. It calls for self-purification, estrangement from and counter-identification with the sense of self one inherits from the old bourgeois order—in particular with individualism. The new humans of socialism must show the inner strength to imitate and internalize—with the prospect of subsequent identification—models of subjectivity and of social behavior that might initially seem alien, politically flawed, or even dangerous to them. They must trust that imitation of these models will transform them and revolutionize their subjectivity.

Chapter 3, "The Testifying Orphan," focuses on a film that rejects the optimistic and self-denying model of socialist-realist subject production. It is a film of the 1960s, a time when, to a certain extent, the radicalism of the previous decade has been questioned. The film gestures toward one of the obstacles that stand in the way of modern functionalist subject production and its call to uncritical trust in the discourse of the party. This counter-element is trauma. *Dita Saxová* (Antonín Moskalyk, Czechoslovakia, 1967) employs a Holocaust survivor as protagonist and shows how the irreparable emotional and intellectual damage caused by the death camp experience affects the identification of the subject with any proposed model of self. The Auschwitz orphan cannot embrace the sanguine mood of postwar internal and external reconstruction. She views history with melancholy. She exposes an incurable unhappy consciousness, haunted by the guilt of survival and discomforted by her contemporaries' lack of interest in her testimony about the nightmarish forms of exploitation modern politics perpetrated in the camps. Her experience throws light on what might be called posttraumatic subject production, which not only takes into account the unconscious dimensions of human mental behavior, but also relates hesitantly to narratives of progress that anchor the present in the future and envision the subject as a means to achieving political goals.

Chapter 4, "Children of the Revolution," focuses on a film that raises concerns regarding the consequences of revolutionary subject production. It addresses, in fact, subject *reproduction*, asking how socialist consciousness can change itself. Continuous transformation of the self reflects the dialectics at the core of Marxism-Leninism. The orphan protagonist of Krzysztof Kieślowski's *Camera Buff* (Poland, 1979) is a fully socialized subject of the New Order who feels that the world he dwells in no longer lives up to the revolutionary promises of communist discourse and no longer motivates him to participate in the improvement of himself. While previous films presented more or less successful processes of creating the socialist subject, *Camera Buff* puts socialism's new man on display and suggests that the world he has been prepared for has not developed as rapidly and radically as he has. Inspired by the revisionist thinking of the 1960s and 1970s, the film presents a critique of socialist modernization from a leftist position. For the hero of *Camera Buff*, socialism has lost its revolutionary edge, and has become yet another static form of government that favors control over transformation. Consequently, he has to learn how to preserve his progressive thinking and disentangle his perceptions of social and political activism from the blurry images put on display by the pragmatic governance of the Gierek regime in 1970s Poland. Self-governance and participation in alternative public spheres become the meaningful political practices of his time, stimulating him to continue developing his political consciousness.

Chapter 5, "The Family of Victims," introduces another reactive subject, one who refers to the past in order to question the present. The film analyzed in this chapter reveals the importance of memory in assessing the political role and social and psychological effects of modern discourses of subject production. Márta Mészáros's *Diary for My Children* (Hungary, 1984) revisits Eastern Europe's Stalinist terror era of the late 1940s and early 1950s from the perspective of the 1980s in order to understand how damaging the radicalism of those years has been for socialism. Instead of revolutionary enthusiasm, accelerated development has produced a general sentiment of sweeping insecurity and the rule of terror. Like trauma, memory serves here as a challenging element to socialist mobilizing discourses and as a certitude in a world caught up in a too sweeping metamorphosis. More than trauma, which produces a melancholic subject desiring to testify about the horrors it experienced, memory enables the articulation of counter-discourses. And unlike trauma, memory is an important element of development because it signals the repetitions of history. Family ties, whose influence in subject production communism aimed to downplay, regain a central role for the subject's sense of self. As the title of the film suggests, they create a community of memory and a network of resistance against often brutally articulated narratives of political change.

"The Abandoned Offspring of Late Socialism," the book's epilogue, investigates not a willing but a forced political re-orphaning of the subject in the last decade of the socialist experience, the 1980s. It concentrates on the Romanian film *Sand Dunes* (Dan Piţa, 1983) and aims to reveal the paradoxes that riddled the stagnant late years of the socialist experience. While the official discourse of the Romanian Communist Party resurrected the radicalist rhetoric of the Stalinist 1950s, the everyday governing practices of socialism distanced individuals further and further from revolutionary practice. The whole project of transferring leadership from the party to the multitude via subject production seemed to have been abandoned. In spite of its ardent revolutionary rhetoric, the party seemed no longer interested in interacting with active subjects instrumental in transforming social and political structures, but in ruling over obedient individuals, whose main duty toward socialism was not to call into question the decisions of the party and the legitimacy of its leadership. In the late days of socialism, the radicalism of the 1950s returned as a caricature, as a spectacle of itself, cancelling any chance of achieving individual or collective fulfillment through participation in the socialist project. Narratives of happiness are cast from the political realm into the unmapped territory of the private, which becomes the locus of overcoming political alienation. Unlike the hero of *Camera Buff,* for whom alternative public spheres and collective forms of resistance existed, Pița's protagonist is all by himself. His predicament harks back to what Vaclav Havel in *The Power of the Powerless* imagined as the post-totalitarian subject and his constraint to seek life in truth only in the private sphere (2009, 137–138). Exiled from public life, the protagonist of Pița's film searches for meanings in and under the radar of existence. The possibility of a dialogue between citizens and state is no longer envisionable in the 1980s, when socialism has become a purely oppressive structure. It has transformed into a callous and arrogant plutocracy with its back to its subjects. The orphan of this film embodies the betrayed *demos* of Eastern Europe, which is no longer ruled by a revolutionary government, but by an elite whose sole purpose is to preserve its grip on power and expand its privileges.[7]

* * *

This volume captures subject production in the framework of a rise-and-fall narrative—the rise and fall of socialism in Eastern Europe. But this rise-and-fall structure also refers to a certain understanding of social and political transformation, specific to modernity and, more importantly, indicative of the political potential of Marxism and communism. From this perspective, the films I analyze here address not only a certain temporally and spatially informed subject production (the Eastern European experience), but also, in more general terms, the Marxist and socialist project of changing the world. If communism still is, as Alain Badiou claims, the most reasonable political hypothesis of the twenty-first century and the "failures" of the regimes in Eastern Europe represent (only) "stages" in its development, then this book imagines itself as a progressive discussion of these stages. If the Eastern European experience can be also regarded, again as Badiou suggests, as being in fact "the history of the proof of the [communist] hypothesis" (2010, 7), then its study only opens the consideration of socialism and not closes it, as intellectuals and scholars in thrall to Cold War thinking have argued (the trash can of history or the end of history arguments).

The Eastern European experience must not be simply put aside as a historical mishap, viewed only as totalitarianism, and referred to in a similar way as one refers to fascism. This book follows Bruno Bosteels's call to remember the Eastern European experience as a form of communism that is worth talking about and which produced informative intellectual insights and social experimentation (2011, 12). Yet the twenty-first-century Left often seems to ignore it and to regard Eastern European socialism as an embarrassment and orientalize it in the same way it does with North Korea or China. Instead, it prefers the more comfortable choice of focusing on communism as an oppositional discourse, preferring to deal with Western-grown Eurocommunism, which Eastern European governments denounced as a Western invention aimed at deradicalizing the workers' movement, intellectualizing it and infusing it with bourgeois values. The Western Left sees more revolutionary potential in the 1968 student revolts, in Maoist, Trotskyist, or anarchist student factions located in European capitals or in the guerrilla wars of the red messiahs of the third world.

What it forgets is that socialism means the taking of power, mobilization, organization, and governance. It is not Marxist revolutionary theory that the world is missing; there is plenty of literature written on this topic. As Bosteels puts it, the re-opening of the intellectual debates on Eastern Europe channels the thinking of the Left toward envisioning "communism [only] as a beautiful soul refusing to bother with the inscription, here and now, of its noble idea in a concrete historical program" (2011, 7). In other words, what the Left lacks is insightful and updated thought on communist taking power and governing. And since communism was the official doctrine of Eastern Europe for more than four decades and since the Soviet Union and Eastern Europe were examples of an effort to put its insights into practice, the study of Eastern European political culture from a leftist perspective caters to this need and fills a large lacuna. The Left must learn from their experience because, as Slavoj Žižek argues in a 2011 interview on *Charlie Rose* for the U.S. Public Broadcast Service (PBS), socialism in general and Stalinism in particular remain moments in history so arcane that "we do not have a theory for [them] yet and a real understanding of what went wrong."[8]

* * *

As primary sources, the films analyzed in this book bear witness to a leftist political experiment. To better understand their message one needs to consider the conditions in which each of them was articulated. The films reflect history twice. They are not only set in socialist times but also produced in them. They present aspects of life and subject production in socialism and the gaze socialism cast upon itself. This "seeing act" (just as Searle's speech act) is performative, as Judith Butler would have it.[9] It performs and thus highlights the intellectual discourses and artistic trends of its era, the demands from its sponsor (the Communist Party), and the interventions of censorship. It enters a dialogue with them that reveals how power operates upon representation. The films inquire into socialist subject production as deeply and as critically as they could and were allowed to—and the extent to which these performances see or represent socialism reveals these limits. The socialist state was interested neither in freedom of speech nor in aesthetic innovations. It regarded art as a discourse in the service of politics. What could and could not be presented testifies to a continuous negotiation between artists, viewers, and power. The negotiation pertained to content and style, and to the very role cinema was expected to play in society. The performative dimension of these films refers also to that which they could not see or show.

On the other hand, from the early days of total commitment to the revolution, the cinema of Eastern Europe also slowly gained more independence from Communist Party politics, and increasingly performed the social functions of art that were characteristic of the pre-socialist era. Often it became loaded with nationalist rhetoric, imitated Hollywood genres, popularized history, experimented stylistically, and hosted intellectual debates on relevant issues of the time. At times, the state suppressed deviations from revolutionary poetics, but at times it condoned and even encouraged them. The reasons were multiple, sometimes logical, sometimes not, and they included anything from true concern with social dialogue, censorship's lack of vigilance, socialism's stake in branding itself as sophisticated on the international scene, and pecuniary interests—since co-productions and oppositional films received international distribution and brought in much-needed foreign currency.

The analysis of the political, awareness-raising function of socialist film thus needs to take these contingencies into account. It is not clear if and how those in power listened to the criticism or the suggestions articulated in the films of their time (and in the arts in general). The logic and functioning of artistic censorship in Eastern Europe is also not fully elucidated—if censorship ever had a detailed consistent logic. Especially in the late years of socialism, which also coincide with the rise of its art-house cinema, the Communist Party might have condoned controlled intellectualist or formalist cinematic dissent. As in the case of other highbrow arts, such as poetry, jazz, and theater, tolerating esoteric dissent could have served party interests. It could have been instrumental in harnessing the frustrations of the educated. The arts could have been used to compensate for the absence, in the socialist polis, of an uncensored public sphere and to constitute a small and irrelevant substitute in which some social frustration and (veiled) dissent could be aired, creating the illusion of a public dialogue. For two hours, in the dark environment of the movie theater, the unhappy consciousness of socialism would feel that his or her dilemmas had been addressed onscreen, would experience some degree of civic catharsis, and then go on with his or her life, continue playing by the rules, causing no trouble in the more effective public arenas such as the street, the workplace, or the Communist Party meeting.

A more cynical reason for the state's tolerance of the articulation of dissent in the arts was its interest in gaining international prestige. Revisionist political films attracted the interest of selection committees of international festivals. *Somewhere in Europe* was acclaimed in Cannes. *Dita Saxová* received the Silver Seashell in San Sebastian. *Camera Buff* won awards in the United States (Chicago) and West Berlin, and *Diary for My Children* was awarded in Cannes and nominated in Chicago.[10] These awards indirectly endorsed the socialist state too, as an artistically and intellectually talent-breeding environment, and proved to those who spoke of totalitarianism that socialist governments tolerated counter-discourses. Homemade critiques of socialism also yielded Western currency—not much, but enough to persuade the state to distribute political films internationally.[11]

* * *

Viewed historically, each film discussed in this book speaks of a certain change in the way in which Eastern Europe perceived its revolutionary transformation. These visions are informed by competing discourses on communist governance. *Somewhere in Europe*, the film analyzed in the first chapter, envisions a political transformation of postwar Europe inspired by Rosa Luxemburg's revolutionary tactics.[12] As the influential Marxist cultural theorist Georg (György) Lukács put it in a text that inspired *Somewhere in Europe*, Luxemburg grasped and built her theory of political praxis on the "spontaneous nature of revolutionary mass actions." She argued (against Leninism) that "organization is much more likely to be the effect than the cause of the revolutionary process" (Lukács 1923). The community of orphans in *Somewhere in Europe* exemplifies this assumption. The orphans rebuild their continent and let the act of rebuilding (work) organize them as a community.

While the political visions of socialism in *Somewhere in Europe* are symptomatic of its pioneering moments, those in *Story of a Young Couple*, under scrutiny in the second chapter, mark a change in the understanding of socialism. In the universe of this film, party discipline and rigorous organization are the sole way to achieve revolutionary goals. Its plot presents the viewer with a socialism engaged in an effort to purge society of remnants of fascism, to educate its subjects, and to fight to persuade the West of the superiority of socialism. *Story of a Young Couple* was produced and took place during a period in the development of socialism that bears the name of Stalinism, and the film itself includes homages to the liberating role of the Soviet Union and to its genius leader, comrade Stalin. But the film also shows that Stalinism was not a monolithic intellectual phenomenon. At least its German avatar bears the imprint of the place of its articulation and dialogues with the long and complex tradition of the interwar German communist movement.

Analyzed in chapter 3, *Dita Saxová* relativizes the socialist project and cautions it (and perhaps also against it). Like fascism, socialism has produced its own camps. Accelerated transformations engender not only spectacular and positive social change, but also radical countercurrents, radical others, radical opponents, and radical procedures to restrain them. From this point of view, socialism is just one tormentor of history among others, another bully of modernity. The film speaks, then, from and for an age in which socialism aimed to distance itself from its own record of brutality and frantic development and sought to restructure itself in order to avoid engendering antagonisms. Subtle ironic statements accompany the reformist self-scrutiny stance of *Dita Saxová*. Is utopia truly possible? the film's Holocaust survivor asks. Will optimism be forever mandatory? Can humans pretend to be able to keep at bay the murderous drives that lurk in the shadows of civilization?

Camera Buff, in chapter 5, brings the discussion of reformism to a more mundane level. In its day, socialism had already become Janus-faced. It had split into state socialism and revisionism. The former represents the transformation of socialism by the practice of government, while the latter takes over the abandoned revolutionary activity the former claimed to monopolize, brings it underground—where theoretical writings, alternative forms of organization, and an updated class-struggle tactic are envisioned. *Camera Buff* reopens the discussion on political alienation and puts forward an assumption that would later inspire theorists such as Slavoj Žižek, Michael Hardt, and Antonio Negri: Soviet and Eastern European communism was not able to revolutionize the state, and it let the state crush it. This failure forced socialism to preserve various premodern or capitalist organizational structures and practices, which, in the long run, perverted its development.[13]

Though produced in the 1970s and released in the 1980s, *Diary for My Children,* discussed in chapter 5, anticipates the era of glasnost and perestroika (launched in 1985 in the Soviet Union with the coming to power of the reformist Communist Party leader Mikhail Gorbachev) and its assumption that socialism will not survive unless it undergoes a thorough and continuous process of self-evaluation. *Diary for My Children* is also indicative of the changes that happened in Eastern European politics in the aftermath of the Helsinki (1975) and Belgrade (1977) conferences, which spurred the human rights debate in Europe. The position of the Hungarian government, in contrast to that of other socialist states, stated that self-criticism was a necessary tactic for the survival of socialism. It would make it stronger and more prepared to face the challenges of the late twentieth century. *Diary for My Children* follows this suggestion and addresses a topic criticism of which was most acceptable in its time: the era of Stalinism (the 1956 revolution was taboo). It confronts Stalinism from the perspective of another age of socialism, one which puts more emphasis on respecting individuality and human imperfection. Passions, small pleasures, mundane desires, sentimental love, memories, and the unconscious, all aspects of the human psyche that the revolution aimed to ignore, transform, or repress, are now given consideration. Indeed, melancholia might hinder a person's total commitment to the revolution, and love might distract one's attention from duties. But experience shows that such passions, if not properly taken into consideration and accepted as such, might develop into reactionary and counter-revolutionary drives or even forces.

The pernicious transformation of socialism by its practice of government is also thematized by the film analyzed in the last chapter. *Sand Dunes*'s vision is nevertheless bleaker. It no longer presumes that the Eastern European socialism of the 1980s, mostly economically bankrupt and politically isolated, can establish a social dialogue or tolerate reformist impulses. The unequivocal repression of the Charter 77 movement in Czechoslovakia, the imposition of martial law in Poland, and the return to Stalinist practices in Romania demonstrated it. *Sand Dunes* presents socialism as a political practice that has lost touch with its ideals and compromised its transformational potency. It has squandered its popular support, wasted its power to redefine itself, and become a fully perverted dictatorship. The implosion of socialism is anticipated in the film. It suggests that power elites can maintain their privileges only by employing force and the threat of using it. But their arrogance will also bring them down.

The book's concluding remarks reflect on the denouement of the rise-and-fall narrative of socialism and stress one of the pernicious legacies of socialism in the post-1989 era: the radical divorce and distrust between citizens and their states. A new era of transformation commences for East Europeans, but one which shows even better that the state is nothing but an instrument used by a few to exploit the many. The only thing that has changed is its procedures, which mark a shift from the political to the economic. A new generation of political orphans comes into being in Eastern Europe's post-socialist era. They long for state protection but no longer receive any in the neoliberal jungle. They are much freer than their predecessors, but are not prepared to function as free and immune subjects, and end up in other forms of servitude specific to the post-1989 political and economic world.

This brief presentation of Eastern European socialism will not surprise readers who are familiar with the history of the region and of revolutionary political experiments. In films of the 1940s and 1950s, political, social, and economic transformation was more tightly linked to the transformation of the subject. The later films of socialism displayed more individualistic visions. The subject's social network shrunk. It was no longer the entire political community (sometimes national, sometimes even international—as the communist revolution imagined itself until the settlement of the Cold War). The networks that built the community of the subjects of the later films narrowed to that of friends, family, and co-workers, culminating with the solitary hero of *Sand Dunes*, imagining his quest for happiness as an individual enterprise.

The act of looking back at lost political and social configurations also gained more importance in these films. Prewar orphans were creatures without a past since both fascism and bourgeois socialization were supposed to be erased from their vitae. In the more inquisitive and revisionist productions of the post-1968 era, the past, as a repository of repressed traditions, and of alternatives to or solutions for present problems, gained more importance. The films studied in this book engage memory through the figure of the orphan in five ways. First, there are the orphans without memory, who participate in the building of political structures inspired only by grassroots democratic impulses originating in their present economic and social predicament. Second, there are the orphans who have memories but are willing to alienate themselves from them. They identify with the role the New Order assigns them in a future-anchored scenario of revolutionary transformation of self. Third, there are orphans who try to work through their memories but can't. They are too tightly linked to the past by trauma. Fourth, there are orphans who struggle to keep their memories alive against repeated calls to forget, as memories constitute one of their main weapons in fighting the repetitions of history. And fifth, there are the orphans with new memories, produced by their exposure to the New Order's promises of revolution, but which are betrayed by the realities they live in.

* * *

Plato's words in the epigraph to this introduction gesture toward the way in which socialism claimed to regard its orphans. Following the Soviet model, Eastern Europe tried to make sure they were all cared for and educated for the revolution by their second parent, the state, through its institutions. But the idea of a second birth, not within an individual body, but within the body of the community, was a common theme of Christian discourse too. The New Testament promised the world: "I will not leave you orphans" (John 14:18). In its early days, Christianity disregarded the family. St. Paul's epistles promoted celibacy and stated that the subject's primary relation of subordination was neither to the natural nor even to the social parent (the father), but to the religious one. Christianity, as John assures his ecclesia, would not leave any orphans uncared for. Christianity's internationalist and exoteric writings, dogmas, and institutions targeted anyone regardless of provenance, race, or income. The emerging church accepted everybody in its large family of believers as long as, through baptism (the second birth), they accepted its faith.

Internationalist socialism took on a similar stance and even followed some of Christianity's transformations. It also initially disregarded the institution of the (bourgeois) family and opened its doors to all biological and political orphans of the world.[14] One of communism's early theorists argued that "the family is ceasing to be a necessity for the state: on the contrary, it is worse than useless, since it needlessly holds back the female workers from more productive and far more serious work" (Kollontai 1992, 115). Like the church, communism also sent thousands of missionaries all around the world, organizing them under the umbrella of three Socialist Internationals in order to better spread its message and bring the orphans from everywhere into the community of believers. And if missionary practice and gentle persuasion did not work, the armies of socialism—in particular those of the Soviet Union—would sometimes invade the lands of those resisting it in its twentieth-century crusades.

But the discussion around the figure of the orphan also reveals the heavy-handed governance of socialism in Eastern Europe, which perpetrated one of the biggest miscalculations of modernity. Socialism trusted discourse and education too much. It overestimated their enlightening, mobilizing, and transforming powers. In its quest to change the world, socialism ended up privileging institutions and multitudes over the individual and thus produced new forms of alienation and oppression. The figure of the orphan brings this aspect of socialism to light. Perhaps because they have no families and can be reeducated and "re-born" in various contexts, orphans also function as tropes of freedom and, as we have already seen, of hope. They may be the disciplined soldiers building a new order, but they can also embody individualities living in a radical here and now, desiring happiness and control over their lives.

This introduction must end with an alert to the reader. The above presentation may have already suggested that the book's allegiances are not limited to the history of Eastern European cinema. No doubt, it aims to provide close readings of a group of films that I consider commendable, along with an evaluation of their style and intellectual value. It talks about film schools, production issues, trends in cinema, foreign influences, acting style, and the work of directors. But of all this information, first and foremost the larger interest is in depicting Eastern European political culture and drawing conclusions about its view of subject production and about social processes specific to modernity and to accelerated and radical development. All the issues of film style and history discussed in this book are relevant insofar as they reflect social and political visions and transformations. Films are here definitely used as intelligent windows into the past and the past as an introduction to the future.

1 Creatures of the Event

Subject Production
in the Reconstruction Era

The unconscious is an orphan and produces within itself the identity of nature
of man.

—Gilles Deleuze and Felix Guattari, *Anti-Oedipus*

The Postwar Desert

At the end of World War II, most of Eastern and Central Europe was in ruins.
Prague had been spared Allied bombing, but not Budapest; and Berlin and Warsaw were both mazes of rubble. War had been fought on their streets. Even Bucharest had been hit. The images of the collapsed Danube bridges of Budapest
have become a staple element of the Hungarian collective memory. Photographs
of postwar Warsaw and Berlin are even more disturbing. They present eerie urban landscapes, with entire neighborhoods consisting of hollow buildings. Everywhere uninhabitable houses, lacking roofs and windows, stories and stair-
cases. The streets overflow with debris and are blocked by burned vehicles. Any of
the still-standing facades might collapse. Landmark buildings and squares have
become unrecognizable, and even the German Reichstag seems to stand only
for the purpose of having a Soviet soldier place the flag of Eastern Europe's new
rulers on it.

The human landscape looks similar. Cities are deserted. The few men and
women appearing in pictures of the rubble era seem to wander, puzzled and aim-
less, in the post-apocalyptic landscape. Most images are not representations of
despair or horror. They don't present the Warsaw Ghetto, which during its days of
maximum occupancy had corpses lying on the streets. Resignation is the prevalent postwar mood. People's presence in the bombed city seems to be as useless

as that of the buildings that still stand. Ruined lives among ruined dwellings. The rags they wear and their slim bodies match the decor. Some rummage in the debris for scrap; others just pose for the camera, contemplating together with those who take the pictures the strangeness of the architectural remnants. In an uncanny way, their presentation and their body language reminds the viewer of today of other images of hopelessness. The precariat of the third world comes to mind, atop the garbage mounds of twenty-first-century metropolises—maybe even more hopeless-looking than the Europeans of 1945.

A famous photograph of the rubble era shows a skinny Warsaw boy siting pensively on a pile of debris. Many similar images survive from then—children alone in front of an imploded building. Their young flesh, recently emerged into the world, contrasting with the crumbling scenery. While looking at the image of the boy, viewers might ask themselves what his story is. Where does he come from? Is he on his way somewhere? It seems like a warm day; he wears shorts, keeps a hand on one of his knees, and stares into the ground. What does he feel or think? Is there a connection between him and the collapsed building in the background? Does his family lie dead under the wreckage? Or is he just resting, hungry, tired, disappointed, or lost?

Perhaps he has no purpose. He is neither tired nor sad. He thinks of nothing, feels nothing; just stares into the ground with the sleepiness of the undernourished. Perhaps he just waits for something to happen, which was a widespread attitude of everyday men and women of 1945. War had brought into the realm of the everyday not only death, suffering, hunger, and exhaustion, but also disorientation, lack of perspective, and idleness. After taking in the staggering landscape of destruction which marks the conclusion of the war—a perceptive experience that reminds one of overwhelming exposure to the sublime—the postwar subjects, like the boy in the picture, lower their heads. Theorists of the sublime argue that the hugeness and the overpowering effect of the object of contemplation shatter the inner cohesion of the subject. The positive outcome of such an inner commotion is, Immanuel Kant argues, a rediscovery of oneself, as self, for and with oneself—and the viewer can speculate that the pensive pose of the Warsaw boy catches exactly this process of self-reconstitution. The negative aspects are two. One is the disintegration of the self in a post-traumatic scenario, which will generate social recklessness; the other is resignation and deep skepticism, the sources of existential powerlessness and passivity.

The same experience of 1945 bafflement, about how confusing the last months of war and the first months of peace were, is presented in Primo Levi's novel *The Truce* (*La tregua;* published in the United States as *The Reawakening*), and in its brilliant 1977 screen adaptation by Francesco Rosi. Their protagonist is an Auschwitz survivor (assumed to be Levi himself). The book depicts his picaresque nine-month journey returning from Auschwitz to northern Italy through almost all the countries of Eastern Europe. To the gaze of an individual who thought he had seen everything in Auschwitz, similarly perplexing urban and human landscapes reveal themselves here: the devastated cities, the hungry homeless, the discharged soldiers, the Red Army checkpoints, the soup kitchens, the displaced persons' camps, the columns of armored vehicles and army trucks acclaimed by the masses as they pass through the centers of provincial towns, collaborators arrested, Nazi symbols dismantled and replaced with pictures of the ideologues of the New Order (Marx, Lenin, Stalin); improvised shelters for the sick, traveling refugees, overcrowded hospitals, packed trains, the ever-present flea markets (where a gold watch might be exchanged for a few potatoes), scenes of generosity and horrifying villainy, but also the first gestures of returning to normality, to life as it was remembered from before the war: the reopening of a bakery, of a coffee shop or of a movie theater; men courting women, children playing on the streets, people looking for work and bonding in cooperative social relations.

The central theme of Levi's book and the film is the return home. Every character in the film embarks on this journey, even when the chances are high that it will become a long odyssey or that home no longer exists. Returning home is the metaphor for the postwar predicament of the continent, the first step in the effort to rebuild its civilization. For Levi's character, returning home means the (slightly illusory) desire of reconnecting with friends and family and starting his prewar life again. Returning home means putting an end to a state of existential hovering, to disorientation and purposelessness. Home is thus, perhaps even for the Warsaw child in the photo, not a place, not a family nest, not a house, a room in it, or some other form of shelter. Many of these might have been obliterated by the war. Home is a condition. It marks a closure, the end of a terrible journey, and, most importantly, it becomes a place from which one can start over (or imagine starting over), and reverse the course of history from destruction to reconstruction, from contemplating devastation to developing opportunities. Home means life lived for more than survival; it assumes a return of reason to the center of social life.

The Ultimate Poor

Written by Béla Balázs and directed by Géza Radványi, *Somewhere in Europe* (original Hungarian title, *Valahol európában*), the film analyzed in this chapter, thematizes the postwar experiences described above, from disorientation and reckless survival acts to the rediscovery of home and commencement of the reconstruction process. It presents the same landscape of devastation, the chaos, the famine, the purposelessness, and the villainies of 1945 recorded in Levi's book. But it articulates a more developed and more pregnant message of optimism than *The Truce*. It presents the conditions, the opportunities, and the beginning of the slow and difficult but essential rebirth of community in postwar Eastern Europe.

Somewhere in Europe was among the first postwar Hungarian film productions. Shot during 1947 and premiering on January 1, 1948, the film articulates a vision of the political future of the continent.[1] It is, however, not a world seen by individual consciousness, but by one of a collectivity, and it is not one of grownups, but of children, who have been turned into orphans by the war. They are the cinematic avatars of the Warsaw boy in the photograph, their story an interpretation of the boy's whereabouts, a reading of his hopes, fears, and desires. The opening of the film on New Year's Day of 1948 was meant to herald—politically, cinematically—a new beginning, a moment of rebirth in the continent's history. Europeans were called on to envision themselves as orphans—to radically break away from the past, liberate themselves from discursive forms of control, experiment with new forms of social organization, create collective property, and relearn political life. The opening date also suggested that the main social functions assumed by reconstruction films of the late 1940s were to provide an interpretation of the war, to establish reliable criteria for defining guilt (antifascism), to depict the tough reality of the postwar situation, and to articulate a narrative of a return to political life.[2]

Somewhere in Europe draws on the premise that a bodily connection exists between its protagonists and the devastation produced by the war. The voiceover in the opening scene announces that the film is dedicated to the war's orphans: "We dedicate this film to the nameless child, to all those children who met the same fate on the highroads of historical times." The boys and girls whose story it is set to tell are shown as emerging from the rubble. They are its children and successors. They have inherited the debris from the previous generations. It is theirs to have and change. The film fashions them as the agents of Europe's reconstruction. They have the generational legitimacy, the moral entitlement, the vital energy, and the nihilistic freedom from outdated legal and ethical constraints to become the new leading force of the continent and create a more just political and economic order. *Somewhere in Europe* shows how from a famished, antisocial, and apolitical condition—their poverty—these children of the debris organize into a democratic community, building literally "from scratch" a New Order.

War orphans were a common figure of the postwar landscape. Historical statistics show that tens of thousands of them roamed through each European country (Judt 2005, 21). They were also visible in rubble and reconstruction films, and in newsreels and documentaries of the time. But in spite of their omnipresence, no film prior to *Somewhere in Europe* granted them a central cinematic and political role. Other reconstruction films confer this role on other postwar figures, such as the concentration camp survivor (*The Murderers Are among Us* [*Die Mörder sind unter uns*], Wolfgang Staudte, Germany, 1945); the war veteran (*Somewhere in Berlin* [*Irgendwo in Berlin*], Gerhardt Lamprecht, Germany, 1946); or the resistance fighter (*Rome, Open City* [*Roma città aperta*] and *Paisan* [*Paisa*],

Roberto Rossellini, Italy, 1945 and 1946, respectively). In other words, they focus on adults, on characters with a past, socially more integrated and thus politically less unpredictable or revolutionary than a gang of orphans.

In *Somewhere in Europe*, orphans bear a revolutionary impetus that is similar to the one envisioned by theoreticians of the Left in the aftermath of World War I. They have the advantage of coming from nowhere. They have nothing, not even biographical baggage or family bonds. They are not inscribed in any way by civilization. They are the ultimate poor. The film shows how, one by one, they build a gang that roams a desertified land identified as "somewhere in Europe." Their revolutionary potential rests not only in the fact that they lack basic necessities, property, parents, care, and education, but especially in their immunity to mechanisms of discursive coercion, such as laws, hegemonic morality, religion, and education—laws that have lost their legitimacy because they were of the Old Order. Orphans are barbarians, total outsiders of the polis, who don't recognize the discourses that protected, reinforced, and naturalized privilege and unjust economic relations in the past. They bear the revolutionary potential of having nothing:

> For what does poverty of experience do for the barbarian? It forces him to start from scratch; to make a new start; to make a little go a long way; to begin with a little and build up further. (Walter Benjamin as quoted in Hardt and Negri 2009, xi)

Described by film historians as a "shattering indictment of the world's [belligerent] antihumanism" (Liehm and Liehm 1977, 147) and as depicting the predicament of a "whole generation of youth betrayed by the war" (Cunningham 2004, 68), *Somewhere in Europe* shows how its orphans progress from vagrancy to political consciousness. Initially they make use of their poverty to call into question all rules of civilization. They steal, pillage, and even kill for survival as they wander through a world in ruins, where "they have never encountered anything but contempt for the right to live and disrespect for human dignity." Even after they settle in a bombed-out fortress and, inspired by a Socratic figure, engage in changing their way of living, "society rejects them and does everything in its power to hamper their struggle for the future" (Liehm and Liehm 1977, 147). But once bound to a place, the children refuse to return to their barbarian or nomadic life, and decide to defend what they have gained, the common they have created.

This is the moment when they gain a home—the one Primo Levi's characters were looking for. The film exemplifies how this home is mostly condition—not a place one returns to, but a starting point, the foundation for building a common. Once the home is established, the reconstruction process can begin, materially, psychologically, socially, politically—the particle "re-" in "reconstruction" referring not to the re-surrection of a predicament from the past, but to transforma-

Figure 1.1. War orphans, barbarians, agents of reconstruction (*Somewhere in Europe*).

tion, to the overcoming of the state of postwar perplexity and chaos. It marks a re-turn to being human. And this is the humanism articulated in *Somewhere in Europe*. To be human is tantamount to building the common.

The orphans decide to give up their nomadic predicament and remain in the fortress. They organize their lives in it, rebuild it, and fight against the reactionary militia attacking them at the cost of some of their lives. Their sacrifice, however, is not in vain, since they obtain, in the words of another commentator, a "certificate from the new [antifascist] government that the [fortress] will be developed as a home for orphans—the first sign of the rebuilding that will usher in a new future" (Cunningham 2004, 68). In other words, they acquire recognition, sovereignty. The common they have built is recognized as theirs together with the principles that underpin it: collective property and direct democracy. Moreover, it is hoped that this new form of organization developed in this "somewhere" of Europe will spread out all over the continent.[3]

Introducing the Orphans

Somewhere in Europe is organized in three parts, which address the past, the present, and the future of its orphan protagonists. The past, the shortest section of the film, is narrated in Soviet montage style and aims to describe, on the one hand, the way in which the war has produced orphans and, on the other, the orphans' intimate relationship to it, to the unthinkable devastation (and death) it caused, which I will refer in the following as "the Event." A series of cinematic vignettes illustrate the horrors of war through dramatic lighting and camera angles. Soldiers' boots march resolutely to the sound of army drums. A plane bombs a village. Terrified partisans await execution near a mass grave. The wheels of a freight train roll eastward on a journey from which there is no return. An air raid sets an amusement park on fire. Inside the haunted house, among the skeletons and monsters, a wax statue of Hitler catches fire, its slow melting, against the background of eerie music, suggesting the end of fascist Europe.

These vignettes also introduce the protagonists of the film, the orphans, and the violence that links them intimately to the Event. A child steps into the bombed house and sees the corpses of his parents, killed in a recent air raid. A Jewish boy escapes through the narrow window of a *Reichsbahn* train heading to a death camp as the rest of his family continues their trip to the gas chamber. A schoolgirl helplessly watches the execution of her partisan father. A six-year-old kid takes refuge inside the burning haunted house and stares in terror at its monsters and the melting Hitler. Two adolescents emerge from the rubble of a youth detention center, shell-shocked, but passionate to be alive and free.

The first part of *Somewhere in Europe* condemns the horrors of the war, but simultaneously views the disaster with a gaze reminiscent of religious awe. Alienating framing and dynamic editing gesture not only toward unfathomable destruction, but also to a bewildering and perhaps auspicious interruption of history. The war is sublime terror. *Somewhere in Europe* interprets it in an eschatological tradition, envisioning it as the violent conclusion of a chapter in human history and as an event that both creates a historical opening and gives birth to the creatures that will inhabit it. Orphans relate corporeally and immanently to the Event. The survival of the two adolescents from the detention center shows how the Event has ruptured any relationship they had to the Old Order and has bonded them intimately, almost mystically, to violence and death. They literally emerge from the debris. They have, in a sense, factually been rubble, but have been resurrected. Returning from the dead, they are now total strangers to civilization. Death has revealed to them one of the best-kept secrets of modern political life: the arbitrary foundation and values of civilization. As radical others, they return to the present and crisscross it with a question: the question of the ultimate goals of European collective existence.[4] Which way are we heading? How? With whose help?

The act of answering these questions starts by considering what is left, in the aftermath of disaster, from the understanding of man in the twentieth century. As creatures of the Event, the orphans show that, after the crimes of World

War II, "man, a certain determined concept of man, is finished, [and that] the true humanity of man, of the *other man*, of man *as other* begins or has finally the chance of heralding itself—of promising itself in an apparently inhuman or else a-human fashion" (Derrida 2006, 73). This is why the interruption in the past of the orphans is so relevant. They are transformed into the "other man" or "man as other." The Event gives them the legitimacy to embody the alternative. Eschatologically, they are "the chosen ones"; biologically, they are the fittest; and existentially, they have experienced the ultimate horror. As the bearers of a personal loss, they are morally superior to ordinary survivors and to those who helped bring about the devastation; biographically, they are creatures without a past; ideologically, they are anarchic (a-human), as the Event has exploded the symbolic order that constructed man in the past.[5]

Unlike other films of its time, *Somewhere in Europe* is unsentimental in its presentation of the orphans. The two adolescents emerging from the rubble are not innocent beings but delinquents. The gang of children that gathers around them (and around their anarchic impulse) behaves similarly. They engage in looting, robbing, and even murder. The second part of *Somewhere in Europe* depicts in realist visual style how the orphans perform their lawless actions. They roam barefoot through a countryside whose landscapes are barren, crops scarce, settlements in ruin, and human relations suspicious and violent. The gang has grown to more than twenty; it is hungry and unscrupulous; wanders through the postwar desert, plunders fields, attacks households and the roads, both killing and being killed. No romanticized depiction of orphanhood here: their rags are as menacing as their intentions. For the gang, civilization has returned to a Hobbesian state of war of all against all. They find themselves, like postwar Europe in general, in a pre-political condition.

The depiction of the postwar landscape in the film receives confirmation in Tony Judt's account of the period. Like Levi's *The Truce*, Judt stresses that, along with the unimaginable devastation of human life and property, another defining feature of postwar Europe is migration. Europe of that moment is characterized by movement: a continent without inner borders, traveled by victims fleeing persecution, by homeless people looking for a new place to live, and by nomads caught in a disoriented exodus. Humankind provides, in Judt's evocative words, a spectacle of "shaven-headed deportees and concentration-camp inmates in striped pajamas [who] stare listlessly at the camera," a "pitiful stream of helpless civilians," wandering among the rubble (2005, 13).

Both Judt's depiction of the postwar predicament and the plot of the film show that this postwar traffic acquires a political dimension. For Levi, the journey bordered on the absurd, its only meaningful aspect being its end, the arrival, the regaining of a home as a condition to start over. In contrast, the second part of *Somewhere in Europe* recuperates movement positively. The pace of the editing slows, and attention concentrates on the whereabouts of the gang—how it assembles and breaks apart; how it travels, what it looks for, how it fights, and how it interacts with the remnants of the Old Order. The film aims to draw a diagram of Europe's political predicament and present how it breaks—articulating a radical questioning—away from everything that represented the values of the continent. This is why, until this moment, it has refrained from contouring characters and has preserved an impersonal, almost sociological, perspective on its subjects. There is something beneficial in Europe's unsettlement. The continent is searching for a political vision and practice through which it can redefine itself.

The way the gang moves suggests its political potential. It crisscrosses the land aimlessly. Orphans come from nowhere; have no home understood either as past or as destination. The Event has rendered impossible such a return home. The orphans are creatures of the present, nomads. Thus, politically speaking, there is no viable project for them in the past which they can claim as origin or to which they can return. Moreover, as children, they don't have a political consciousness yet. In this phase of their development, their sole desire is focused on the present. They are what Agamben calls "bare life": life unreflected, apolitical, without a project; life of the eternal nomad, the delinquent, the excluded, the ultimate poor. But paradoxically, it is exactly as the excluded, as bare life, that they play a central role in modern European political thought and practice, as the product not (only) of power, but mostly of the Event.[6] A community at a crossroads in a state of exception recuperates bare life as a figure of political thought, as included exclusion.[7] Bare life is life that can be killed, as the villagers can kill the orphans, but not sacrificed, as the final scenes of *Somewhere in Europe* demonstrate.

Identifying the orphans with bare life allows one "to uncover an originary *political* structure that is located in a zone prior to the distinction between sacred and profane, religious and juridical" (Agamben 1998, 74). *Somewhere in Europe* exemplifies how reconstruction films employ figures of bare life to reenact an inaugural political predicament.[8] The first part of the film has shown how the war causes the mass production of bare life: the killing of the parents is the primal exclusion. The second depicts the interstitial existence of bare life as included exclusion and life limited to the present. But this second part also shows that bare life can overcome its passivity and transform, as barbarian, into a political subject: that it can be not only an *included* exclusion (referred to in the passive voice, as Agamben sees it), but also an exclusion that *includes* (in the active voice), that produces a liberated biopolitical space (as Hardt and Negri [2009, 5], following Foucault, see the barbarian). The orphans are not only the exception upon which the sovereign power decides (to paraphrase Carl Schmitt's definition of sovereignty), but also, in a different approach to the political, the exception that imposes a new regime of sovereignty—an immanentist one.

Somewhere in Europe seems to suggest that true political change, revolutionary or not, can only come about from such vagrants who fully experience their status as bare life. From this perspective, the political predicament of the orphans is "creaturely," as Eric Santner (developing Agamben's theory) puts it, since they are both objects of limitless oppression and sacred agents of a political renewal (2006, 9).[9] Put otherwise, they are bare life with a twist.[10] The twist is the Event, which has changed their ontological status and facilitated their transition from passive to active subjects of history. To conclude this dialogue with Agamben's concepts, the orphans are the exception to the exception, lifted to this status by their corporeal relationship to something that transcends the discursive, and which, for a leftist project such as *Somewhere in Europe*, is the pre-symbolic determinism of the body (matter). It is, however, not the body alone (as in Foucauldian biopolitics), but the body "touched" by the Event that prepares the terrain for a radical transformation of Eastern Europe, which, as we shall see, follows a Marxist direction.

Forgetting

The orphans embody another characteristic with the potential to elevate bare life from its passive political predicament: radical forgetting. Their unresponsiveness to everything the Old Order represents recalls Nietzsche's celebration of forgetting as a precondition for political satisfaction:

> In the smallest and greatest happiness there is always one thing that makes it happiness: the power of forgetting, or, in more learned phrase, the capacity of feeling "unhistorically" throughout its duration. One who cannot leave himself behind on the threshold of the moment and forget the past, who cannot stand on a single point, like a goddess of victory, without fear or giddiness, will never know what happiness is; and, worse still, will never do anything to make others happy. (Nietzsche 2005, 6)[11]

In a courtroom scene towards the end of *Somewhere in Europe*, an ex-fascist policeman (acting simultaneously as judge) asks the orphans who they are. He wants to identify them as subjects of the Old Order so that he can put them on trial according to the requisite laws. He asks for their last names. The orphans shrug their shoulders and giggle: they have none, or have forgotten them. The judge wants to know who their parents are. His question spurs more hilarity. With grotesque humor, one of the boys describes the only thing he remembers about his father: a hand, its contorted fingers emerging from the debris. The orphans have forgotten everything else. The judge, however, does not give up his effort to identify them, and orders them angrily to disclose where they come from and where their home is. But his request evinces similar responses. The orphans explain that their home, if they ever had one, no longer exists. They have no memory, and no history (yet).

The orphans of *Somewhere in Europe* have forgotten not only their identity, but also a sense of humanity constructed by disciplinary discourses of the Old Order. The film narrates the consequences. The orphans plunder farms not only because they are hungry, but also because private property, one of the foundational values of the modern liberal-capitalist state and of the Old Order, no longer means anything to them. Yet it is important to notice that they do not reject the law in the dialectical form of antithesis. The film is careful not to portray its protagonists as evil. Like the Event, they are agents of rupture. They *break* the law, but do not articulate its negation. Their delinquency is not an act of choice, but the effect of their forgetting. Their conflict with the past order does not result from antagonism, but represents the collision between moving bodies and the obstacles blocking their way. As nomads, the orphans do not confront the old world with a purpose; they challenge it incidentally. Further, as nomads or *bricoleurs* (as Derrida would call them) existing in a non-dialogic relationship to the structures of power, they experiment with new forms of being that can lay the groundwork of a different political order (1978, 360–361).

Territorialization

Nomadism, however, is inherently an interstitial predicament, one in which the rupture with the Old Order is performed and the experimentation that prepares the New Order practiced. The narrative of the film shifts in the middle of the second part (that is, in the part addressing the postwar future, after the orphans' past and present predicament has been depicted). This shift introduces a focus on the orphans' initiation into political life (the Aristotelian good life).[12] Hunted by the peasants, the orphans take refuge in a fortress. Initially, they believe it is deserted, but later they discover that someone else lives there. The orphans' act of settling in the fortress and their encounter with its inhabitant trigger their transformation from nomads into citizens, from outlaws into inhabitants of the law (of their laws), and from exceptions to the Old Order into builders of the new one.

Their assistant in this transformation, an adult named Peter Simon, is a Socratic figure. Their interaction introduces another feature of the rubble and reconstruction film: the uneasiness of children with men who have caused and perpetrated the war. In *Somewhere in Europe*, the generational hiatus separating the orphans from the elderly Simon is evident. Men between the ages of eighteen and sixty do not play a progressive role in the film, but rather act as the children's antagonists. Adult men are the villagers who form the militia attacking the fortress and the former fascist officials who still lead them. Politically, these figures are still captive subjects in the structures of the Old Order. But neither the children nor Simon is.

Simon connects the present to an imagined political experience located in the era before the rise of fascism—to a democratic political impulse that has been dormant in Europe during the war. In inner exile in the fortress, the old man has preserved it. He embodies memory. But even if his statements hark back to past progressive politics, he is neither the embodiment of the New Order nor its outright preacher. The New Order, *Somewhere in Europe* suggests, is the creation of the orphans, produced in and from the present, oblivious of the past and thus not a return to a paradise lost. The orphans' interaction with Simon does not involve a transfer of knowledge. From the beginning, Simon is the one who is in their power (they almost have him killed). If the children learn anything from him, it is only because they are willing and prepared to listen.

But the orphans' transformation into builders of the New Order can begin only after their settlement. In order to become a political body, they need to inhabit a territory they claim as their own. *Somewhere in Europe* reinforces here an archetype of European political thought: the necessary conjunction between sovereignty and territory, order and political identity. In the modern political imaginary, a sovereign community can exist only if it is tied to a place. It is only in relation to a place, to a material "otherness," that this community can claim political agency. Anticipating that the villagers will come to hunt them, the settled orphans rebuild the walls of the fortress, and the work put into improving their security tightens the inner fabric of their community and sense of sovereignty. The walls of the fortress delineate the common, a collective self. Territorial defense becomes self-defense, but also self-edification.

Somewhere in Europe depicts the development of the orphans' political consciousness by literally verticalizing their productive activity. Prior to settling down, they have roamed as nomads on a two-dimensional surface. Once localized, the protagonists' trajectories change. The camera must tilt vertically to capture their new itineraries: up and down the hill on which the fortress stands (to haul food or wood from the forest); up and down scaffolds (as they rebuild the defenses and roof of the fortress), up and down the walls (as they prepare to fight the militia), and up and down the stairs inside the fortress as inhabitants of it. This vertical movement and the act of inhabiting and rebuilding become metaphors for their discovery of political life, a life that, from now on, is concerned not only with survival (the horizontal axis), but also with the improvement of one's condition (the vertical axis).

Once they have become territorialized, the orphans' perception of time changes as well. As nomads they existed only in the present. But once bound to a place, they experience the passage of time as accumulation. The layers of the present that have previously been lost in migration begin to pile up, creating a palimpsest. Territorialization splits their previously indiscriminate experience of time. Once settled, they start to envision life in notions of the past, the present, and the future. The passage of time becomes visibly inscribed in their material surroundings, as their community shapes and transforms them. Layered time creates awareness of change and historical consciousness.

The transformation in the orphans' perception of time brings a sense not only of accumulation but also of teleology to their world. Life, decisions, and

Figure 1.2. Orphans rebuilding the fortress (*Somewhere in Europe*).

actions become integrated into a historical, and, in a Hegelian sense, spiritu-al, project of self-emancipation. Time underpins development; it becomes the framework of transformation. Land ownership (collective property) and settle-ment constitute the basis of the transition from natural freedom, the freedom of the nomad, to a freedom defined by limitation (*Beschränkung*). Limitation en-ables the materialization of the self (spirit/*Geist*) in an otherness through which one fulfills oneself. This is the establishment of a home (*zu Hause*), of a limitation that grants the subject persistence to itself (*sich-auf-sich-selbst-beziehen*), as op-posed to nomadic wasting (*Zerstreuung*). Territorialization frees the subject from responding only to transcendent challenges—challenges that originate in the en-vironment—and offers it the possibility of articulating its own projects. These are challenges emerging from one's territory, within the limits of a chosen scope of self-realization (Hegel 1998, 304, 374, 582).

The territorialization of the orphans (and their final showdown with the vil-lagers) engenders the establishment of a sovereign community within the for-tress. On the top of a hill and surrounded by strong defense walls, the orphans organize themselves for a better life, assert their right to self-determination, and stand out as a unitary body against their antagonists. In both the narrative and the ideological economy of the film, the role of the conflict between orphans and villagers is to accelerate the orphans' gaining of political consciousness. Conflict is also an important ingredient in a scenario that generates political identity. After resisting the villagers' assault, the orphans become owners of the ruined fortress. At the end of the film, a newly established legal authority grants them property rights and recognizes them as a sovereign subject. Collective ownership becomes the central means enabling them to return not only to history, but, as Simon himself emphasizes, to freedom.

Marxism

In one of his disputes with the orphans, Simon asks: "What is freedom?" When he receives no answer, he continues in the vein of an apparently Hegelian logic. Freedom is contingent on limitation (*Beschränkung*). He asks, rhetorically again: "Freedom to do what you want to do, lawlessness?" Or is freedom linked to the idea of a home, to an act of settling? The orphans listen to him distrustfully, so Simon makes his point clearer: "You were never free," he tells them, referring to their nomadic existence. Free individuals give up their natural privilege of unrestricted movement in order to gain access to a superior form of existence, signing a contract of coexistence with each other and with a place. So far, the orphans were driven by the quest for basic needs, but were not engaged in superior human activities: "You had to roam around, to steal and rob; otherwise you'd have died of hunger," he tells them.

Thus far, Simon sounds Hegelian. Yet his next statement discreetly reveals the Marxist inspiration of *Somewhere in Europe* (as does the film's emphasis on collective property). Simon's words anchor the Hegelian dialectic in materiality and class identity—which, as Hiroshi Uchida points out, constitutes one of the crucial transformations of Hegelian into Marxist thought (1988, 42). Political change does not result from the voyage of the (bourgeois) spirit through the world, but emerges from objective material and economic realities. Simon outlines the causes of the orphans' criminal acts: "The worst captivity is poverty, hunger." The lesson stops here; the rest is shown: poverty can be overcome by communal effort, within a radical democracy built on non-discriminatory relations of production, in which every member of the community co-owns the land and all means of production.

This is the development model the film envisions for Eastern Europe, a non-authoritarian, direct democracy, based on collective property, limited division of labor, and enthusiastic and unalienated production of wealth. Béla Balázs, who wrote the screenplay and helped produce the film, was, unlike Radványi, a declared Marxist who had lived in political exile (in Moscow, among other places) since the early interwar period. He had been part of the Budapest Sunday Circle, a group of leftist intellectuals who promoted a brand of communism inspired by the writings of Rosa Luxemburg. The group included the sociologist Karl Mannheim, the art historian Arnold Hauser, the writer Anna Lesznai, and the musicians Béla Bartók and Zoltán Kodály. Perhaps the most prominent member of this circle was Georg Lukács, who was also a good friend of Balázs until Lukács endorsed Stalinism. His seminal work, *Geschichte und Klassenbewusstsein (History and Class Consciousness, 1923)*—a mixture of Hegelianism and utopian Marxism—constitutes a central inspiration for the strain of Marxism expressed in *Somewhere in Europe.*[13]

What Balázs had in mind, however, was not Soviet-style communism, but a form of proto-communism true to the notions of the Budapest Circle. For example, the song Simon teaches the orphans is the "Marseillaise" rather than the "International," which would have been the appropriate choice if one wanted to please the Comintern. *Somewhere in Europe* lacks references to the liberating role of the Red Army, the dictatorship of the proletariat, and the genius of Stalin. The agents of reconstruction as portrayed in the film do not require the guidance of a party. They are political orphans who organize and reorganize themselves continuously, autonomously, and spontaneously from the bottom up. The orphans' movement in space is "the movement" in the political sense. This movement preserves its immanence, regardless of Simon's assistance.

Grounded in this utopian faith in the spontaneous organization of the masses, Balázs's Marxism must have appeared old-fashioned to the new generation of Lenin- and Stalin-inspired communists who were leading the Hungarian Communist Party (HCP) in the late 1940s, and to his friend and former mentor, Lukács. Consequently, the vision of the reconstruction of the European polis presented in the film was not appreciated by the pro-Stalinist HCP, although it funded the film. HCP publications criticized Balázs's work and even insisted that he not be referred to as a communist (Zsuffa 1987, 337). This non-Stalinist vision of socialism also shows how the situation in Hungary and Eastern Europe remained at least partially open between 1945 and 1947. Just a few months after the premiere of the film, the political climate in Hungary changed radically: spontaneous workers' movements and alternative forms of Marxism were no longer tolerated. The Stalinization of the film industry turned the poetics of Hungarian and Eastern European film in a different direction, which is discussed in the next chapter. Radványi's return to exile (first to Italy and then to Germany) and Balázs's death, in 1948, were also symbolic markers of this changed situation.

The Non-Authoritarian Path to Community: A Comparison to Nikolai Ekk's *Road to Life*

That the movement of the orphans' bodies draws Peter Simon into the plot reveals his limited pedagogical role and non-authoritative political schooling. It also emphasizes the materialist approach to subject production of the film: it is not ideas that make the transformation of consciousness and revolution possible, but bodies, their activity and their desires. The other adults in the film, captive to an outdated present, regard the children as dangerous vagrants. Simon, however, is able to connect with the orphans because he recognizes their agency. He understands their predicament, their potential, and understands that it would be superfluous to ask them where they come from or indeed anything else about their past. His task is to bring them back into the polis (to "include" them) and then to let them change the polis and themselves according to an inner dynamic that is out of his control.

Language plays an important role in this process. Before Simon enters the story, *Somewhere in Europe* unfolds almost like a silent film. Dialogue is minimal and communication occurs primarily through gestures. For example, when two gangs cross paths and start a fistfight (the preamble of their merger), one of the gang leaders comments: "They are getting to know each other." But once the orphans become engaged in organizing work in the fortress or discussing the common good, they become reliant upon language. The discussions between Simon and the children and among the children themselves address their present condition, plan future actions, express dreams, and precede decisions. The increased significance of language shifts the emphasis of the story from what Agamben terms life as *zoë* (bare life) to life as *bios* (life for the common good). The use of language (and through it, the division of labor) is thus a crucial step in the orphans' political emancipation.[14]

Only when Simon enters the stage, one might say, does *Somewhere in Europe* truly become a talking film. Yet his verbal interventions do not assume an authoritarian position. He hardly teaches or gives orders. He is a musician, a composer—thus a mind fluent in non-linguistic structures. He performs language. Besides words, he brings inspiring rhythms and harmonic arrangements into the narrative. Much of the orphans' political awakening takes place around Simon's piano (this is where they first listen to the "Marseillaise"). Like bodies, music escapes the realm of the symbolic and creates a framework or disposition in which the articulation of the truths of the New Order becomes possible. His words create openings. Here the film clearly echoes Marx's thesis about the humanizing mission of art. Re-becoming human, becoming political, escaping from the cage of transcendent necessity, imply understanding the aesthetics of social cooperation.[15]

Simon's pedagogic practice once more emphasizes the film's radical political project and its distance from Soviet-style communism. The complexity and originality of the political vision in *Somewhere in Europe* stands forth even more clearly through comparison to a Soviet film that also addresses the predicament of war orphans. It is a classic of Soviet cinema, Nikolai Ekk's 1931 *Road to Life* (*Putevka v zhizn'*, sometimes translated as *Ticket to Life*), the first Soviet talkie. As a film critic and as an author of children's books, Balázs would undoubtedly have seen Ekk's film more than once during his exile in the Soviet Union. Radványi would likely have been exposed to it as well, since *Road to Life* proved a success throughout Europe. Its notoriety was spurred by the fact that it took inspiration from the writings of the most influential Soviet pedagogue of the time, Anton Makarenko, who worked with orphaned and neglected children between 1920 and 1935, and created (with the help of the Cheka, the early Soviet secret police) several colonies devoted to "rehabilitation through work."[16] Ekk's film also took inspiration from M. S. Pogrebinskii's *The OGPU Labor Commune* (1928) and *People Factory* (1929), two other books reporting on attempts to socially integrate minors and manufacture revolutionary subjects, as the title of the latter text suggests (Dobrenko 2007, 221). The film aimed to synthesize the most influential perspectives on social work and political reeducation before the Great Terror.[17]

There are revealing similarities between *Somewhere in Europe* and *Road to Life*. The Soviet Union after World War I, like Europe after World War II, was a territory crowded with vagrant children. The two films also depict an analogous historical moment, the eve of a period of political radicalism. *Road to Life* appeared shortly before Stalin's Great Terror, and *Somewhere in Europe* shortly before the Soviet takeover and subsequent Stalinization of Hungary and Eastern Europe (coupled with a regime of terror). The plot of *Road to Life* develops "from the relatively specific problem of liquidating homelessness [to] a larger theme about the birth of the new man," as one reviewer observed (quoted in Dobrenko 2007, 223)—an observation that could apply to *Somewhere in Europe* as well. Both films respond to the predicament of the *besprizorniki*, the "untended ones," as criminalized orphaned children were called by the Soviet authorities.[18] The two films also reject punitive solutions for controlling vagrancy.[19]

Yet, unlike Ekk's film and the Soviet Union's policy on orphans, *Somewhere in Europe* does not tell a tale of reeducation; its orphans are not presented as a "problem." The questions of guilt and of education remain undecided, and more complex, in *Somewhere in Europe*. While *Road to Life* portrays the orphans' vagrancy as a sign of social dysfunction requiring repair (caused by the war and the policies of the NEP),[20] *Somewhere in Europe* tells a story that starts from a historical zero hour in which all political relations need to be rearticulated; the "common good" as such requires reconsideration, and all political institutions need to be reorganized. Reeducation—understood in the Soviet context—is thus impossible in the worldview of *Somewhere in Europe*. In its post-Event world, there are no preexisting values, either transcendent or discursively transcendentalized, in which to ground reeducation, and no legitimate leaders and institutions to put reeducation into practice. Such institutions, the state itself, must be rebuilt from scratch, and in *Somewhere in Europe* the orphans themselves form the avant-garde of this reconstruction process. In spite of their criminal behavior, they are exempt from guilt: in the aftermath of the war, there is no legitimate moral or legal instance to condemn them. They cannot be put on trial by the institutions of the Old Order, because the Old Order itself was criminal (a statement that *Road to Life* could not have made about the Bolshevik political order in the Soviet Union), and the children's offenses prove insignificant when compared to the organized murder perpetrated by those responsible for the war.

The positive depiction of the orphans' revolutionary impulse in *Somewhere in Europe* is a vision that could not have been accommodated in a Soviet-era film like Ekk's. The political avant-garde of the Soviet Union (and its leading role) had already been defined by Lenin's writings and the October Revolution (and, eventually, by Stalin's purges). The Communist Party was the sole originator of coherent revolutionary action. Accordingly, *Somewhere in Europe* and *Road to Life* put forward conflicting views of political agency. *Road to Life* effectively states that there is much revolutionary work "to be done" in the Soviet Union, but that the future is not open to spontaneous reorganization, as it is in the Europe depicted in *Somewhere in Europe*. The vagrants in *Road to Life* are not immanently driven by the Event. Once out of their family milieu, another institution captures them. First they are drawn into organized crime, and later they are reeducated by state institutions, but at no point do they constitute a self-determining collective body. Ekk's orphans thus lack the political agency of Balázs and Radványi's, and do not act as the channel through which the Event can establish the present. Their "road to life," which leads to the Soviet polis and state communism, has already been mapped: the Soviet orphans just have to follow the yellow brick road.

Dobrenko claims that *Road to Life* "realizes the classic socialist-realist model of progression: from [lack of revolutionary] consciousness ("déclassé elements," orphans, robber gangs, depravity, drunkenness) toward consciousness (children's educational colony, railroad construction) (Dobrenko 2007, 222). But comparison with *Somewhere in Europe* shows that Dobrenko's observation, though accurate, is incomplete.[21] The influence of Soviet-style communism in *Road to Life* is visible in the way the film interpellates the object of reeducation or *Bildung*—the orphan—and envisions the dynamics of power between educator and educated. The Soviet Weltanschauung only permits the question of *how* to reeducate criminalized orphans. The question of *whether* reeducation is the appropriate response to the orphans' delinquency, and, by extrapolation, to civic dissent or other forms of spontaneous political expression, cannot even be formulated. Nor can one question whether it is ethically appropriate and politically operative to regard collective subjects as a passive and malleable mass that can "be educated."

For Cristina Vatulescu, this dilemma reflects the fact that both *Road to Life* and the actual reeducation camp the film refers to had been set up by the Soviet Cheka, the secret police. In fact, Felix Dzerzhinsky himself, the head of the Cheka, regarded the "solving of this problem" as a top national priority (Vatulescu

2010, 135). Vatulescu's point is that even the apparently liberal pedagogical measures taken in the camps served the party's political purposes, and that behind the apparently liberal motivation for the camps lay "quintessentially secret police tactics" (142).

The children of *Road to Life* are brought to a camp located in a former monastery and are given the chance to work their way to civic consciousness. The camp is not a prison: "You can leave whenever you want," says the camp instructor Sergeev, pointedly flagging his belief that humans are essentially good and will reach appropriate decisions without coercion. *Road to Life* thus ostensibly aims to demonstrate that liberal reeducation methods work (at least with children), and, more broadly, that despite competing political projects Soviet communism is the system that best fits human nature. But there is an addendum to this credo, which reveals the authoritarian impulse of the Soviet system. People will choose the right "road to life" as long as the political game of competing projects is "played correctly" and by "honest" rules, that is, as long as human nature is not seduced or intoxicated by self-sabotaging projects. But authoritarian regimes assume that the enemy never plays by honest rules. (The spy paranoia that infected the politics of the first years of the Cold War illustrates this well.) The violence of Soviet-style socialism, then, in the Soviet Union and throughout postwar Eastern Europe, is the inevitable result of the construction of the political competitor as a conspirator and cheater.

The ideological differences between *Somewhere in Europe* and *Road to Life* can be pinpointed with more precision through the dialectic between "consciousness and spontaneity" that Katerina Clark identifies within Soviet communism and Marxist thinking in general. The dialectic operates between, on the one hand, planned and institutionally controlled social and political action, and, on the other, "actions that are not guided by complete political awareness" and that are "either sporadic, uncoordinated, even anarchic . . . or can be attributed to the workings of vast impersonal historical forces rather than to deliberated actions" (2000, 15). Clark emphasizes that Leninist theory regards this conflict as the driving force of history, which leads to the end of history in communism: "The ultimate stage of historical development, communism, is reached in a final synthesis, which . . . will result in the triumph of 'consciousness,' but the form of 'consciousness' will then be such that it will no longer be in opposition to 'spontaneity'; there will no longer be a conflict between the natural responses of the people and the best interest of society" (16).

Though her study focuses on literary texts, Clark's conclusions can be applied to cinematic productions, in particular the ritualistic aspect of Soviet and Soviet-influenced community-building narratives. The master plot of these narratives, Clark argues, is not so much the *Bildung* plot Dobrenko describes or the description of a struggle between class enemies (leading to social reconciliation), but rather an account of the Marxist-Leninist idea of historical progress: the staging of a grand settlement between consciousness and spontaneity achieved through the ritualism of the novel (15). From this perspective, *Somewhere in Europe* deviates from the Soviet master plot not so much in its setup (consciousness vs. spontaneity, which remains a central theme even in contemporary Marxist thought), but more in the significance granted to spontaneity in social action. This significance can be explained by reference to Balázs's Budapest-circle Marxism, which, influenced by the writings of Rosa Luxemburg, favored spontaneity, while Leninism and real-life Soviet socialism favored consciousness (23). But, in *Somewhere in Europe*, consciousness is compromised by a more general distrust in any form of centralized political action. For this reason, the film aims to promote communism as a natural choice of community, oblivious to preestablished road maps towards political organization.

Political Rituals and Manipulation

Despite distancing itself from Soviet cinematic language, *Somewhere in Europe* contains a few ritualistic moments that unite "otherwise diffuse cultural energies" and use a formula of reconciliation to resolve various antagonisms. One such ritualistic moment, personalizing "abstract cultural meanings and turn[ing] them into a comprehensible narrative," shared by *Road to Life* and *Somewhere in Europe* is the sacrificial episode that concludes each film (Clark 2000, 9). In *Somewhere in Europe*, during the final confrontation with the villagers, the youngest member of the gang, Kuksi (one of the few children in the film who has a name) is mortally wounded. In *Road to Life*, the most dedicated member of the work colony, Mustafa, is also killed. In both films, the death of the child is intended to make the audience identify with the orphans and their pledge.

In the logic of dramatic film, the murderer of a child is always an antagonist. The sacrifice of the child thus draws a clear line between good and evil; it bolsters the intensity of the showdown and, consequently, of the viewer's catharsis. It also propels the plot into the realm of ritual, suggesting an allegorical or mythological reading. An adorned railway engine carries Mustafa's body back to the colony. The mortally wounded Kuksi speaks his last words surrounded by teary-eyed comrades. These ritual deaths also mark moments of reconciliation, and thus function as inaugural sacrifices. The community not only mourns its dead, but commits itself (and bonds), in the name of this sacrifice, to build a better world—and here lies the mythopoeic moment—in which such killings will never happen again.

Many critics expressed unease regarding the use made in these films of such dramatic cinematic tropes. Although the ritual of death and rebirth is a prime motif of the Soviet-style narratives of *Bildung* (marking the passage from boyhood to manhood, or from spontaneity to consciousness), several Soviet critics responded negatively to the tactics of persuasion used in *Road to Life* (Clark 2000, 9). They criticized Mustafa's death and, more generally, the film's "melodramatic humanism," "romantic-dramatic sentimentalism," "sensitive declamation," and reliance on manipulative tropes (Dobrenko 2007, 223–224). Among the film's detractors was the leading Marxist theoretician Karl Radek, who regarded such ritualistic and sentimental tactics as an irrational obfuscation of the social conflicts that caused juvenile criminality. "The class aspect of homeless children," Radek wrote, "their anti-bourgeois character that eases a return to public labor under the conditions of the proletarian dictatorship is not revealed; nor is the social character of the struggle against homelessness shown, and its difference from bourgeois philanthropy and petty-bourgeois sentimental humanism" (223).

Radek's objections are of interest here because they help reveal how *Somewhere in Europe* attempts both to distance itself from the Weltanschauung of socialist realism and to attract large audiences. In his criticism, Radek (later a vigorous promoter of socialist realism) takes a stance not only within debates on "genuinely Marxist" art, but also against commercial cinematic practices that shape popular film in general and their employment in didactic, proto-socialist-realist Soviet productions. At the time he wrote his article, Radek still envisioned the political role of cinema in line with the Soviet avant-garde of Eisenstein and Pudovkin. This position is partially continued by Balázs and Radványi, who—as the film's prologue shows—pay cautious tribute to Soviet agitprop. But following Balázs's biographer, Joseph Zsuffa, we can safely assume that their fidelity to Soviet intellectualism was limited. *Somewhere in Europe* was a film for the people, and the goal of reaching a mass audience seemed unattainable without playing by the rules of commercial filmmaking, which are always formalized and ritualized. Moreover, as a film lover, Balázs had a soft spot for sentimental, emotional, and mythological devices: the value of *Somewhere in Europe* lay, he claimed, in its "ancient instinct for human solidarity" (Zsuffa 1987, 341).

Another trope both films borrow from commercial cinema is the third-act showdown, the final confrontation between antagonists. In *Road to Life*, the antagonists are defeated and punished; in *Somewhere in Europe*, the orphans successfully defend the fortress against the militia. Yet the more complex and inclusive approach in *Somewhere in Europe* to the issue of war guilt, and the emphasis on creative forgetting, means that nobody gets punished at the end. Violence, however, is necessary not only to forge identity and assert sovereignty, but also, as Robert Rosenstone demonstrates, to mark political moments of change: to lend them the requisite drama to propel the birth of the new polis into the mythological sphere. In this sense, "drama" evokes a certain violence of the sacred spectacle and injects extreme affects (such as divine terror) into the representation of an event. Real revolutions, Rosenstone argues, are often banal or even bizarre transfers of power. Eisenstein knew this when he fabricated the story of the storming of the Winter Palace in *October* (Rosenstone 2006, 66–69). But representations of radical change must construct a tumultuous event in such a way as to endow the New Order with a transcendent legitimacy.

Violence and sacrifice are thus key moments in narratives of political passage. The third-act violence in *Somewhere in Europe* marks the orphans' symbolic transition from a condition of bare life to the status of legitimate members of the polis. Bare life, as was discussed earlier, can be killed but not sacrificed. Kuksi's death—he is shot by one of the villagers during the showdown—marks the end of the orphans' life as *zoē*, and their acceptance within the space of the law (*bios*). It comes as no surprise that, as Kuksi is dying, a legal confrontation over the orphans' political inclusion takes place in the adjacent room. Kuksi's death is simultaneously the final act of killing perpetrated by the Old Order, and the first sacrifice in the new one. As the tribunal pronounces the orphans' acquittal and acknowledges that, from now on, there is no court of law within the Old Order that has the legitimacy to put them on trial—which is tantamount to acknowledging the sovereignty of the community in the fortress—the spectator witnesses the birth of the new European subject.[22]

Yet the use of such manipulative cinematic devices in *Somewhere in Europe* also suggests that the film does not always "play correctly" in its relationship to its audience, that is, by rules that allow rational choice. But this critical observation calls for some contextualization. The obvious manipulative tactics in *Somewhere in Europe* need to be understood as a function of its aim to become a popular film and of its effort to articulate a statement about the postwar rebirth of Hungarian (and European) cinema. If well-crafted dramatic endings characterize cinematic products of major film industries, *Somewhere in Europe*, as an inaugural film on the Hungarian postwar screen, had to demonstrate that it possessed the artistic muscle to produce something similar to this quality.

The European Context: Rebuilding a Film Industry

Above I used the comparison with Ekk's *Road to Life* in order to reveal the way in which *Somewhere in Europe* forged a vision of European communism distinct from the representations of political agency produced in the Soviet Union. In the final part of this chapter, I aim to establish the position of *Somewhere in Europe* within the Hungarian and European cinematic landscape and outline the film's didactic aspirations—with its own ambition of participating in the production of the postwar subject. In this context it needs to be emphasized that, while *Somewhere in Europe* was saturated with communist ideas and borrowed cinematic tropes from both Soviet and commercial cinema, critics generally perceived it as an art film, and often compared it to Italian neorealism. It was regarded as a film of the Left anchored in a European tradition of socially concerned cinema.[23] Influential names in film history such as Alexander Korda and Guido Aristarco praised it (Zsuffa 1987, 340–341). *Variety* magazine saluted it as "a good, artistic attempt" that touched "with great skill and ability on many of the most important problems of Europe" ("Valahol Europabon" 1948), and even the film theorist André Bazin, whose response I will discuss later, had some positive things to say about it. These contemporary responses reverberate in the works of later film historians such as István Nemeskürty, Antonin and Mira Liehm, and Graham Petrie (Petrie 1980, 7).

Histories of Hungarian and Eastern European cinema recognize *Somewhere in Europe*, together with *Song from the Cornfields* (*Ének a búzamezőkről*—a film directed by István Szőts in the same year but not released due to the newly imposed Stalinist censorship), as landmark productions of the postwar Hungarian screen. These two major films marked the postwar rebirth of Hungarian cinema, and as John Cunningham points out, they were a far cry from the "melodramas and romance-comedies of the inter-war and war years" (2004, 68). The audiovisual strategies of *Somewhere in Europe* must be viewed in this context. The character of Peter Simon is, once again, key to understanding the form of the film—its relationship to commercial filmmaking—as well as its role in the development of Hungarian and Eastern European cinema.

Both Balázs and Radványi were, in a sense, Peter Simon figures. Like their character, they spent the war in exile, and, like many other Hungarian and European intellectuals, returned to their countries to take part in the postwar reconstruction process. But they were no longer young talents—Balázs was in his sixties, Radványi in his forties—and they did not regard themselves as agents of radical change in film aesthetics. Rather, they were helpers, as is Simon in the film: not the new face of Hungarian filmmaking, but a link to prewar Hungarian and European cinematic tradition. With *Somewhere in Europe*, they aspired to bring the true protagonists of change, Hungary's young filmmakers, into contact with a cinematic language and tradition that fascism and the war had made seem distant. Balázs was, after all, the leading figure of the Hungarian film academy that was established in 1945 and a promoter of Hungarian film abroad. Therefore, the stylistic eclecticism of his film, its dramatic ending, and, more generally, its complicity with the cinematic Old Order have to be judged from this perspective.

The film aims to bestow the Hungarian cinematic polis with a vocabulary to express itself. Unlike other films emerging in the postwar era, such as the German rubble films or Italian neorealism, *Somewhere in Europe* assumes the task not only of defining a new vision of the past, but also—in contrast to those other movements—of participating through its very form in the reconstruction of an orphaned industry. It makes no claim to articulate new "maps of the sensible" or new "trajectories between doing and saying," something that Szőts's *Song from the Cornfields* could be understood to be attempting, but instead offers those true audiovisual innovators—the coming generation of filmmakers of liberated

Hungary and Europe—a compilation of various cinematic traditions (Rancière 2004, 39).[24]

In addition to the visual Soviet montage tropes in its prologue (and some elements in the battle scenes) and the narrative devices from commercial cinema in its final scenes, the stylistic toolbox of *Somewhere in Europe* includes figures from German expressionism and Italian neorealism. The second part of the film depicts the postwar present through the cinematic language of the latter: outdoor sets, on-location filming, naturally lit frames, protagonists played by amateur actors (possibly authentic orphans), and minimal dialogue. The marked emphasis on visual elements led many critics to compare Radványi to Roberto Rossellini and Vittorio De Sica. But commentators have less often remarked upon the tropes borrowed from German expressionism that enrich the stylistic palette of the film. This employment of German expressionist style should not come as a surprise since it offered Hungarian cinema, as well as other Central European cinemas, a means to distance itself from Hollywood and commercial filmmaking in the interwar era.[25]

References to German expressionism are identifiable in the first part of *Somewhere in Europe*, such as in the haunted house scene, when the camera distortion appears to create a subjective perspective on reality in a manner reminiscent of Friedrich Wilhelm Murnau's *Der letzte Mann* (translated as *The Last Laugh*, 1924). But the most obvious reference to expressionist technique occurs in the second part of the film, in the sole flashback scene. One of the two female members of the gang recalls how she was sexually abused by an SS officer. Of interest here is the association of an expressionist visual reference with a German or Nazi character—such as the melting Hitler statue in the haunted house sequence—which would suggest that the makers of *Somewhere in Europe* shared Georg Lukács's thesis that there was something inherently politically dangerous (leading to fascist consciousness) in expressionist imagery.[26] The girl's flashback is a pastiche of Murnau's *Nosferatu* (1922), another German expressionist classic. As the SS officer approaches her, we do not see his hand reaching out for her, but (similar to Count Nosferatu's attack on his helpless female prey) only the shadow of his body and arm on the wall.

This stylistic contrast between the prologue and what might be called the film's Nosferatu scene shows that *Somewhere in Europe* posits two distinct ways of relating to the past. The allusion to Soviet montage in the prologue is progressive and underscores the orphans' radical break with the old world. The later expressionist flashback is a symptom of war-induced melancholy. While all the other gang members in *Somewhere in Europe* have broken with their past, the abused girl remains captive to it (and the gender marker should not go unnoticed).[27] No surprise then that, before the final showdown, the leader of the gang asks her to let go of her memory. Forgetting, a precondition for writing the heroic history of the New Order, is the best thing she can do for herself and for her companions. The New Order, both rubble and socialist-realist films suggest, cannot be built by melancholic subjects haunted by the past.

Somewhere in Europe also draws upon Italian neorealist imagery, which, in contrast to German expressionism, focuses on rendering the present sensible, and thus rarely includes flashbacks. At the time *Somewhere in Europe* was released, the influence of Italian neorealism was felt throughout Europe.[28] Many of the visual and narrative devices in *Somewhere in Europe* are drawn from the neorealist toolbox. But to expect in postwar Eastern Europe a cinematic and visual style that consistently imitates Italian neorealism, as some critics have done, misses both the pedagogic leftist mission of *Somewhere in Europe* and the tumultuous political predicament of this part of the continent. For this reason, André Bazin's critique of *Somewhere in Europe* seems biased, at least from today's perspective.

The comparison to neorealism brings us back to consideration of manipulative devices in the film. In a review of Rossellini's *Germania anno zero* (*Germany Year Zero*, 1948), Bazin draws a contrast to what he regards as the scheming cinematic aesthetics of *Somewhere in Europe*. As John O. Thompson points out, this comparison inspired Bazin to define realism against manipulative cinematic practices, as a particular (and particularly democratic) way of addressing the viewer as citizen. Rossellini's cinema, Bazin argues, empowers its spectators to draw their own conclusions about what they see on the screen, "instead of manipulating [them] into accepting someone else's interpretation" (as *Somewhere in Europe* allegedly does).[29] Bazin further criticizes *Somewhere in Europe* for its portrayal of children. They speak and act more like adults.

According to Bazin, realist filmmakers must respect and cultivate otherness, and children are such others to the adult world. Yet in *Somewhere in Europe*, he argues, this does not hold. This observation raises questions about the film's ability to support stylistically its radical progressive political statements. It suggests that orphans are only adults in costume and that the foreignness imprinted upon them by the Event and their legitimacy to change the political order of the continent are limited to a melodramatic simulacrum. Bazin regards *Somewhere in Europe* as another film that treats childhood "as if it were open to our understanding and empathy" like a Shirley Temple movie (Bazin 1997, 121).[30]

The representation of children in *Somewhere in Europe* as tame and obedient adults, Bazin's argument continues, reflects political anxiety and fear of the future (in other words, a reactionary vision) and thus undermines the film's political project:

> Mystery continues to frighten us and we want to be reassured against it by the face of children; we thoughtlessly ask of these faces that they reflect feelings we know very well because they are our own. We demand of them signs of complicity, and the audiences quickly become enraptured and teary when children show feelings that are usually associated with grown-ups. We are thus seeking to contemplate ourselves in them. (Bazin 1997, 121)

Figure 1.3. Kuksi's sacrifice (*Somewhere in Europe*).

Kuksi's death, Bazin concludes, best illustrates this thesis. In his view, Rossellini's *Germany Year Zero* proves more skilled in constructing the otherness of the child. Rossellini also portrays the death of a child. But, according to Bazin, this death is less easily reduced to the logic of sacrifice than is Kuksi's. Regarding Kuksi, Bazin remarks: "I can't help seeing that the death of the ten-year-old boy who is shot down while playing the 'Marseillaise' on his harmonica is so moving because it confirms our adult conception of heroism" (121–122). In Rossellini's film, the psychology of the child remains untranslatable, closer to the photographs of children among the rubble discussed earlier. Kuksi, however, embodies an aesthetic and political déjà vu.

Bazin interprets *Somewhere in Europe* as a socialist-realist production and misses the film's antiauthoritarian and anti-Soviet message. *Somewhere in Europe* is not neorealist, but, in this context, a didactic film, anthologizing the main cinematic styles of the prewar era and belonging to a film industry more modest than the Italian one. While raising an important question regarding the ideology of form, Bazin's exclusive focus on it overlooks how the plot of *Somewhere in Europe* articulates a clear statement that an unbridgeable gap and an alienating distance separate the children, and their political universe, from the adults. Precisely the otherness of the orphans (their "mystery") bestows upon them the political legitimacy to lead the reconstruction process. This political premise makes the plot of *Somewhere in Europe* stand out among films of the reconstruction period.

* * *

At the end of *Somewhere in Europe*, Simon leaves the fortress, letting the orphans take control of their destiny. Gathered in front of the gate, they whistle the "Marseillaise" as they wave to him. As Simon walks down the hill and is about to exit the frame, the viewer expects the camera to stay focused on the orphans and, implicitly, the future. But it follows the old man—surprisingly and ominously. Simon's exit anticipates that of his makers and their film from the Hungarian stage. *Somewhere in Europe* was the final project both Balázs and Radványi made in Hungary. It was a transitional film, produced by filmmakers schooled under the Old Order with the didactic mission of sketching a project for Europe's postwar political and cinematic reconstruction. Yet the transformation envisioned in *Somewhere in Europe* never really took place. Stalinism, a centralized and authoritarian order, replaced, in politics, the direct democracy it envisioned. Socialist realism, mostly an import from the Soviet Union and not a homegrown style, became the hegemonic style in the arts. Both Stalinism and socialist realism did bring a radical break in their realms, but different in values and style than what *Somewhere in Europe* envisioned, and both the political and the cinematic orphans of Eastern Europe were denied the opportunity to choose how to build their polis.

Yet when Simon tells the children earlier in the film that "the future belongs to you, but you don't know it yet," he is not totally mistaken. Stalinism and socialist realism failed to offer Eastern Europeans a political or aesthetic refuge, and both were soon denounced and abandoned. The homelessness and political orphanhood of the continent continued and even became its normal state of ideological being, thus turning the exception into the rule. Communism survived as compromise, and the dream of an immanentist subject production within, or alongside, a radical democratic community continued to haunt the Hungarian and Eastern European political imaginary. Hungarian filmmakers responded, took up the legacy of *Somewhere in Europe*, and focused on the figure of the orphan. As Melinda Szaloky shows, Hungarian cinema demonstrated a peculiar preoccupation with this figure, producing several political films that had orphans as protagonists (2005, 81–102). One of them, *Diary for My Children*, is analyzed in chapter 5 of this book.

2 Producing Revolutionary Consciousness in the Times of Radical Socialism

Notes on Socialist Realism

In the 1948–1951 period, Soviet-style communism is introduced in Eastern Europe. Under the supervision of the Soviet Union, the political order of the region is transformed. Soviet-style workers' states emerge—with new elites, rewritten laws, redefined priorities, a revamped ethos, and a radically new political culture. The period of indecision and experimentation that characterized the immediate postwar era is over. The Zhdanovist two-camp rhetoric, followed by increased hostility towards the West, the Tito-Stalin split of 1948, the espionage and anti-Zionist paranoia, the Communist Party purges and show trials all over Eastern Europe, create a climate of heightened political mobilization and an increased sense of class conflict (sometimes real, sometimes imagined). The collectivization of agriculture (or, in some cases, its attempt) also plays an important role in the radicalization of political culture. Most Eastern European countries—Romania, Hungary, Bulgaria, and Poland—had predominantly agrarian economies, and class consciousness and revolutionary spirit had to be spread to the rural majority of the population, turning it into the rural proletariat.

The catchword of the times, perhaps one not so new, is "revolution." Everything has to be revolutionary or revolutionized, from the functioning of the economy to education, from the arts to family life. Consciousness, perception, and understanding of reality have to be transformed, and cinema is expected to give this process a hand, especially in the new context of nationalization of the industry and the establishment of national studios. Thus, in the years to come, until the late 1950s, the cinema of Eastern Europe will closely coordinate its discourse with the interest of the Communist Party (and the state, its main sponsor) with the goal of producing socialist reality. Moreover, as around 1950 the antagonism between East and West, between socialism and capitalism, sharpens, the political cinema of Eastern Europe will also respond to the call to participate in what David Caute has termed the "the struggle for cultural supremacy during the Cold War"[1]—that is, to promote the socialist project internationally, develop the antifascist discourse, and discredit the competing U.S.-sponsored liberal-capitalist democracy.

Scholarship on Eastern European film views the 1948–1956 period as one informed by the poetics of Soviet-style socialist realism. For good reasons, all histories of Eastern European cinema regard socialist realism as an artistic formula (a method, as some of its Soviet promoters also called it)[2] alien to the cinematic traditions of the region, and imposed, like Soviet-style governments, by the Red Army. Socialist realism inspired uninteresting art. It was mere propaganda that muzzled authentic talent and bred a generation of uneducated artist-apparatchiks. It did not contribute to the development of artistic discourse and, from a present perspective, it should be regarded as an oddity, an accident, or perhaps an aberration in the normal development of art.

This chapter calls into question these assumptions. It closely analyzes a cinematic product of socialist realism, the 1952 East German film *Story of a Young Couple (Roman einer jungen Ehe)*,[3] aiming to reveal that what has been by default designated as "socialist realism" is much more diverse and meaningful a discourse than is usually assumed. It is not as alien to leftist (and avant-garde) European cultural traditions, being perhaps even their most legitimate continuation. Instead of indulging in more of the same patronizing approaches that delight in uncovering hackneyed formulas, sterile character types, propaganda schematas, streams of ideology, and imitations of Soviet models—as even contemporary writing on *Story* still does[4]—this chapter follows Dennis Tate's observation that GDR socialist art developed in part independently from Muscovite models, as its origins are also to be found in the cultural debates of the late Weimar era about the nature of a committed socialist art, "which took a markedly different course to the debate in the Soviet Union" (1988, 60).

In order to emphasize this diversity and divergence from the socialist-realist "method," this chapter will use the term "socialist film" to refer to the cinematic phenomenon of the early Eastern European cinema (commonly labeled as "socialist realism" or "Stalinist cinema"). The term refers to all films made in this period that are dedicated to the building of a socialist society, opposed to, among other things, what might be called "bourgeois film," with its different political horizon, but also with its different (and hegemonic) aesthetics, within which mainstream film criticism and history still articulate their judgments today. The goal of this chapter is to propose a nuanced approach to the umbrella term "socialist realism," coined in 1932, which echoes a suggestion voiced by Thomas Lahusen in his introductory chapter to a volume on socialist-realist aesthetic production that he co-edited with another prominent scholar in the field, Evgeny Dobrenko (whose work has already been cited in chapter 1). Lahusen argues that a new perspective in the study of socialist realism is needed in order to record the historical openness of both the theoretical writings and the artistic effort that falls into this category (1997, 6–7). This openness—neglected in most scholarly representations—is triggered by the dialectical-materialist underpinnings of socialist art (socialist realism). Its very definition in the *Large Soviet Encyclopedia* emphasizes that it is "connected with the spread of socialist ideas in various countries [and] with the development of the revolutionary, working class. . . . It constantly widens frontiers, acquiring the significance of the leading artistic method of the contemporary epoch" (as quoted in Porter 1988, 49). Similarly, Lahusen quotes Soviet theoreticians, such as Evgeny Makarov, who also insist that socialist realism is a "historically *open* aesthetic system" of representation of life (1997, 6; my emphasis). Lahusen refers to other research on Soviet artistic production (mostly literature) revealing that "the cultural field was . . . far from rigid" even during the high Stalinism of the 1940s (18).

In my opinion, studies that see in socialist art only formula, propaganda, and dogmatic artistic translation of dialectical materialism, and theorize it as such suffer from a series of intellectual shortcomings:

1. They mostly center on literature—in particular, on novels—and thus don't take into account the stylistic, auctorial, and economic hybridity of other media and formats, such as the higher-budget feature film.
2. They center on the Soviet Union, are less attentive to the cultures and traditions of Eastern and Central Europe, and assume that Eastern and Central European artistic production of 1948–1956 was an unreflexive replication of the "method" established in the literary congresses and production studios of the Soviet Union of the Great Terror era, that is, the mid-1930s.
3. They conflate socialist art with the main *political* discourse of the period—Stalinism (and Stalin's personality cult)—and thus uncritically transfer the concept of "Stalinism" from political to cultural analysis, from the study of the economy to that of documentary and fictional representations of society.
4. They employ textual-analysis methods, such as Russian formalism and structuralism, which are positivistic in purpose and identitarian in outcome (and hegemonic in Slavic studies during the Cold War era), and are prone to reveal "formulas," "functions," "types," and so on.
5. They are biased with regard to the human value of the communist project and to the fundamentally political and educational role of art in socialist society, and they evaluate socialist art (especially until the 1980s) by looking for aesthetic beauty and realism as defined by norms naturalized by what Peter Bürger calls the "bourgeois institution of art" (1984, 22).
6. They often forget that socialist art theory was formulated (and practiced), as Boris Groys demonstrates, "by well-educated and experienced elites who

had the experience of the avant-garde and been brought to socialist realism by the internal logic of the avant-garde method itself" (1992, 9).

The Orphans of Socialist Film

Story of a Young Couple, the film analyzed in this chapter, is a thought-provoking vehicle to approach the diverse and complex intellectual grounding of socialist poetics. It thematizes artistic production, the life of actors, directors, and producers; and their activity in the cinema, theater, and new artistic formats specific to proletarian life in the immediate postwar era. The film targets the German and European intelligentsia, who, on the one hand, remembered the late years of the Weimar era and the Nazi period, and, on the other, were familiar with the contemporary political landscape and cultural policies in both the eastern and western occupation zones of Germany. But *Story of a Young Couple* is of interest here also because it has an orphan as protagonist, and thus articulates visions of the production of the subject in a radical period of socialism ("Stalinization" in Soviet studies lingo). The film rearticulates the utopian vision of the immediate postwar era expressed in *Somewhere in Europe,* but in the new context of the Zhdanovite two-camp Weltanschauung. In this confrontational context, the immanentist and spontaneous visions of creating a New Order expressed in *Somewhere in Europe* no longer seem realistic. Revolutionary impulses need to be negotiated with the discipline required to produce a convergent collective discourse that will be able to counter capitalist propaganda and spread the socialist message around the world. Socialism is no longer produced only by a community in quest for a better life, but by citizen-soldiers fighting an international battle against the organized barbarism on the other side of the Iron Curtain.

Unlike rubble and reconstruction films, several socialist productions of the Cold War era have orphans as main characters,[5] and, indeed, most of their stories are *Bildung* stories narrating the becoming-socialist of their protagonists (Dobrenko 2007, 219).[6] What is specific to *Story of a Young Couple* is the way in which it envisions this becoming, the *Bildung.* Its orphan protagonist is an actress, and her conversion to socialism differs from mainstream narrative film situations (whether socialist or not), which rely much more on internal development. Her transformation into a socialist subject is the result of performing socialism. It is linked to learning and interpreting parts. Her acting, her transpositions into other identities, in particular, the imitation of their biomechanical movement, construct her, from surface to interior, as subject.

This, the film suggests, is the proletarian, communist way of self-transformation, ideologically inspired by the Marxist assumption that praxis—often understood as work, and more often work in a collective environment—serves as the motor for the change of consciousness. It stands in contrast to mainstream models of envisioning persuasion, which are more centered on the individual and are, communists believed, the product of bourgeois humanism. Persuasion is conceived of as a psychological operation that changes, via rational and emotional arguments, thoughts and feelings independently of the materiality of the body. This interior entity, the soul, then conditions the subject's behavior (the body and its expression) and triggers an emotional and intellectual metamorphosis, externalizing the character's "change of mind." Action follows persuasion, the exterior follows the interior. First, the rational subject acknowledges the values of the new discourse, internalizes them, lets this internalization reshuffle his or her priorities, and then turns them into bodily output.

One of the intellectual stakes of *Story of a Young Couple* is to challenge this model and demonstrate that, in a socialist context, revolutionary persuasion works differently. First action, then persuasion. The body conditions consciousness, or better put, consciousness cannot be separated from the body and its actions, and imitation and identification with a model precede rational decision. *Story of a Young Couple* develops a psychological and political scenario started in *Somewhere in Europe* but gives it a twist. In Radványi and Balázs's film, music (mood and enthusiasm) and collective work produce subjectivity and political vision. *Story of a Young Couple* borrows this materialist approach. Even if it is a film that features artists and intellectuals, it offers primacy to the body, to its movement and manifestation—that is, to surfaces and matter. In addition, by making reference to parts played by actors, it asserts the virtues of imitation and experimentation as forms of persuasion and subject production appropriate to a world constructed on proletarian materialist ethics. This is the twist. Behavior, gesture, intonation, disposition, and looks create the psyche, as the latter develops through body movement and the biomechanics of social exchanges. Socialism is thus not "ideology" understood as set of tenets and explanation of the world. Socialism is a corporeal style, a way of speaking, moving, looking, and interacting: a performance, which is to be learned via imitation.

The Transformation of Agnes

DEFA[7] produced *Story of a Young Couple* at the height of the Stalin era in Eastern Europe and during tense moments in the history of the Cold War. Its main character is an aspiring twenty-year-old actress,[8] Agnes Sailer (played by Ivonne Merin), who arrives—future-oriented, optimistic—in Berlin to start a career in the theater. The film is framed as a long flashback. Agnes moves to Berlin on December 31, 1946, but tells her story from the perspective of 1952. In this interval, not only she, but also the emerging workers' republic she lives in (the GDR), transform. Critical historical events that mark this period are: the emergence of socialist states all over Eastern Europe (1947–1955), the Tito-Stalin split (1948–1955), the introduction of the Marshall Plan (April 1948), the introduction of the (Western) deutsche mark (1948), the Berlin Blockade (June 1948–May 1949), the coming into

Figure 2.1. Agnes Sailer—embodiment of socialism (*Story of a Young Couple*).

being of NATO (April 1949), the founding of the two German states (the Federal Republic of Germany and the German Democratic Republic on March 23, 1949, and October 7, 1949, respectively), the increasing tolerance shown to Nazi war criminals by U.S. and West German authorities (since 1948), the West German economic miracle (becoming visible in 1950), the Korean War (1950–1953), and the building of the internal German border (since 1945, but stricter from 1947 on).

All these events are referred to in the film and affect Agnes's destiny and her development as a soldier of socialism. When Agnes settles in Berlin, the city's artistic and ideological climate is one of cohabitation. People freely express competing political views; East and West are still in dialogue. Actors commute between the various theatrical stages of the occupation zones, and hope for reconciliation between the two camps is still manifest and believable. But as the plot develops and the Cold War sets in, the Berlin stage (both theatrical and political) becomes more polarized, talent more partisan, artistic and intellectual dialogue more confrontational, and reconciliation—artistic and ideological—looks more and more like a myth or a propaganda tool. As the film ends, in late 1951, the differences between East and West have transformed into overt antagonism, and allegiance to one means incompatibility with the other.

Polarization affects Agnes's personal life. Soon after arriving in Berlin, she meets her future husband, Jochen Karsten (played by Hans-Peter Thielen), also an aspiring actor, but a West Berliner. They marry and work on the Berlin stage. Agnes is more drawn toward the militant art produced in the East; Jochen looks for less politicized involvement, as he still believes in the independence of art from politics. But as the world around them changes, their artistic praxis becomes political allegiance, and triggers disagreement in the couple. Eventually divergences lead to separation. On her own, Agnes emerges as one of the stars of the new art of socialism, with successful performances on the screen and on avant-garde construction-site venues, such as the ones on the Stalinallee (Stalin Avenue). Jochen continues his activity on the Western stage, in bourgeois theater and in the recently introduced genre of the Cold War espionage movie. Eventually, he realizes that his belief in the autonomy of art and subject makes him easy prey for political manipulation. In the end, the couple is reunited, and since *Story of a Young Couple* is a film made in East Germany, Jochen concedes that Agnes's artistic and political allegiance is superior to his and follows her to East Berlin and, we assume, accepts a part in the socialist reconstruction of Germany.

Agnes's relation to her past, her orphanhood, her predicament as ideologically adoptable subject, is established in the first shots of the film. She is shown emerging, to an ominous musical score, from the landscape of bombed Berlin (a common opening of rubble films), carrying two suitcases on a street without traffic. Three monumental edifices rise behind her: a church, a theater, and a government building—all three symbols of power, all destroyed by the war and objects of reconstruction within the framework of a new political order. This suggestion that change is on its way is reinforced by a close-up of a sign displaying a street name. Its old name, Kaiser Wilhelm, is crossed out. Written on top is its new name, Karl Liebknecht, the name of one of the founders of the German Communist Party.

The other element that establishes Agnes's relationship to her past is the disclosure, also in the early minutes of film, of her place of origin. She comes from Dresden, the city obliterated by Allied air raids. This calamity resets her biography. Her family and her past remain under the rubble, silenced, like the suffering caused by the war, like Nazi Germany, Hitler, collaboration, and the entire Old Order. The only thing that matters for her is to start over, to be challenged, and the stage on which she can play a reconstruction role is Berlin. The destruction of the city does not intimidate her. Agnes herself tells us that its ruins look "exactly like the ones my mother was buried under." From this *Stunde Null* in her biography, Agnes's rebirth as socialist subject commences. The date of her arrival is suggestive: New Year's Eve 1946. The second act of the film starts at a New Year's party, as it is here she meets Jochen and two of her other initiators into socialist life.[9]

Directors of Agnes's Performance

Each of these initiators or paternal figures in Agnes's biography represents a distinct and competing political position within the early Cold War and the GDR, a position on the role of art in society, and a discourse on the method and goals of subject production. Each of them offers Agnes parts to act in, and each tries to direct her performance (understood here both artistically and politically). But none of these directors she meets at the New Year's party becomes her ultimate initiator. They only prepare her, with their honest but limited political vision, for the meeting with her ultimate mentor, whose influence (discussed later in this chapter) will conclude Agnes's artistic and political education. Presenting the contrast between these various visions of subject production and, certainly, demonstrating why one of them is superior constitute the central intellectual message of the film.

Agnes's first initiator is the film director Burmeister, who invited Agnes to Berlin to act in one of his movies. The invitation, we find out, was made out of solidarity with Agnes's deceased mother, who seems to have been a well-known theater actress of the interwar stage. Burmeister's appearance is that of an intellectual of the Proletkult movement. He is in his forties, athletic, energetic, firm in body language, with a proletarian artist haircut and a socialist pin on his more modest New Year's Eve party suit. He is forthcoming and professional; he talks with enthusiasm about his projects and the future. He represents the cultural socialism of the Weimar era, combined with postwar antifascism and Soviet Proletkult.

At the party, Jochen introduces Agnes to her other mentor, the esteemed theater director Moebius, whom he describes, admiringly, as a "gray-haired fireball" (*Feuerkopf*), a reference to the artistic personality associated with romantic conceptions of genius and autonomous art. Moebius directs at the Westend Theater, mostly classics, a preference initially shared by the cultural policy makers of both Soviet- and Allied-occupied Berlin. The biography of the actor playing Moebius, Martin Hellberg, explicates that of his character. He was a writer and director himself. His career was put on hold during the Nazi era (so he had the antifascist credentials), but in the GDR, he directed several film adaptations of the German bourgeois drama of the eighteenth century such as *Emilia Galotti* (1958), where Thielen (the actor playing Jochen) had the lead. He also directed adaptations of *Kabale und Liebe* (1959) and *Minna von Barnhelm* (1962).[10]

The East and the West shared the view that classics denazified, but in different ways. The Americans believed that they inculcated not only foundational anti-Hitlerist values, but also anticommunist ones. Documents of the American administration reveal that the staging of classics was employed as part of "an educational and informational program to explain to the German people the basic concepts of democracy as opposed to the communist system" (as quoted in Caute 2005, 253). For the administrators of East Germany, especially for the main articulator of the cultural policies of its early period, Johannes R. Becher (who was also a promoter of radical socialist are), the classics were instrumental in forging an antifascist, but also anticapitalist humanist ethos because they fostered the "belief in the equality of human beings and peoples" (as quoted in Nothnagle 1999, 47). In his popular primer *Education for Freedom*, Becher adapted Lenin's theory that socialist art should synthesize all the progressive trends of human culture, and advocated a critical return to the "liberal traditions of our people" in the context of a creative use of Marxism (47).

These observations reveal the importance in subject production given to art in those days on both sides of the Curtain. Unlike Burmeister, whose antifascism is overt and militant, Moebius advocates a more mellow approach. He talks about his plays in the lingo of Aristotelian poetics. His productions seek catharsis. He tells a group of friends that with his last play he made his audience feel relief, *Entspannung* (that is, catharsis): a moral and psychological discharge from the memory of the war and the dire predicament of the postwar era. The point here is not that art is entertainment, which could also be a translation of the German *Entspannung,* but that relief and compassion are the best ground for sustainable reconstruction efforts.[11]

Moebius invites Agnes to perform in such a humanist construal of life. He offers her the role of Recha in his new production of Lessing's *Nathan der Weise,* a classic about the reconciliation between the three main monotheistic religions. Recha is also an orphan, a child, like Agnes, saved from the fire, and one adopted and reeducated by the sagest man of her times, Nathan. In a rehearsal scene, Moebius tells Agnes/Recha to act as if she is instrumental in fostering "mutual understanding and humanity" and in persuading the powerful to act humbly, peacefully, forgivingly, and openheartedly. In the cold physical environment of the theater—the winter of 1946–1947 was one of extreme cold and starvation— Moebius asks Agnes to picture herself in the warm climate of the Mediterranean, whose soft air nurtures tranquillity and sympathetic human interaction. Imagining herself in a different place will improve her performance.[12] As he talks to Agnes, stagehands carrying a piece of scenery painted with palm trees (*Nathan* takes place in Jerusalem) complain about the never-ending winter, throwing an ironic light on Moebius's words, on his denial of the reality he and the people around him live in, and, more generally, on the escapist dimension of his conception of art.

Agnes accepts Moebius's directions and softens her acting style. In a later discussion with Jochen, she admits that, indeed, her acting needs to improve along the lines that Moebius indicates. The fact that she has adopted Moebius's suggestions becomes even more evident in a discussion she has with her other mentor, Burmeister, who demands a different acting style from her. With Burmeister, Agnes shoots an antifascist film. Also in a rehearsal scene, but one on a film site (and on the eastern side of Berlin, where it is not so cold!), an even more proletarian-looking Burmeister explains to Agnes that she is not to embody a passive female character from the past. The reference here is made to the fragile women of the German eighteenth- and nineteenth-century stage (such as Recha), but also—yet only partly accurately—to the passive and maternal image of women produced by fascist melodrama.[13] She is not to be a "Gretchen," a reference to the lead female character of Goethe's *Faust* (also an orphan) and a more general reference to the sensitive female leads of the German bourgeois drama (*das bürgerliche Trauerspiel*). She is not to be the innocent and gullible beauty who, through the power of forgiveness, saves the soul of one who has signed a pact with the devil. The woman of the New Order must act uncompromisingly, follow socialism's campaign to marginalize from public life the men and women who have cooperated with the devil (that is, the fascists and their supporters).

Under the influence of Moebius, Agnes doubts Burmeister's suggestions. They are too confrontational. She argues that the demeanor of the new woman he envisions is improperly "aggressive," and "unfeminine" (*unweiblich*). "I'm here not to hate, but to love," she explains. Love is the key to European peace. But the antifascist Burmeister sees things differently. The adequate way to deal with Nazi war criminals is with a spirit of justice, not reconciliation. Tolerance is their ticket to return to power. As Agnes insists that "art should make us forget about these issues," forgetting being foundational to reconstruction, and not obsessively revisit collaborationist guilt, Burmeister details the need for intransigence. Art, he argues, cannot be a distraction from the burning issues of the time. In the postwar and post-Auschwitz context, advocating compromise through art is criminal.

The overall East German perspective on fascism was, as Judt points out, that "Nazism was not just a trick perpetrated on an innocent German proletariat. The German working class, like the German bourgeoisie, had failed in its responsibilities" (2005, 59). Thus bourgeois culture could no longer be, as Burmeister puts it in his dialogue with Agnes, a torch enlightening the way to the future. The triumph of Nazism demonstrated the powerlessness of the bourgeoisie, and the outdated character of its understanding of the functioning of politics (liberalism). And especially because its practices could not keep up with the times, the leaders of the Communist Party argued, "it would be more, not less likely to adapt itself to Communist goals, given the right combination of stick and carrot" (Judt 2005, 60). They had to be taught that normality in postwar politics was militant spirit along the Zhdanovist doctrine of international confrontation between the West and the East—or, in Zhdanov's propagandistic language, between imperialism and democratic forces.

The next scene supports Burmeister's point. At the premiere of his *Nathan*, just before the rise of the curtain, Moebius's stance about the reconciliatory function of art faces a major challenge. As the performance is about to begin, he notices with excitement that representatives of all occupation forces are present in the audience—Brits, Frenchmen, Americans, and, of course, Soviets—creating the impression that art can bring Europeans together as it transcends national boundaries and ideological disagreements. But in the spirit of tolerance and forgiveness, an acclaimed director of the Nazi era and maker of its propaganda movies, Hartmann, also exercises, in the house's spirit of tolerance, his right to attend the opening. His presence in the theater triggers a commotion. The antifascist Burmeister is the first to react and to point out the presence of the "war criminal" in the room. His work of hatred against racial and ethnic others has nothing in common, Burmeister shouts, with the tolerance message of *Nathan*. The audience chimes in, but Hartmann refuses to leave the venue. He has purchased tickets to the show. In the logic of tolerance and capitalism, he has the right to sit there just like anybody else. Moebius himself has to intervene. As he escorts Hartmann to the door, he sees himself as contradicting his reconciliatory proselytization.[14]

Hartmann's name has already been mentioned during the New Year's Eve party, when Burmeister and the theater critic Frank recall with indignation his public appearances. "Hartmann" is the screen reference to the actual Nazi-era director Veit Harlan. Though the director's name is changed, the references to Harlan's films, the anti-Semitic hate film *Jew Süss* (*Jud Süß*, 1940) and the pro-war epic *Kolberg* (1945) are verbatim.[15] Other references to Harlan's work and biography are included later in *Story of a Young Couple*. He serves as a key character in the questioning of Moebius's discourse on reconciliation and in condemning the tolerant attitude of the Allies and the Adenauer regime of West Germany toward former Nazi officials (including troubling amnesties of war criminals during the 1950s and the silence on the war crimes committed on the eastern front [Judt 2005, 270–271]). *Story of a Young Couple* even presents a reenactment of one of Harlan's trials for his complicity with the Nazi regime in crimes against humanity, a trial that ends with his acquittal.[16]

Construction-Site Art

The third paternal figure in Agnes's path to gaining revolutionary consciousness is the most important. Though he is in charge of directing Agnes's appearances, he is not active in established artistic formats, such as theater and film. He directs action on a new type of stage, specific to the socialist era and central to socialist poetics: the construction site. His name, Father Dulz, is suggestively paternal, and the performances he is directing as a foreman are of brigades of workers building the Stalinallee. This giant construction project in the workers' district of Berlin commences in the same year that *Story of a Young Couple* is shot, and its progress is intertwined with the film's production and distribution: on November 1951, the GDR government decides on the opening of the Stalinallee construction site; on February 3, 1952, the *Grundsteinlegung* takes place (the official foundation-stone laying); and the January 18, 1952, Berlin premiere of *Story of a Young Couple* is followed, the very next day, by a celebration marking the completion of a prototype building for the architecture of the Stalinallee (Allen 2011, 255–256).[17]

Under Dulz's mentorship, Agnes no longer appears in theaters and films (or on the radio),[18] but in eclectic festive events taking place at workplaces. Stages are mounted on construction sites, or construction sites are turned into stages that host performances aiming to break away from bourgeois art contexts. These shows avoid the locations and formats established by the Old Order—the black box theater hall, the opera house, or the ninety-minute feature film—in order to liberate artistic expression from established conventions of presentation and reception, and from its separation from reality-building (productive) human activity. Construction-site venues articulate the material link between performance, exhibition, and socioeconomic context. They redefine the social function of art, as they contribute to socialism's project to blur the distinction between labor and leisure, productive and creative work, performer and spectator. Their productions are no longer mirrors reflecting independently (or autonomously) the "realities" of the world, but are vigorous (symbolic) contributions to building these realities, just like any other human productive activity. They intertwine art with life, infuse the present with utopia, and are instrumental in merging the economic use of physical work with its aesthetic value, labor with labor's choreography.

By including these construction-site performances in its diegesis, *Story of a Young Couple* dialogues critically with previous artistic projects of the Left. It comments on the interwar effort of both the German mainstream Left to create "cultural socialism" and on the project of the avant-garde to destabilize bourgeois art. This commentary is even more appropriate when it comes from a film whose plot takes place in Berlin, where, in the interwar era, both the avant-garde and the popular communist movement were the most influential outside the Soviet Union. Visual artists such as George Grosz and John Heartfield, writers such as Ernst Toller and Walter Benjamin, and theater and film directors such as Bertolt Brecht, Erwin Piscator, and Slatan Dudow fought (on the communist side) in the cultural confrontations of the interwar era (Eley 2002, 209). Postwar socialist art aims, on the one hand, to avoid the shortcomings of Weimar cultural socialism and to disentangle itself from the poetics of bourgeois art, and, on the other, inspired by Soviet Proletkult, to rethink the avant-garde in order to put it in the service of the workers. Because it was not radical enough, cultural socialism, Geoff Eley explains, fell into the trap of the culture industry, as its administrators made the mistake of separating work from leisure and life from art, bracketing "precisely the arenas—workplace, party-political structures, family—where the new values needed to be most tenaciously pursued" (215).

Instead, learning from the avant-garde, postwar socialist art aims to articulate something different in terms of function, form, exhibition, and reception, something alien to bourgeois taste and worldview. Given its antibourgeois stance, its acknowledgment of the political relevance of art, and its emphasis on undermining institutionalized values and perceptions of reality, some theoreticians of postwar socialist art and socialist realism considered it a legitimate heir to the avant-garde of the interwar era. For Valery Tiupa, the socialist realism of the 1930s and 1950s was the righteous continuator of the avant-garde and "left" art (Lahusen 1997, 21). Boris Groys suggests that socialist art be viewed not only as a continuator of the avant-garde in the socialist society but also as a version—however, a very particular one—"of the global modernist culture" (1997, 76).

But the avant-garde model had its limitations, and socialist art had to overcome them. The most evident shortcomings that builders of the New Order noticed in the discourse of the avant-garde were its negativity, its inability to articulate the new, and its restricted audience. Limited interest was a problem for cultural socialism too. In the interwar era, "workers turned only partially to the socialist cultural organizations yet flocked in masses to capitalist-organized commercial entertainment" (Eley 2002, 216). Consequently, socialist art had to find a way to convey a progressive message without becoming uninteresting or elitist. "Going to the pictures" was a central fixture of working-class life, popular culture's real location, and socialist art of the postwar era had to bridge the "gap between socialist ideas of cultural progress and actual workers' behaviors" (216).

This is why another important task of socialist art was to rediscover affirmation and render its discourse popular without being preachy. This imperative is assumed by Maetzig, who regarded filmmakers as popular artists. In "Film as Art," an essay written during the making of *Story of a Young Couple*, he emphasizes that the cinema is a bridge between the higher arts and the people, as it is meant to be watched by thousands of workers (Maetzig and Agde 1987, 218). He writes these lines in a period in which he wants to distance himself from the fascist melodrama and capitalism-informed Hollywood constructions of individual happiness and social fulfillment. But he also criticizes the Frankfurt School and Brecht, who, in his opinion, argued that entertainment films were as dangerous as Nazi films (219).

Several critics of the Weimar era thought that producing affirmative, democratic, non-bourgeois art was achievable only in revolutionized social and political contexts, in which capitalist relations of production had been abolished.[19] Postwar socialist art starts from this premise: that it functions in a new social and political context, where the articulation of a worker's interests and worldview is possible.[20] But *Story of a Young Couple* tells us that the struggle is not over, and the values of the Old Order are still influencing artistic choices, taste, and the understanding of the role of art in society. Moreover, in the Cold War context, a militant stance is even more needed, since the bourgeois view on life and human relations is promoted aggressively with money, insight, and military muscle by anticommunist forces on the other side of the Curtain. Thus the project of affirming a new perception of reality, of repairing the alienated senses (and consciousness) of workers exposed for decades to hegemonic bourgeois artistic discourse remains in jeopardy.

The critique of socialist art coming from the capitalist camp in this period focuses on revealing its lack of taste (kitsch) and its didacticism (propaganda). The former judgment drew on naturalized (inherited) bourgeois aesthetic expectations, the latter on the premise that socialist art was not in the service of enlightening workers, but was instrumental in their exploitation and in establishing a society that lacked arenas for the expression of dissent. Skeptical of the artistic affirmation, the social synergy, and the convergence of art and politics, critics denounced socialist art as producing what Hannah Arendt, among others, called the homeless (uprooted) modern mass-subject of twentieth-century totalitarian society.[21] Socialist totalitarian art articulates not only partisan visions of reality (misrepresentations), but, under the illusion of empowering subjects as a collectivity, disenfranchises them as individuals and diminishes their resistance to manipulation (the immunization of self generated by critical thinking). This counterfeit empowerment creates addiction to an illusion and a subject "in a situation of spiritual and social homelessness," "longing for fiction," willing to deny "common sense perceptions of reality," "the plausibilities of the world," and to believe instead in fabrications (Arendt 1962, 352). These fabrications, which are smoothed and rationalized views of the world, produce existential comfort as they deprive reality of its "accidental," "incomprehensible," "individual," and "uncontrollable" aspects, and offer quick and comprehensible solutions to control it (352).[22]

By feeding its public what Arendt calls "outrageous insults to common sense" (352), socialist art aims to propel consciousness in a post-bourgeois humanist context. This recontextualization might be a virtue for the avant-garde but not for the anticommunist ideologues on the Western side of the Curtain. For them, socialist art demolishes the natural ties of the world in order to reorganize it for totalitarian rule. It produces a domain of political orphans, of subjects who are ready to reject what they have acquired via tradition, within their families, and through what they perceive as their natural interests. The totalitarian subject internalizes the precept that reality and the self are produced discursively and that "common sense," "plausibilities," and individual faculties of perception and organization of knowledge can offer them only limited guidance in the modern world. They can access truth only as collective subjects (the proletariat) or mediated by supra-individual ones (the Communist Party, Stalin) and by scientific discourse (dialectical materialism).[23]

But Maetzig imagined himself as a champion of realism. He definitely wanted to bond with the public and not bring "outrageous insults to its common sense" (Maetzig and Agde 1987, 223).[24] In the period of making *Story of a Young Couple*, he wrote articles and manifestos with titles such as "Against Formalism, Kitsch and Schematism" ("Gegen Formalismus, Kitsch und Schematismus") and "On Partisanship in Film Directing" ("Über Parteilichkeit in der Spielfilmregie"). For him, socialist realism is not an alienating artistic formula. Formulas are just uninspired, politically ineffectual art. In the spirit of dialectical materialism, there are no eternally valid forms. Content determines form, and in 1951 filmmakers were still looking for the appropriate form to fit the revolutionary context of their times—one that is not schematic (221). For Maetzig, the paragon of formalism was the fascist entertainment film (especially the melodrama).

In *Story of a Young Couple*, Agnes's acting receives criticism when she performs a lead role in one of Burmeister's antifascist films. Her first and most vehement critic is her husband, Jochen. A few years have passed since 1947, and they are both more experienced actors. The Marshall Plan is in operation, the Berlin Airlift is under way, the tension between East and West has increased, and Burmeister is now more than ever dedicated to the Soviet communist cause (he is also shown directing one of the darlings of the Soviet occupation, Simonov's play *The Russian Question*). Jochen's disapproval of Agnes's performance, which leads to the couple's separation, is preceded by other episodes in which husband and wife criticize each other along East and West lines. Agnes is dissatisfied when Jochen plays the lead in Carl Zuckmayer's *The Devil's General*, with its redemptive message regarding the Wehrmacht—a very popular play in West Berlin. In another episode, Agnes triggers controversy when she refuses to accept a part in another famous play of the era, also staged in the West, Sartre's *Dirty Hands*, which she regards as anticommunist (as it was mistakenly regarded at the time).[25]

The fact that the political function of art is to control what is experienced as real, natural, and commonsensical is illustrated in a conflict between Agnes and Jochen. Agnes is given an important part in Burmeister's next film. Initially, Jochen shows excitement at Agnes's chance to play a lead character. But when he takes a random look at the script and stops at a line in which Agnes's character argues that the socialist competition (*Wettbewerb*) is different than the capitalist one (*Konkurrenz*), he becomes dubious. "It sounds odd . . . ," he comments, "this construction pathos [*Aufbaupathos*]." He then recommends: "You will have to tone it down." But Agnes doesn't seem persuaded, and wonders whether for other people, people who live in the East, like Dulz's daughter, such statements do not sound unnatural, but have become part of their everyday explanation of their predicament. Jochen disagrees, and since Agnes remains unconvinced, he continues: "No human [*kein Mensch*] speaks like that!" But his appeal to the universal human, the *Mensch*, can't persuade Agnes. Her attitude seems to suggest that it is exactly the post-human, a post-bourgeois construction of the subject, a cyborg whose actions and consciousness intertwine natural with ideological impulses, that draws her attention. She is about to grasp that the universal and universalizing idea of *Mensch* is class-constructed as a tool of social control.

Their disagreement reaches its peak in the cinema after the opening of the film. It takes place, like *Story of a Young Couple*'s premiere, at the Babylon Theater in East Berlin. As the music swells, marking the conclusion of the film, Jochen refuses to join the standing ovation of the audience. "This is unbearable," he exclaims, after having the opportunity not only to read but also to see how the socialist human speaks. He leaves the box where he has been sitting with Agnes. She follows him into the lobby, where he vents his frustration. He has expected her to tone down the *Aufbau*-rhetoric, but through her acting, her body, voice, and expression, she has done exactly the opposite. She has insulted art, a phrase that is reiterated by Frank in his review of the film, printed not surprisingly in the West German newspaper *Der Tagesspiegel*. The review labels the film as "misuse of art" and "blatant black-and-white propaganda" flawed by "tedious construction pathos," and Agnes as nothing but a stale reproducer of communist slogans.[26]

Dulz's Directing Style

The confrontation between Agnes and Jochen is interrupted by Burmeister, who defends his actress.

> BURMEISTER: "Jochen was *machen* Sie denn mit Ihr?" [What are you doing / making out of her?]
>
> JOCHEN: "Was *Sie* aus ihr *machen*, Herr Burmiester, das ist verantwortungslos." [What *you* have done to her / made out of her that is irresponsible.]

But their conflict about art-*making* is not the central one for *Story of a Young Couple*. What each of Agnes's mentors—the ones discussed so far, Burmeister, Moebius, and Jochen—*does* to Agnes is to prepare her for her true adoption, for her work with her ultimate director, Father Dulz—that is, for her ultimate transformation into a socialist subject. None could form her totally, because they all (even the progressive Burmeister) function within the traditional institutional context of bourgeois art, theater, and cinema (as well as old-fashioned formats of political thought and practice). They show their productions in locations with names such as Westend, Urania, and Babylon. They work within specific production and financing schemes, follow its rituals of promotion (the poster with the star's face on it), exhibition (the grand opening), valuation (focusing on the credibility of the actors' performances), and reception (the expert's review). As

Figure 2.2. Agnes "made" on the poster of Burmeister's film (*Story of a Young Couple*).

an actress, Agnes remains a product of a reactionary division of labor, and her activity is organized and assessed according to norms that are specific to the old institution of art.

The Burmeister-Jochen confrontation, with its focus on the word *machen* (to make), echoes a dialogue that Agnes has with Dulz before the premiere of her film. Dulz approaches Agnes in order to invite her to participate in the art that he is interested in "making"—the one on and of the Stalinallee. As he waits for her in the hallway, he looks at the poster of the film, which highlights Agnes's face. The shot lingers long enough on Dulz's act of looking to suggest that, when the real Agnes appears, Dulz, and with him the spectator, will make a comparison between her and the representation on the poster, between actress and character, between the person and her construction. The dialogue between Agnes and Dulz individualizes the latter's "directing." The verb *machen* appears here too, but with a different meaning. In the Burmeister-Jochen exchange the verb is used in the passive voice: what has been made out of Agnes by her mentors. Dulz uses the reflexive: "Ach, Agnes sie haben *sich* gemacht" (my emphasis). The sentence can be literally translated as "Agnes, you have made yourself," indicating that it is she and not others who control her transformation.

Because Dulz comes from a locus where the present has met the future and where, liberated from bourgeois confinements, art belongs to the workers, his direction focuses less on prescription and traditional persuasion, but offers primacy to bodily motion and imitation. Dulz's invitation suggests that, after her apprenticeship in the traditional artistic formats of the interwar era (theater, film, and radio), Agnes is prepared to participate in revolutionized forms of artistic expression, where, as Georg Fuchs, the German theater theoretician of the early twentieth century, argued, art and productive human activity interlace as festival with the purpose of forging revolutionized social bonds.[27] Dulz's praise and his reference to *machen* also suggest that Agnes's transgression, even if not complete, has been achieved through performance. The parts she played may have been alien to her in the beginning, but, by identifying with them (and we shall see what kind of identification Dulz has in mind), she was able to transform herself. She has become her image (the poster) by struggling to embody the alien, the non-bourgeois *Mensch* of Burmeister's film.

Dulz's praise emphasizes socialism's productionist and post-human understanding of subjectivity, which grounds individual emancipation in the rejection of and the working through of the inherited and the natural. He doesn't tell Agnes how to act, like Moebius, Burmeister, or Jochen did. His method is different. He takes Agnes to the construction site on Stalinallee and lets her take its spirit in. On the Stalinallee, reality and utopia become indistinguishable. Its liberated relations of production and the dynamic of the bodies of the protagonists of this stage should inspire her. She is to absorb the way these bodies move and rest, the tasks they perform, the way they relate to each other, and the energy they expend. As actress and political subject she should internalize them and let them transform her. She should imitate them and gain a better understanding of the New Order and the social function of its art. Her artistic performances will then refine these movements into a choreography that synthesizes their transformative power and monumentalizes them as the corporeal style of the New Order.

Agnes also receives guidance and help in her transformation from another character who will accompany her in most key scenes of her conversion to socialist corporeality. This character functions as her double, anticipating not only how a fully emancipated Agnes will one day speak, move, and gesture, but also the overlap between Agnes the private person and Agnes the actress, between inherited self and its political (re-)construction. It also addresses Agnes's status as orphan, showing what it means to be a fully adopted subject of socialism—no longer daughter of a natural parent but of a chosen, ideological one. This character is herself a daughter, Dulz's, Brigitte.[28]

There are several moments in the film that present the relation between Brigitte and Agnes, the merger of the self with the image. Usually the two women are shown together with Dulz—one on one side of the father, the other on the

Figure 2.3. Brigitte, Father Dulz, and Agnes on the Stalinallee construction site (*Story of a Young Couple*).

other, suggesting the specular method of Dulz's directing style. He mediates, is an interface, a mirror through which, as in the scene where Dulz compares Agnes to her image on the poster, Agnes is confronted with her utopian representation, the one that she, the real person, has to imitate. References to Dulz's adoptive role abound in the film. From the initial situation in which Agnes calls him "father," to a sequence on the construction site in which Brigitte, catching up with Dulz and Agnes on the scaffolds, asks him jokingly who is in fact his real daughter, she or Agnes. She asks this question because she thinks Dulz has never shown her the construction site so thoroughly. As Brigitte approaches them, Dulz happily embraces both and answers that they are both his daughters. His reply suggests that it is not biological ties and blood that underpin the family of the New Order, but the flow of the same discourse through one's political veins; the same perception of reality and the same political goals. In a later scene, after Agnes separates from Jochen, Dulz even suggests she share a room with Brigitte.

Denaturalizing Performance

In a key scene of Andrzej Wajda's 1976 *Man of Marble*, a film reflecting on the same era as *Story of a Young Couple*, the protagonist, Birkut, opens an exhibit that displays the new art of socialism. The exhibit includes, as in Agnes's case, an artistic image of him. Yet it is not a poster or a stage performance, but a large marble sculpture. The actual person has become a model, his body a representation of the healthy and liberated corporeality of socialism. The mission of socialist art is to produce such models. It has to monumentalize a new look and corporeal style inspired from the activity of workers. *Story of a Young Couple* conveys a similar message. But unlike Wajda's film, which was made in the 1970s and which reflects critically on the past, *Story of a Young Couple* also aims to become itself a sample of such revolutionized art. It hopes to be perceived not only as a film *about* socialist poetics, one engaged in persuading its audience of the superiority of its tropes, but also as a model and a monument itself: as its own double.

Representations of work on construction sites serve this purpose. They show the reality that should inspire socialist artists and the New Order's relevant challenges and actors—the proletariat. The insertion of samples of the politically acceptable performances of the protagonists of the film, in particular the extensive presentation of the celebrations on the Stalinallee—including Agnes's delivery of two patriotic poems there—aim to show the direction that emancipated art should adopt. In Agnes's performances on the Stalinallee, monumentalist interpretation and *Aufbaupathos* reach their peak. They mark the completion of her artistic and political education—the transformation of her consciousness, its liberation from reactive thinking and embracing of the revolutionary demands of enthusiastic affirmation.

But the Stalinallee inserts clash with the more traditional cinematic style of the film—something that has not gone unnoticed by critics attentive to stylistic continuity. In fact, this clash is visible even in Merin's interpretation of Agnes. Her character looks, acts, and speaks differently than any other in the film. Her verbal expression is more declamatory, her gesticulation slightly rigid, and her feelings, her sensuality, and her female seductive powers downplayed in favor of a more rationalistic and politically committed attitude. She is definitely beautiful, but she comes through as untouchable, as if alien, from another world (order). The aesthetic and intellectual purpose of her hybrid performance is to demonstrate how and why the acting of socialist cinema should depart from realism. The other actors (with Jochen in the lead) perform, more or less skillfully, in accordance with established conventions of realistic cinematic acting of their time, most of them conventions that were in place during both the Weimar and the Nazi eras.[29] In contrast, with every part Agnes performs in the film, Merin's visual appearance, demeanor, and verbal articulation transgress into a postnaturalistic style.

Merin's interpretation suggests that the role of art is not to describe the everyday present, but to produce models that will help the process of changing it. From this perspective, her acting aims to be affirmative, to create visions of the future, and to continue the project of education through art as envisioned by interwar cultural socialism. *Story of a Young Couple* is committed to demonstrating that affirmation and political emancipation through cinema are no longer an unrealizable project, but have become its very role in the New Order. But in the tradition of the avant-garde, Merin's acting also performs a denaturalizing function, upsetting (derealizing) bourgeois conventions of representation. Merin's "implausible acting," misunderstood by critics of her own time and subsequently as well (maybe because there was an erotic connection between her and Maetzig), is also designed to gesture toward the fact that characters (and reality) are, like Agnes, *made*.[30] Monumental acting is expected to draw attention not only to the values of the New Order, but also to the staged character of theatrical and cinematic performances, and to call into question established conventions of reception.

Merin's noticeably disingenuous performance demands a different process of audience identification than the traditional ones, which assume the transparency of the medium. Her character does not hide its different ontological status. Since it feels alien to the world of the spectator, it calls for a conscious, self-imposed identification, against one's natural aesthetic drive towards the believable. If representation is discursively produced, its understanding must also include mediation. Socialist cinema-going is not only entertainment, but also learning and an emancipating experience. In order to accept Agnes as a meaningful character, the audience needs to question its own taste, overrule inherited aesthetic expectations, and accept that a reaction like Jochen's "No one speaks like that!" is related to a certain ideological context. The reality referred to in representation—the way one speaks—and what is believable or not are themselves constructed, very often by art (and cinema) itself. Thus they are not descriptive, but normative, and their normative function is the perpetuation of a bourgeois worldview.

Socialist cinema aims to counter the normative function of inherited aesthetic expectations and their production of the believable and the natural. Socialist political discourse aims to do the same. The poetics of socialist art throw thus light on mechanisms of political identification with the New Order. A similar denaturalizing challenge faces, at the political level, the postwar subjects. In the same way, they have to accept the unfamiliar nature of Agnes's demeanor, the subjects of socialism have to coax themselves into getting in tune with the New Order. Revolutionizing one's worldview, especially in the context of departing from fascism, presupposes casting a defamiliarizing glance at established political values and practices—to the extent of refuting "plausibilities" and "common sense." What is important to mention here—something that questions Arendt's reflections on totalitarianism—is that, as hinted at in *Story of a Young Couple*, this inner dialectic is not induced via brainwashing, propaganda, or force. *Story of a Young Couple* presents this call to open towards the unfamiliar as similar to a Kierkegaardian leap of faith. This leap of faith and this identification with an implausible otherness are, in the communist political imaginary of the times, preconditions of revolution. A New Order cannot be developed as result of a gradual rational transition from one "way of speaking" and acting to another. Radical change, both individual and collective (revolution), can take place only as a result of a dialectical process, like the one mentioned above. It involves, on the one hand, defamiliarization and disidentification from naturalized habits, and, on the other, a reidentification with the unfamiliar new. Once this radical new is internalized and performed or imitated, its otherness transforms the subject's perspective on his- or herself and the political and becomes the motor of the New Order. This is *Story of a Young Couple*'s (and socialism's) view of persuasion.

Maetzig's Poetics

By documenting the exposure of its protagonist to various directorial styles, Maetzig aims to articulate his own vision on socialist "making" of characters and subjects. *Story of a Young Couple* includes hints that contextualize his poetics, which are completed by his declarations and recollections. The latter need, however, to be taken with a grain of salt. Some belong to a young director who still struggles to understand the political dimension of his work, so they represent mainly a process of working through the aesthetic challenges of the era. At the same time, his declarations are made in times of radical and radicalist cultural policies, when an inappropriate statement could cost filmmakers their careers.[31] Consequently, Maetzig's reflections on filmmaking negotiate between what he wanted to say and what he could say. Moreover, such statements might have been rendered even more ambiguous or conformist because they were made in a period in which the cultural policies of the GDR itself were uncertain. The country's leadership was unable to express a coherent perspective on progressive art, one that would overcome, at the same time, bourgeois naturalism, remainders of Nazi entertainment, and auteurist and "formalist" temptations.[32]

For all these reasons, Maetzig ciphers his interest in experimenting with acting styles. In order to encode his position on realism, he chooses "Sailer" as Agnes's last name. "Sailer" is an anagram of the Latin *realis*, and suggests that the film and her acting aim to put a twist on realism. In order to individualize his poetics, Maetzig makes several allusions to various artistic venues and real-life artists of the time. He also hints at the complex and sometimes heated debates on art and its social function taking place under the radar in the GDR. For example, his casting of the actor-director Martin Hellberg as Moebius (see note 10) suggests Maetzig's intention to differentiate his directorial vision from the tradition of the classical theater. The fact that Carla, the "fallen" woman in the film, is played by the only performer among the cast of *Story of a Young Couple* who had a career during the Nazi era, Hilde Sessak, also expresses a stylistic intention.[33] But the most pregnant allusion *Story of a Young Couple* makes—and the boldest—is that of choosing "Meyerhold" as the last name of Agnes's deceased mother.

The reference is to one of the most influential theater innovators of the twentieth century, Vsevolod Meyerhold, who was killed during the war, not by Allied bombs but by firing squad.[34] Maetzig aims to link his directorial experimentation and socialist art's poetics to the leftist interwar avant-garde of both the Soviet Union and Germany. Before he became a theater innovator, Meyerhold was a famous actor and, influenced by Georg Fuchs,[35] aimed at crafting a new way of theatrical artistic representation. Moreover, he was of German origin, but a German who, at the age of nineteen, rejected his ethnicity and joined the Soviet revolution (Williams 1977, 87). In the interwar era, Meyerhold became the champion of antinaturalist theater and the theorizer of the biomechanic acting technique. He believed that the actor's central expressive means was the body, whose perfected motor functions could inspire the spectator's feelings and emotions (Kiebuzinska 1996, 521). Meyerhold also developed the concept of theatricality: "the audience never for a moment forgets that [it faces] actors acting, nor the actors that they have before them an audience, beneath their feet a stage and on each side a set" (Hoover 1965, 237).

The boldness of having Agnes referred to early in the film as "the daughter of Meyerhold" is caused by the taboo in the early 1950s on uttering Meyerhold's name. His rehabilitation began only in 1956. But the reference to Meyerhold and Agnes's twisting of the "realis" becomes even more revealing when we remember that, as an actor, Meyerhold worked himself out of the realist tradition. The transparency of representation, the blurring of the fact that actors act and spectators watch, was one of the main conventions of bourgeois theater. The biomechanic technique he developed, based on the principle that one learns by imitation, and lets the exterior condition the interior, was also directed against realism and transparency in acting. It challenged especially the acting technique theorized and perfected by another innovator of the theater, Konstantin Stanislavsky, whose method, as practiced by the Moscow Art Theater, was the only one that benefited from full acceptance in the Soviet Union after avant-gardists like Meyerhold were marginalized (and even murdered). Stanislavsky's acting tenets prioritized intense emotions and identification between actor and character, on the one hand, and between audience and protagonists on the other. A good Stanislavskian interpretation required exploration of psychological depths, which, in his view, determined corporeal signifiers. His approach constructed the psychological interiority that a good performance was able to link with the exterior.[36]

In the context of materialist thinking, Stanislavskian method becomes problematic because what it calls "the interior" transcends material determination and looks uncannily like the concept of the bourgeois soul. At the same time, in a revolutionary context such as that in which *Story of a Young Couple* develops, the interior seems also to overlap with the internalized, with the effects of hegemonic discourse on the subject—in other words, with exactly what needs to be defamiliarized by revolutionary dialectics. As "Meyerhold's daughter," Agnes is expected to be built and persuaded differently. Dulz's way of teaching Agnes how to act emphasizes it, especially if compared to the more Stanislavskian approaches of Moebius and Burmeister. Taking Agnes to the Stalinallee construction site and letting her learn from the effort of the workers is Dulz's tribute to biomechanics. He places the body and its movement before the psyche and ignores the depths of the bourgeois self. He refrains from telling Agnes what to feel or think, and lets her "interior" be transformed by imitating the "exterior" choreography of the working body.

With regard to theatricality, and Agnes's denaturalizing and self-reflexive acting, Maetzig's memoirs invoke the name of another innovator of the theater: Bertolt Brecht.[37] Brecht was the most unofficially esteemed German director of the 1950s; he had just returned to the GDR from exile, and his theories of the epic theater and alienation were strongly influenced by Meyerhold's (Hoover 1965, 235). Maetzig recalls that his encounter with Brecht took place in a period when he was struggling to understand the politics of socialist art.[38] Before meeting Brecht, he argued in an interview that content was more important than form in spreading socialist messages and education through art.[39] But by the time he was making *Story of a Young Couple,* his ideas were already changing, and the plot of the film and its emphasis on how messages should be delivered contradict his earlier statements.

Maetzig declares, post-factum, that he admired Brecht, in particular for the latter's project of defascization of the German theater and his ability to manage the emotions of a performance.[40] Brecht was invited to see a rerun of Maetzig's successful *Marriage in the Shadows* (on a special showing arranged by DEFA) soon after his return from exile. Maetzig recalls that Brecht saw it and disliked it. One wishes one had more details as to why Brecht disliked it. Maetzig speculates that it was the melodramatic Ufa pathos still present in his film that set Brecht off. Brecht's pronouncement was unequivocal: "Was für ein schrecklicher Kitsch!" (What terrible kitsch!) But Brecht seemed to know what Maetzig and socialist art needed in order to improve their message and liberate themselves from the traps of bourgeois art (and maybe also from the Ufa remnants). He sent Maetzig his recently published *Organon for the Theater* (which briefly presents his theories on the epic theater). Maetzig might find in this short book the advice he needed; that is, how to construct a noncathartic plot, and how to avoid bourgeois naturalist acting via *Verfremdung* (alienation or defamiliarization).[41]

Maetzig called Brecht's critique a "very productive impulse" and admitted that "irony and distantiation" were useful aesthetic devices to undermine commercial cinematic tropes (Maetzig and Agde 1987, 37).[42] Meyerhold's concept of theatricality and Brecht's of *Verfremdung* are also recognizable, though in a transformed way, in Yvonne Merin's denaturalizing monumentalism. While it is self-reflexive and dialogic in its relationship with the spectator in a different way than the epic theater or the biomechanical (mostly comical) theater of Meyerhold, it grows on the same intellectual scaffold, of the estrangement of theater from life. Monumentalism, the statuary posterlike attitude of Agnes and the pathos of her expression, is not expected to trigger awe or deceive the audience. It is meant to produce *Verfremdung* as well. It suggests that a character does not exist in the present, in the real world. Agnes looks and sounds fake and has no psychological depth because she comes from another ontological milieu.[43] She has descended from the future, from a (still) strange world in which humans have liberated themselves from self-exploitation.

* * *

If one does not regard *Story of a Young Couple* as a socialist political film, it falls in the category of films with a rags-to-riches plot. Agnes emerges from the rubble of obliterated Dresden and ends up reciting patriotic poems in front of enthusiastic masses on shiny, state-of-the-art buildings on the Stalinallee. Initially lonely and insecure, she grows into an esteemed and self-confident woman in a modern marriage. The first scenes show her homeless in a hostile and deceiving world. The final ones present her completely integrated and being offered a key to an apartment in the neighborhood she helped build. The socialist twist on the rags-to-riches story is that its protagonist's success is not individual. Socialism grows communities, not individuals. It is not only Agnes's quality of life that surges, but also that of the whole society around her. The rapid and collective development of her world reflects the way in which socialism in Eastern Europe liked to represent itself: as an accelerated process of modernization, radically transforming landscapes (rural to urban, rubble to new buildings), social and economic relations, and of course, consciousness.

When, at the end of the film, Agnes is offered an apartment, she receives it in the company of two other symbolic figures of the reconstruction era. Next to her stand the Stakhanovite bricklayer, whose production record performance and destiny will be scrutinized in Andrzej Wajda's *Man of Marble*. Her second companion is a *Trümmerfrau*, a rubble woman, herself a key figure of East German postwar proletarian consciousness. The question is, what makes Agnes stand out in this company, besides her merits as performer and those of being the protagonist of the film? The answer that this chapter has given is that she stands out because her story is representative of how radical Soviet-style communism understood subject production. When the final credits roll, she is no longer an orphan, because the lack with which she entered the narrative has been compensated for; her missing family relations have been replaced by superior social ones.

Agnes's successful socialization story is expected to reinforce theories of revolutionary child-rearing. True communist subjects, Soviet theorists argued, were not raised within the nuclear family, which was either too busy with building socialism or suspected of preserving reactionary values or social relations. "Not the family of the past, petty and narrow, with its quarrels between parents, will *mould* for us the man of the society of tomorrow," Alexandra Kollontai wrote. "Our new man, in our new society, is to be moulded by socialist organizations . . . Intelligent educators will make of him a communist who is conscious of the greatness of this sacred motto: solidarity, comradeship, mutual aid, devotion to collective life" (2000, 65; my emphasis).

Agnes convincingly embodies the values highlighted by Kollontai. In addition, she personifies the new woman Kollontai was envisioning: not only one that is strong, independent, socially and politically active, and a professional and political equal of men, but also a well-groomed and beautiful woman, a model for the new type of female beauty, proletarian style. But what is most revealing in the quote above is that these human values are imagined as the result of a productive process. "To mold" is the key verb here. It brings to the fore how deeply rooted in modernity socialism's understanding of the subject was. Agnes stands next to the Stakhanovite worker and the *Trümmerfrau* because she is a success story of the socialist productionist worldview. She is rewarded for proving so "moldable."

This is why the orphan becomes a key figure of the radical reconstruction era *Story of a Young Couple* presents and represents. Socialist social engineering, and, more generally, the social engineering of the modern world, needed moldable raw material, creatures whose transformation would not be hindered by biographical baggage or psychological inertia. As creatures without a past, without a family, without strong loyalties to counter-socialist discourses—that is, linked to nothing that could generate resistance to the New Order's plan to produce the "new man"—orphans become symbols of life infinitely transformable through symbolic and political praxis. Being or becoming orphan—if not by fate, then by leap of faith—seemed almost the prerequisite to becoming revolutionary ("moldable"). What is specific and thought-provoking about *Story of a Young Couple* is that its vision of "molding" is more liberal than one would expect from a pro-Soviet propaganda film. One also molds oneself. One learns and transforms oneself by imitating and performing this imitation. In addition, nowhere in the film is it specified that the imitation has to be *identical* to the model. The workers on the Stalinallee or Father Dulz just inspire. The faithfulness of *Story of a Young Couple* to dialectical materialism comes here to the fore, as does the inclusion of difference in its view of the New Order.

3 The Testifying Orphan

Rethinking Modernity's Optimism

Times of Contestation

Dita Saxová, a 1968 Czechoslovak film directed by Antonín Moskalyk, thematizes the destiny of the Holocaust orphan. The film shows how radical socialist subject production and its demand for total commitment and affirmation faces a major challenge: the reactive (or divergent) manifestations triggered by uncontrollable dimensions of the human psyche, the unconscious. Unlike the films analyzed in the previous chapters, *Dita Saxová* does not tell an optimistic story about political or personal opportunities in the early postwar era. Its orphan protagonist questions any form of enthusiasm about civilization from the perspective of her camp experience, and with a vivid memory of the fact that the Third Reich had also aimed to radically change the world. Her story is one of melancholia: the film presents her inability to blend in with normal life and the reconstruction discourse.

Dita Saxová is a visual document of the 1960s, produced in times of contestation. When the film started production, Soviet-style socialism in Eastern Europe had already accumulated twenty years of political experience, not all of it positive. It had already gone through a few phases, during which questions had been raised, mistakes acknowledged, rethinking articulated, and some reshuffling of political elites enforced. The most important year in the transformation of political discourse in Eastern Europe had been 1956. Three years after the death of Stalin, the leadership of the Communist Party of the Soviet Union officially denounced the former Soviet leader's policies. Socialism's self-critical gesture triggered a variety of reactions in Eastern Europe in the following five years and seemed to signal changes in the discourse on Eastern European socialist development. Some party leaders fell, and even vocal contestations of the Soviet Union's hegemony in the region were articulated. The most radical attempt to transform socialism took place the same year in Hungary: the Hungarian Revolution of

1956. But the affirmation of a national (Hungarian) road to socialism showed the limits of how much a Soviet-style regime could rethink itself and refurbish its political actions. Soviet tanks rolled into Budapest in the fall of that year, sending a message of caution to the entire Eastern European bloc, which limited the scope of attempts to move away from the Moscow model.

Dita Saxová premiered in 1968, in a year whose resonance for the history of Eastern European socialism equals that of 1956.[1] This year of European (and global) unrest finds its most dramatic Eastern European expression in Czechoslovakia. The effort to reform Soviet-style socialism that takes place here bears the name "the Prague Spring," and is associated with the Action Program of Alexander Dubček, the newly installed communist leader, which called for political and economic decentralization and increased national independence from Moscow. It is also associated with the phrase "socialism with a human face," which meant the abandonment of the Leninist concept of the dictatorship of the proletariat, deradicalization of subject production (the deconstruction of the post-human discussed in the previous chapter), and socialism's absorption of some "humane" or "humanist" values from Western liberal democracy and its emphasis on the freely deciding individual, immune to political manipulation.

Even if the Prague Spring, like the Hungarian Revolution of 1956, lasted only a few months, its influence on Eastern European socialism was more than palpable. On the one hand, it triggered another military reaction—this time not only from the Soviet Union, but also from a coalition of Warsaw Pact states of the socialist bloc, including Bulgaria, East Germany, Hungary, and Poland (the exceptions were Romania and Albania). Their armies invaded Czechoslovakia on 20 August 1968, and soon afterwards the Brezhnev Doctrine of limited tolerance of independent roads to socialism was formulated.[2] On the other hand, it spurred the articulation of various appeals to "humanizing" socialism and reformism all over Eastern Europe, with Poland in the lead (a topic discussed in the next chapter). Most importantly, as Tony Judt emphasizes, 1968 marked an important turning point in the history of socialism,

> even more than the Hungarian tragedy of 1956. The illusion that Communism was reformable, that Stalinism had been a wrong turning, a mistake that could still be corrected, that the core ideals of democratic pluralism might somehow still be compatible with the structures of Marxist collectivism: that illusion was crushed under the tanks on August 21st 1968 and it never recovered. (2005, 447)

For Judt, the Prague Spring was not a beginning but an end, marking an irreparable cleft between the state and its citizens, after which a climate of distrust and outright pessimism would set in. The party was no longer seen as a carrier of progressive social change. What it triggered was an era of more or less passive resistance. "Communism in Eastern Europe staggered on, sustained by an unlikely alliance of foreign loans and Russian bayonets: the rotting carcass was finally carried away only in 1989. But the soul of Communism had died twenty years before: in Prague, in August 1968" (447).

The Prague Spring was preceded and accompanied by a period of intense and creative intellectual and artistic activity, of which Moskalyk's film is part. The Czechoslovak 1960s were times of effervescent intellectual artistic activity, spurred also by the relaxing and even abolition of censorship in 1968. In the 1960s, writers and intellectuals such as Vaclav Havel and Milan Kundera become active alongside a remarkable generation of filmmakers, known as the Czechoslovak New Wave, which included directors such as Milos Forman, Jiří Menzel, Věra Chytilová, Jan Němec, Juraj Jakubisko, and Ján Kadár. Many of the films made in this period were not the most politically correct; some of them, like Menzel's *Larks on a String* (about the Czechoslovak gulag) and Forman's *The Firemen's Ball* (an ironic parable of the gerontocracy plaguing the Communist Party), were banned forever after August 1968.

The Reactive Subject

Dita Saxová was among these uncomfortable films of 1968. Its sin was its eponymous protagonist, a reactive subject. Her story was "unsocialist" in the sense that it presented her as not able to restart her life immediately after the war even with the best of all possible worlds visible on the horizon. While Balázs and Radványi, on the one hand, and Maetzig on the other designed muscular fables of successful institutionalization of the war's orphans, Moskalyk opted for the opposite. His plot deconstructs. It uses the memory of Auschwitz in order to call into question the way in which the twentieth century envisions individual and collective narratives of self-realization. Its orphan, Dita, emerges from the war psychologically and existentially crippled and cannot overcome her handicap. Her social integration cannot heal the wounds of the past. She can no longer march along or invest herself in reconstruction projects. She has become melancholic and self-destructively hedonistic.

Dita Saxová documents a dis-integration that uncannily anticipates the fate of socialism. It investigates the falling apart of a life, of an individual destiny, of hope, of community, but also, in terms of style and in relation to Auschwitz, of cinematic narration and representation itself. Moreover, the film addresses the problematic way in which the postwar world regards women. Beyond the typical cinematic feminization of the Holocaust victim (Kerner 2011, 4), it questions ingrained perceptions of corporeal beauty, erotic desire, companionship, romantic love, charity, and humanism, and gestures toward the barbaric undercurrents that inform them in the modern world. Conundrums of human community addressed by the writings of the German-Jewish philosopher Theodor Adorno are the main themes of the film. How can one conceive of civilization, love, beauty, and poetry after the invention of the death camp?

Played by the Polish actress Krystyna Mikołajewska, Dita has survived Terezin and Auschwitz, where her family perished. After liberation, she lives in a Prague that seems untouched by war. She is in the care of the Jewish community, which, by postwar standards, offers her living conditions that, as one character remarks early in the film, can stir the envy of the average war survivor. She receives room and board, education, medical care, and support to reintegrate socially. Finding a place and a role for herself in life and rediscovering its meaning are the challenges facing her, because not long before she has lived only to survive. As the film begins, Dita, in her last year of high school, celebrates her eighteenth birthday. After graduation, she is expected to leave the shelter—this transitory place between camp and society—and start a "normal life," as her tutors put it.

The film is built of a series of episodes that present Dita's investigation of the life designated as normal outside the institution that has supervised her physical and social recovery. She spends most of her time in what seems to be an upper-class hedonistic companionship and has erotic adventures. As the film advances, Dita's roommates leave the orphanage, most of them via marriage. Dita herself makes a final try to find meaning in life by working for a charity service in Switzerland. But she cannot overcome her melancholia. Nothing in her post-camp existence attracts her. After attending a party in an exclusive villa somewhere in the Swiss Alps, a year after reaching maturity, Dita commits suicide, a gesture not uncommon among Holocaust survivors of various ages and at various points in their post-camp existence.

Dita Saxová is an adaptation of the 1962 eponymous novel by the most influential Holocaust survivor and author of pre-1968 Czechoslovakia, Arnošt Lustig (1926–2011).[3] Lustig's fiction, which also includes *Night and Hope* (1958) and *Prayer for Katerina Horowitzowa* (1964), was the basis of some of the best Holocaust films, all produced during the 1960s, as part of the Czechoslovak New Wave. *Night and Hope* became *Transport from Paradise*, Zbynek Brynych's 1963 brilliant cinematic reflection on the banality of evil. The short story "Darkness Has No Shadows" inspired Jan Němec's haunting, surreal account of two young men's attempt to escape a death camp transport (*Diamonds of the Night*, 1964). Lustig participated actively in the writing of the screenplays of all these films, including *Dita Saxová*.

Eros and Beauty after Auschwitz

Most of the episodes that make up *Dita Saxová* depict the protagonist's encounters with men. Historical evidence shows that marriage and motherhood were the widespread version of post-institutional life for young female Holocaust survivors, enabling them to overcome or escape their predicament of "displaced persons," as homeless survivors were euphemistically called in those days. By the spring of 1946, every third institutionalized woman survivor was either pregnant or had already given birth (Baumel 1999, 236). Marriage was often combined with a migration project to one of the staple destinations for survivors of that time, the United States, Israel, or Latin America.

Dita enters the marriage market too. She is a hot commodity. Her "statuesque beauty,"[4] as one contemporary reviewer puts it, and her mysterious Levantine appearance, reminiscent of Elizabeth Taylor's Cleopatra,[5] attract desiring looks from men of all ages and social standings, Jewish and gentile. But in spite of her charms, her relationships fail to lead to a happy ending in matrimony. From this perspective, the film seems to be built of a series of interrupted melodramatic plots. None becomes the central storyline. In the traumatized psychosocial landscape of postwar Europe, enthusiastic investment of desire, a vital element of melodramatic plot propulsion, suffers syncopations or, even worse, outright perversion. Adorno's pronouncement, articulated in 1949,[6] almost at the same time in which *Dita Saxová*'s plot is set, that it is unacceptable to articulate affect in lyrical registers in the wake of Auschwitz leaves its mark on the narrative rendering of the film. Dita's uncanny encounters with men make the statement that, affected by trauma and marked by lack of trust in civilization, war survivors engage in perverted attempts at bonding that can only mimic human comradeship and love. As love and desire for community are no longer the driving forces that bring people together, their encounters slide into frivolous and sometimes tormenting power games. Consequently, even if there is material wealth and security in Dita's post-Auschwitz world, interior substance is missing or has been damaged. There is social interaction, often intense, but superficial. Cynicism and self-delusion prevail. Beauty is objectified; tenderness serves at best as therapy, and empathy becomes a move in the sport of seduction.[7]

Moskalyk's film uses the perspective of the survivor to dialogue with postwar cinematic narratives of hope and social mobilization, such as the *Aufbaupathos* in *Story of a Young Couple*. His questioning is not grounded primarily in the assumption that trauma cannot be overcome and that, as an absolute trace of the Event, it exerts a damaging influence on modern narratives of community and reconstruction (though the importance of this assumption should not be downplayed).[8] The fact that the film is set before the imposition of the Soviet-style regime in Czechoslovakia helps generalize its commentary on modern civilization. Its criticism aims not only at communism, but also at Eastern Europe's modern postwar development and its way of dealing with its subject. Like *Somewhere in Europe*, it views communism in a broader context of which Soviet-style power is only a facet.[9]

The criticism of the modern productionist envisioning of the subject is best expressed in the most detailed and most explicit of Dita's erotic episodes. The film shows her spending a day with one of her suitors, David Egon, in a luxury hotel in the countryside. The erotic ritual unfolds slowly and hesitatingly in a room that is alienatingly empty and cold. Dita expects David to seduce her. David, a bon vivant who does not ask many questions, gladly accepts the task, gently easing Dita's indecisions with tender embraces and encouraging words. She reacts to David's touches with both pleasure and pain and tells him that their intimacy makes her both happy and sad. Her gaze turns yearningly toward her partner and then pensively away. Erotic pleasure is difficult to achieve because, as Dita admits, she cannot get used to tenderness—neither as a physical experience nor as an idea.

Glimmers of her horrendous past experiences intrude into the present of her erotic game and turn Dita into a discomforted and discomforting lover. Lately, the men who have seen her naked were camp kapos or SS officers. Stripping clothes off was the last thing millions of men and women did before their murder in gas chambers cloaked as showers. When Egon looks at her, Dita feels the overlap of his gaze with that of the camp guards. From this perspective, her sensibility resonates with the way in which Michael Rothberg imagines Walter Benjamin's messianic historian in the post-Holocaust context. Dita seems to set up her *Jetztzeit* (her here-and-now) in such a way as to dialogue (constellate) with the past, thus allowing the latter "to blast open the continuum of history" (Benjamin as quoted in Rothberg 2000, 11), haunt the present and reveal its reifying effects.[10]

Dita's relationship to her body and her perception of others' perception of it are altered by her resurfacing concentration camp memories. She has internalized the Nazi perpetrators' gaze and its crushing power over its victims. In the *Jetztzeit* of the hotel room, this returning gaze disrupts and resignifies the continuum of the erotic relation and the emotional investment that sets the groundwork for both an emotional healing of a victim and the development of a cinematic melodrama. Can her abject body be truly beautiful and desirable? In the camp, the perpetrator's gaze regarded it as racially inferior, parasitic, and dispensable. The camp starved, diseased, overworked, maybe even forced it into prostitution. It reduced it to the depth of bare life, and turned it into the carrier of the message to the outer world that in the camp "it is possible to lose dignity and decency beyond imagination" (Agamben 1999, 69).

In the last paragraph of his camp memoirs, Elie Wiesel recounts this act of seeing himself through the eyes of the perpetrator—the misrecognition of his body as a camp body. He recounts his standing in front of a mirror for the first time after liberation: "I had not seen myself since the ghetto. From the depths of the mirror, a corpse was contemplating me. The look in his eyes as he gazed at me has never left me" (2006, 115). Dita undergoes the same experience. Two years after liberation, declared healthy by her doctors, socially apt by her teachers, beautiful by her suitors, charming and full of wisdom by her friends, she still envisions herself as a living corpse. Her camp body is indelibly associated with her postwar destiny, as is the Auschwitz number tattooed on her arm. She keeps noticing the Muselmann[11] in her, which represents, as Agamben reveals in his readings of Primo Levi's *Survival in Auschwitz*, the experience of reaching not only the threshold between life and death, but also the limit of what it means to be human and dignified (1999, 69).

Dita's camp experience opens, from a different angle, the discussion on humanism started by radical socialist subject production (discussed in chapter 2). When undressing in front of David, as life that wants to live itself and as a desiring subject, Dita struggles to perceive an image of herself different than the Auschwitz-produced living corpse. For a moment, it seems, she succeeds. She manages to chase away the gaze of the Nazi perpetrator constructing her body. After the sexual act is consummated and the atmosphere in the room relaxes, a less-inhibited Dita exposes her naked body to David's eyes and even giggles when she confesses that their hours of lovemaking have been some of those rare moments of happiness when life feels worth living. Like intoxication, her immersion in corporeal pleasure has made her forget the gaze that constructs her as abjection. This is why she looks for intense experiences: they can temporarily relieve her from her demons.

Once the excitement is over, however, the past returns. Even if she seems more cheerful after lovemaking, dark reminiscences soon regain their grip on her. They return, however, as moments not only of despair or melancholy, but also of irony. As she lies naked in front of David, she asks him jokingly whether he thinks she is "well shaped." David, ignorant of the subtext of the question, or pretending to be so, reacts with a baffled gaze: What does she mean? Dita urges him to answer without offering further details. Slightly discomforted by her insistence, maybe psychologizing about her motives—that is, reading her question as an expression of the bodily insecurity of an undressed young woman—he replies reassuringly: "Of course you are." For him, she is the object of an erotic gaze. Nothing more. He refuses to see the other Dita, the corpse, the Muselmann in her, confirming Aldo Capri's pronouncement that the Muselmann is that object or creature from which everybody looks away (Agamben 1999, 52).

Another exchange between Dita and David reinforces that he cannot or is unwilling to notice the other gaze constructing her body. He is intrigued that Dita has taken off all her clothes but has kept a wide golden bracelet on her left wrist. Earlier, the film shows Dita buying it in order to cover her Auschwitz number. Other characters in other contexts also inquire about the bracelet, with the same ignorance—some, such as the shelter's headmaster, Professor Munk, consider it a sign of vainglory. While she is disappointed with Munk's ignorance, Dita seems almost amused with David's. She replies flirtatiously that she has kept it on so that he cannot say she stood totally naked in front of him.[12]

Lustig's novel and Moskalyk's casting construct Dita as an outstandingly beautiful woman. Even if they disagreed on what this beauty should look like,

Figure 3.1. "Am I well shaped?" (*Dita Saxová*).

they both aimed to load it with irony. Yet most of the people who wrote about the film did not notice it, and involuntarily adopted the position of Dita's suitors. Almost all characters in the film and critics from Czechoslovakia of 1968, from today's English-speaking world, and film historians start their description of Dita with a reference to her beauty and without acknowledging that the film frames it in a "paradigm of extermination" (Agamben 1999, 52). They qualify this beauty in various ways. They sometimes exoticize it by emphasizing its "oriental" undertones or mix admiration with pity, but they never become self-reflexive and ask how the abjection of the camp has changed aesthetic discourse.

This extermination paradigm engenders such change. It also opposes and calls into question productionist narratives of modernity, which argue that everything can be transformed. Consequently, dysfunctions can be fixed, damaged parts replaced, abjections and ugliness erased. In the company of men, Dita feels scrutinized by admiring gazes, which means the orphanage has done the job of restoring her to attractiveness. One can theorize that the appearance she has been brought back to is beautiful ("well shaped") because, in a Platonic understanding of beauty, her appearance harks back to an ideal of attractiveness that is appealing to everyone. But Dita's rejection of this admiring gaze, and of all the compliments and proposals she receives, suggests that there is something problematic with such a construction of her as a beautiful woman and of beauty in general.

The problem lies with an aesthetics predicated on conformity, conformity to a norm or idea, and the universalizing claim of aesthetic judgment. In a post-Holocaust context, more exactly, in a context in which modern man has produced the Muselmann, Agamben points out, any ethical discourse—and, I would add, any *aesthetic* one—that is predicated on conformity or adherence to a standard grows suspect of being a carrier of barbarism:

> Auschwitz marks the end and the ruin of every ethics of dignity and confor-
> mity to a norm. The bare life to which human beings were reduced neither
> demands nor conforms to anything. It itself is the only norm; it is absolutely
> immanent. (1999, 69)

Translating Agamben's reflections into the realm of aesthetics reveals that perceiving the beautiful in relation to a norm or an idea becomes problematic because it triggers memories of what in camp jargon was known as *Selektion*. Both
Primo Levi's and Elie Wiesel's testimonies show that the ruling performed by the
Nazi doctor during the *Selektion*—by which he declares an inmate well shaped
enough to live—is uncannily similar in its process of articulation to that of an
aesthetic judgment on the beauty of a body. Only the destination or the use given
to the body after the judgment differs.

The Nazi doctor's pronouncement on the looks of an inmate's body haunts
the act of articulating an aesthetic *Urteil* (judgment) and comments on the social skill of *Urteilskraft* (faculty of judgment). In the context of the camp, *Urteil*
becomes literally an *Ur-teil*; that is, a separation (*teilen*), such as the one that
decided that Dita would live and her mother perish in the gas chamber. The Nazi
doctor rules over the *teilen* of the drowned from the saved (to paraphrase the
title of Primo Levi' last book). The irony invested in Dita's beauty is exactly to
connect the everyday practices of *teilen* (aesthetic and functional) with the selection of the well-shaped body that took place in the camp. Its purpose is to show
not so much that Auschwitz survives after its liberation as a chronic infection of
civilization, but that various human practices, even noble aesthetic ones, the ones
that build civilization, can be reduced to the logic of the camp, the ultimate form
of barbarism.[13]

The judgments Dita's suitors make on her beauty bear such reifying undertones. Her well-shaped looks become her "value" on the erotic market, indicating
her potential for being exploited as an object of desire (and not of hard labor). Her
behavior suggests she assumes there is a connection between beauty, commodifi-
cation, capitalism, and the camp. Her suitors' assessment is reminiscent not only
of the social Darwinism that informs the modern capitalist world, but also of the
way in which the gaze of the Nazi doctor constructs the meaning of life in the
camp. One lives and competes with other inmates for scoring well (better than
others) during the *Selektion*. The *Urteil* of the Nazi doctor not only decides who is
sent to death and who is given a temporary chance to survive, but also separates
the usable Jews (the so-called working Jews [*Arbeitsjuden*]) from the unusable
ones. Survival is thus linked to making oneself useful. It articulates the uncanny
suggestion that the central point of reference of a world constructed on competi-

tion, such as capitalism, can be inhabited by the Nazi doctor. Dita's socialization also assumes that she can make herself useful by marrying. Since she is not able to, she will perish. Wait for a spouse, marry, or die are the only three options the female characters in the film have.

The Testimony and Its Public

Dita's discomfort with some of the core rituals of private and social life in modern secular society—such as making love, socialization, and marriage—puts her in a position to comment on the values on which the modern community is built. In other words, as a Holocaust orphan she bears a testimony for those who have not gone through her experiences, both in private and public life. More than her personal loss and her awareness of the way in which the camp experience haunts the reconstruction process of the postwar world, what troubles Dita is that her contemporaries are not interested in her insights. They care for her suffering, they want to heal her body and reintegrate it socially, but they refuse to listen to her, and its, testimony, to what the camp can teach those who have been spared its experiences. This is the way David has treated her in the hotel room: with caution, as a traumatized subject, but also using her suffering as an excuse not to take seriously into consideration what she has to say.[14]

Moskalyk's film constructs a different (Eastern) Europe than Balázs and Radványi's. While the Europe of *Somewhere in Europe* invites the victims of war to assume a leading position in the reconstruction process, the former's is a continent defending itself from its ghosts. Pogroms against returning Jews—perhaps the most explicit form of rejection of the testimony—took place in Poland, but even a country with no considerable anti-Semitic background such as Czechoslovakia marginalized its returning concentration camp survivors.[15] This marginalization consisted of a series of practices that deradicalized and diminished the ethical and political relevance of their experiences and their message. More important issues were put on the agenda of the administration of collective memory. Self-victimization of the gentile population as war victims served to blur the horror of the camp experience, while postwar nationalism bolstered the heroism and sacrifice of men and women on the front lines, implicitly downplaying the suffering of those persecuted on racial grounds (Lagrou 2005, 16, 22).[16]

The shelters and displaced persons' camps hosting Holocaust survivors also gained such a deradicalizing role. Though aimed at reintegrating survivors socially, they also had the marginalizing effect of displacing the voices of the survivors from the testifying mainstream and interpellating them as traumatized subjects. The survivors' condition was declared abnormal and in need of treatment. Camp persecution was remembered only as suffering and injustice, as an exception with no link to the present order. Survivors were institutionalized, and institutionalization framed their testimony as an individual's effort to work through his or her suffering and not as an exemplary addition to collective memory from which modern civilization could learn something.

In order to address the downplaying of the survivor's testimony, *Dita Saxová* develops an attentive critique of institutions such as the shelter. First, it emphasizes their paradoxical status. Even if they are aimed at helping Jews reintegrate socially and politically, and restore their dignity, they are in a way robbing them of it, by undermining the relevance of their testimony. In that context, the survivor's testimony remains relevant only to doctors, pedagogues, nurses, and counselors, and not to the community at large. The rendering abnormal of the survivors' testimony liberates the postwar subject from the ethical injunction to listen. Shelters, orphanages, and displaced persons' camps protect thus not only survivors from the challenges of postwar existence, but also the larger community from the survivors' truths. Healing offered in institutions functions to erase or render invisible—both symbolically and corporeally—the ghostly image of the camp body that Wiesel sees in the mirror. An uncanny cooperation comes to the fore here: if the racial discourse and policies of the Nazi state sought to render the integrated Jew visible, the role of the shelters became the reversal of this process. Their social and political function was to reassimilate: to produce the healed survivor, whose words, actions, and body would no longer bear the traces of the camp. Put differently: to clean up the Nazi crimes.

The disciplining social role of the shelter confirms Michel Foucault's thesis of the political function of hospitals and institutions of mental and social rehabilitation (2008, 34).[17] The institutional context also complicates the discussion about the survivor's beauty. Various scenes in *Dita Saxová* show how the shelter interpellates the protagonist and her mates as objects of beautification. Beautification is an effect of healing, but also a practice of erasing and forgetting the symbolic and physical violence inflicted upon the survivors' bodies. Yet in the case of women, it is even more problematic because it not only obstructs testimony, but also restores a prewar patriarchal order. The rehabilitation of the Jewish woman is made, *Dita Saxová* tells us, with an eye on the marriage market. The success story of an asylum girl is a quick engagement with a rich and elderly man.[18] One of Dita's suitors (played by the acclaimed director Jiří Menzel), has such an offer for her, which she refuses: an affluent life in El Salvador, comfortable, safe, and far away from the ones who should but refuse to hear her testimony.

Dita Saxová shows that, in the shelter, the female survivor is not prepared for full social integration, but only for her transfer from one institution (the shelter) to another (the family), where the future husband (her new doctor) will continue to monitor and manage her healing (and silencing). The social integration practiced in the shelter aims to bestow the female survivor with the values sought on the marriage market. No surprise then that Dr. Fitz, the physician monitoring the health of the young women, tells one of them that she eats too much and thus might become overweight and not desirable (beautiful) for the marital *Selektion* awaiting her. In the same vein, he assures another inmate that they, the institution, will make a Rita Hayworth of her. He has similar reassuring words for Dita.

The scene presenting Dita's health checkup suggests this double function of the shelter. The examination begins with remarks about her beauty. Dr. Fitz comments that her beauty has eclipsed to such an extent her camp body that it makes a man, even a professional like him, uncomfortable when looking at her. Their dialogue moves then to education, another significant aspect of her reintegration, which Dita neglects. As Fitz listens to her lungs and heartbeat, he talks about her school results and advises her to take life more seriously. The conversation continues by addressing her future. What will Dita do now that she is eighteen? The suggestion is clear: "Think of your beautiful figure. Why not get married?" The institution has prepared her, physically, intellectually, and aesthetically, for marital success: "One smile of yours and the whole world lies at your feet," he continues with professional pride.

Encounters between Dita and the director of the shelter, Professor Munk (the other character referred to with his title in the film), unfold in a similar fashion. He also wants Dita to marry soon. Since he is responsible for her education, he is concerned with her grades. But as chief administrator of the shelter, he is also preoccupied with her sexual activity and promiscuous behavior. They decrease Dita's value on the marriage market and question the socializing effectiveness of the institution headed by him. Munk is also aware that optimism is an important value in the melancholic postwar context. Optimism is what Europe needs, not melancholia. It eases integration and forgetting of the past. On her birthday, Munk brings Dita a record containing marching music, reminiscent of a Soviet revolutionism that Munk finds appealing. As he listens to its upbeat rhythm, he suggests that "we have to forbid hopelessness . . . even if it sounds absurd." Optimism must be a mandatory mood in the postwar world, he continues.

Irony

Dita's response to such calls to optimism is an ironic smile, similar to the one she displays when men flatter her or offer unwanted advice. Irony is thus not only the act of referring to the extermination perspective (countering uncritical optimism), but is also Dita's main weapon to fight postwar Europe's lack of interest in her testimony. Her reaction to Munk's calls to optimism recalls Adorno's diagnosis of the postwar predicament:

> After the Second World War, everything, including a resurrected culture, has been destroyed without realizing it; humankind continues to vegetate, creeping along after events that even the survivors cannot really survive, on a rubbish heap that has made even reflection on one's own damaged state useless. (1991, 244)

Irony works in two ways. First, as we saw above, it undermines and reframes the statements of Dita's interlocutors in an extermination context, revealing the superficial, reifying, or plainly barbaric undertones of their statements and the rituals of forgetting that incorporate them. The second subversive goal of irony is, as Adorno puts it above, to make the "reflection on one's own damaged state useless." Dita aims to redirect the attention of the postwar subject from her suffering to her testimony and smuggle her survivor's message into the present. She has to use this oblique rhetorical strategy because the present is either not willing to listen, or is compromised by its own complicity with the Nazi genocide:

> Family members, friends, neighbors, coworkers, students, teachers, employers, employees, religious leaders, municipal and government officials, real and imagined allies were all potential betrayers or murderers, and it is this dissolution of an entire network of human relations, not just the killing, that constitutes the Holocaust. (Kerner 2011, 7)

A scene in which the young women in the shelter sing with enthusiasm what is presented in the film as a popular song of the reconstruction era is an example of such subversive ironic reframing. The cheery chorus of the song says "We are all stars in the sky." The ironic twist given by the film is the linking of the stars to the girls' experience with anti-Semitic persecution. In an extermination context, the stars gain a different meaning. They no longer shine for a youth confidently facing the future, but hark back to the identification of Jews in ghettoes and camps.[19] As limitation, the sky no longer functions as a metaphor of optimism, but becomes the black horizon of death, which the girls have nearly escaped—an allusion reinforced by the title of the song: "Where Stars Go to Sleep."[20]

The lovemaking scene and the reference to the well-shaped body are examples of the second use of irony, to smuggle the past into the present. Another subversive insertion of testimony takes place in a dialogue Dita has with the shelter's physician, Dr. Fitz. The doctor tells her that she cannot succeed in life if she does not have "a push." When Dita throws him a puzzled look, asking what he means by "push," he tries to clarify his stale word choice: one should have a push, but one should not step, as they say, "over dead bodies." His wording turns Dita's puzzlement into irony. For her, the "dead bodies" have a referent and are not abstract use of language in a coined phrase. She reframes the doctor's words and unravels problematic aspects of everyday semantic practice, the "heaviness of language,"[21] the way in which it is inscribed with the violence of the past.[22]

Dita uses the opportunity created by the doctor's uninspired word choice to make a reference to her predicament, that is, to articulate a testimony. She not only replies with her ironic smile (reframing), but also tells Dr. Fitz that she might consider what he suggested. But in order to follow his advice she must *go over* her own body, which, inscribed with traumatic experiences, stands in her way. Dita's ironical intervention smuggles into the present a statement on her

Figure 3.2. Hieronymus Bosch's *The Last Judgment* (detail, *Dita Saxová*).

predicament: in order to make "a push" in the postwar world, which is not interested in what one stands for, the survivor has to render inconspicuous the traces of the past she bears. She will be listened to when she is integrated, when her testimony is no longer uncomfortable, that is, when she no longer has a message.

Another such assertive use of irony takes place toward the end of the film. Dita is in Switzerland, on a charity mission. Learning that she comes from Prague, two rich Swiss men who want to seduce her ask her whether she knows who Franz Kafka is. With her slow voice, Dita answers, "Like I know myself." Through irony she detours the discussion toward her predicament as witness without an audience, which she sees as Kafkesque.[23] The two men pretend not to understand her insinuation, and a few moments later, they confess that, unlike her, they had a comfortable war experience. As a proof of that, they walk her through their family art collection—parts of which, it is hinted, have been acquired during the war. As they show her the exhibits, they stop in front of what they say is the most valuable piece of the collection, an etching by Hieronymus Bosch (an image that appears in a larger painting titled *The Last Judgment*—another reference to *Selektion* and *Urteil*). The drawing presents a beast from the Inferno swallowing a human body. As Dita looks at it, she replies, similarly to the Kafka reference, "My case." This time the undertones of her remark are grimmer.

The painting harks back to what Dita calls her motto, which she has engraved on her golden bracelet. It reads, "Life is not what we wish to have, but what we have." The motto suggests that she belongs to a group of people who have not chosen their destiny. It was decided for them, as they experienced it embarked in cattle cars heading toward death camps. Dita also suggests that the grotesque predicament of the half-swallowed body mirrors her condition—a reference to both her camp body and her inability to adapt to the post-camp world. The film includes a long close-up of the etching. With its legs in the air, the half-swallowed body reflects the condition of the half-dead and not-listened-to survivor. The fact that the drawing represents the process of swallowing the victim suggests that the Holocaust is not totally over. There is one last aspect of the crime still in the making: the destruction of its memory.

This interstitial condition of the half-dead body allows Dita to identify with the victim in the etching. The upper part of the body is eaten first, which includes the mouth, the organ through which the testimony can be articulated. As in the case of the Muselmann, only the lower, vegetative part of the body remains still visible. If she is not able to testify, Dita's existence becomes as grotesque as the swaying of the victim's legs in the air. This is the Kafkaesque predicament she knows so well, the metamorphosis the Holocaust has inflicted upon her. She experiences the final episode of her post-camp, survivor's existence: the moment when irony is overtaken by despair, when there is nothing more to say. Her suicide takes place in the next scene.

Bosch's image comments, however, not only on Dita's "case," but also on a certain perceptive experience of any viewer of the drawing. Its inclusion in the film challenges the way in which art addresses its consumers. Even if grotesque and uncanny, for the two men, who are art lovers, the violence depicted in Bosch's etching seems to remain confined within the frame of the painting, as abstracted from reality as Dr. Fitz's phrase referring to dead bodies. Gentiles with a comfortable war experience don't perceive its heaviness. The etching is nothing but an aesthetic trophy. For Dita it refers to a real, existing monstrosity; for them artistic representation is not testimony. They appreciate it for its aesthetic value, and maybe, philosophically, for its commentary on the human condition, but not as a medium of memory harking back to an actual situation in the past, one that can return to the present.

The film thus articulates a criticism of art as an injunction on its consumers to appreciate form and not to remember. Beauty—this time artistic and not corporeal—seems to be employed again in the service of forgetting. Dita's perception of the etching suggests that, in the post-Auschwitz context, artistic representation needs to be perceived differently; first and foremost, as an act of memory and history. Her stance anticipates the criticism of art articulated by Berel Lang, who argues that, in an extermination context, art "typically if not invariably aspires to the condition of *history*" (2000, 74).

Disjointed Narrative

The reference to the grotesque also provides viewers with a reading of the film's narrative organization. On the one hand, it calls upon them to notice Dita's *case*, the Kafkaesque condition of the bearer of a testimony in the postwar era, and perhaps even in the 1960s. Adorno's pronouncement that, after Auschwitz art has to reject both lyricism and the temptation to infuse the unthinkable with meaning, had an intimidating effect on the 1960s art dedicated to the Holocaust.[24] The irrecoverably melancholic postwar subject Dita represents experiences itself as grotesquely disjointed by the violence inflicted upon it. Perhaps testimony could reassemble it, coax her to rediscover coherence. But testimony is not possible in Dita's world, and this dead end is reflected in the narrative articulation of the film.

Not only the whereabouts of the protagonist, but also the elliptic and disrupted enunciation of the film reflect the absurd predicament of the survivor, who has to perform as witness in front of an audience that is not interested in listening to her and that might have been an indirect accomplice of the perpetrator. The monstrosity and the incomprehensibility of the Holocaust make its ethical (and truthful) emplotment difficult (White 1992, 37). This explains the fragile, slow-paced, and episodic construction of the film. Artistic testimony aims to organize formally an event that was, at least according to prevalent functionalist (incrementalist) explanations, imagined and planned in its making (Lang 2000, 74). This is why, Lang argues, a disjointed narrative makeup, such as that of the chronicle, is more appropriate to make sense of Holocaust representation.[25]

Disjointed narrative is also ironic narrative, understood as one that thematizes its own dissolution, "the constant possibility of a disruption of narrative intelligibility at every 'point'" (Man 1996, 32). Moreover, following Adorno, irony protects, due to its complicity with meaninglessness, the work of art from the traps of phony realism and sentimentalism as both might render representation instrumental in a ritual of forgetting.[26] This explains some of Moskalyk's artistic choices, such as the film's failed melodramatic subplots, Mikołajewska's non-realist acting, and the estranging cinematography (long shots and use of telephoto lens). Moskalyk seems to follow here Adorno's warning that art as "working through the past"—meaning causality, realism, and management of emotions—removes something from the horror of the Nazi genocide, and "by this alone an injustice is done to the victims" (1992, 103).

Produced in a time when self-reflexivity in filmmaking was at its peak, and within one of the most formally conscientious moments of art cinema, the Czechoslovak New Wave, *Dita Saxová* aims to limit this injustice, and it does its best to avoid what Anton Kaes calls the "unabashed [narrative] commercial exploitation and trivialization of human suffering" (1992, 208). Even at the risk of frustrating aesthetic expectations and alienating his public, Moskalyk's aesthetic choices are at the same time ethical ones. The protagonist's enigmatic behavior, her looks, her disenchantment, the long silences in the film, including its slow pace, its disentangled storytelling, and its pretentious and sometimes conspicuously anti-naturalistic visuals, express the filmmaker's effort to narrate in a non-exploitative way and to grasp the complex effect an atrocious event such as the Holocaust produces on human relations.

Unfortunately, Moskalyk's scrupulous approach to representation did not receive the credit it deserved. *Dita Saxová* collected some polite accolades abroad, but did not enthuse its contemporary Czechoslovak critics. Reviewers from both contemporary Czechoslovakia and later times did not grasp the ethical substratum of Moskalyk's stylistic choices and did much injustice to the film. Overall they saw it as unreasonably stylized, undramatic, with a weak screenplay and uninspired casting. Moskalyk's cinematography, which makes use of the telephoto lens to isolate characters in the shot in order to reveal the survivor's difficult communication situation, was criticized as one example of such excessive formalism. His long shots, both static and tracking, employed in key emotional moments of the film in order to prevent identification and sentimentalism, were also misinterpreted. Reviewers dismissed the slow pace of the narrative, failing to acknowledge Moskalyk's effort to give its audience time to understand the ramifications of Dita's ironic reframings.[27]

But the main source of the critics' frustration seems to have been the performance of the lead actress. Even Lustig expressed disapproval of the casting of Mikołajewska as Dita. He accused Moskalyk of stereotyping. In Lustig's novel, Dita is blonde and blue-eyed, childish and libertine. In Moskalyk's rendering, Dita gains a darker complexion and Mediterranean looks; is melancholic, acts with restraint and talks with subtext. Lustig did not grasp the fact that the film purposively plays with stereotypes, provoking the audience to buy into them and adopt a problematic viewer position that orientalizes Dita. He wondered sarcastically why all Jews need to be presented with a Semitic look. He also failed to notice that the film focuses not only on the story of a survivor but also on that of a community that has to deal with her return from the camp. He considered the film to be too grim and wondered why the cinematic Dita is so mature, ironic, and untransparent.[28]

Czechoslovak critics' unease with Mikołajewska's casting also came to the fore in their objections to the foreignness of the actress. Their emphasis is uncannily reminiscent of the discomfort voiced by the gentile population regarding the returning of "foreigners" from concentration camps in the immediate postwar era. Coupled with objections to Moskalyk's cinematography (isolating individuals in the shot and rendering dialogues into monologues) and with Mikołajewska's acting that rarely makes eye contact with her interlocutors, their condemnation prevented them from noticing the film's project to thematize estrangement. *Dita Saxová* aims not only to show its protagonist's difficulty, as racial stranger and survivor of a strange place with strange experiences, to interact with the postwar world, but also to produce an alienation effect that could challenge and detour ingrained cinematic aesthetic expectations into making more sense of the Holocaust.

Technically, Mikołajewska's foreignness as actress made her perform more with her body, enabling the film's thematization of beauty, the camp body, objectification, and the gentile's refusal to hear the survivor's testimony.[29] But critics did not acknowledge her merits. For them, Mikołajewska's acting seemed provocative and diva-like, as if Moskalyk himself had adopted the perspective of one of his characters, had fallen prey to his lead actress's charms, and had transformed the film into an act of adoration.[30] Without understanding Moskalyk's effort to depart from psychological realism and identification, reviewers rejected Mikołajewska's performance as superficial and exhibitionistic. The overstated concern with her exterior, a critic from *Rude Pravo* argued, led to the obfuscation of the heroine's inner drama.[31]

The comment proves how misunderstood the film was at the time of its premiere. Reviewers did not consider that it intentionally obscured its heroine's inner struggles in order to avoid psychologizing and to argue that the emotional and existential traces of the survivor's traumatic experience are unrepresentable through psychological realist acting. Even English-language film historians of the post-1989 era failed to recognize the stylistic sophistication of *Dita Saxová*. One such example is a 1996 review in *Cineaste*, which is unable to notice Moskalyk's effort to link form (framing, cinematography, and acting) to content. It overlooks the alienation effect the film aims to create and complains that it is "overly decorative," that "every shot . . . is fastidiously structured, and . . . compositions are just too exquisite," all of which is caused by the fact that "Moskalyk has succumbed too easily to the influence of Antonioni's *Eclipse*" (Liebman and Quart 1996).

Just like the reviewers of the 1960s, the *Cineaste* reviewers attack Mikołajewska's acting as "too theatrical and elliptical," declare it "pretentious posturing," and call for realism and psychological investigation.[32] Even Peter Hames, the author of the seminal study *The Czech New Wave*, adopts a similar position. In his more recent survey of Czechoslovak cinema, Hames limits his comments on *Dita Saxová* to only two paragraphs, without taking into account that films about the Holocaust might play by different aesthetic rules (more self-conscious and emphasizing ethics of representation) than ones with less monstrous themes. He also mainly sees in Moskalyk an unskilled imitator of Antonioni, and, in *Dita Saxová*, a film compromised by tedious dialogues and slow-paced narration (2009, 106).

Silence

In *Strangers to Ourselves*, Julia Kristeva insightfully reflects on the stammering voice of the foreigner, on her difficulty to articulate statements about her situation and on the temptation of silence she is facing. *Dita Saxová*'s slow-paced, oblique, and disjointed narrative reflects the foreigner's hesitant enunciations, whose hiatuses become even more loaded when one considers the murderous events that have triggered her estrangement. The film includes not only slow dialogues interrupted by long silent intervals (such as the mute rendering of Dita's suffering after the death of her closest shelter companion, Tonička), but also spatial, temporal, and even logical continuity hiatuses, which create the aforementioned "vacuum" effects and the abstract impression of the film.

Dita Saxová incorporates silence in its (disjointed) cinematic enunciation because it envisions itself as testimony and hints at the lack (the silence, or what Agamben calls "the lacuna" [1999, 39]) that rests at the center of each memorialization of the Holocaust. The acknowledgment of this lack is crucial, because it reminds both the speaker and the listener of the paradoxical nature of testimony, of the fact that those who can speak about the camps are not the ones who have experienced the ultimate consequences of its horror. Those who did have either become Muselmann or have died in gas chambers; have lost either their faculty to understand their predicament or their lives, and thus can no longer testify.

Most Holocaust testimonies thematize their incompleteness. One way of addressing their limits is by dedication, by making reference to a character who has seen it all (and thus can no longer testify), and in the name of whom the survivor speaks. In a contrived way, these invoked victims serve as muses for the performers of the testimony and as an ethical incentive to continue with their effort to testify. For Elie Wiesel, the inspiring voiceless victim is his father; for Primo Levi, it is a young boy called Hurbinek he encounters in Auschwitz. For Dita, it is the nameless girl whose face is shown in the opening shot of the film, and which serves as the background for the rolling of the opening credits: the written text (the word) that replaces the silence of the ultimate witness.

Agamben's analysis of the role Hurbinek plays in Levi's testimony helps one grasp how *Dita Saxová* understands itself as an act of remembering and as the staging of testimony. Levi's Hurbinek is a boy from Auschwitz, named after a famous Czech puppet from the 1920s, Hurvinek, a name that Levi—perhaps purposely—misspells.

> Hurbinek was a nobody, a child of death, a child of Auschwitz. He looked about three years old, no one knew anything of him, he could not speak and had no name; that curious name, Hurbinek, had been given to him by us . . . He was paralyzed from the waist down, with atrophied legs, as thin as sticks; but his eyes, lost in his triangular and wasted face, flashed terribly alive, full of demand, assertion, of the will to break loose, to shatter the tomb of his dumbness. The speech he lacked which no one had bothered to teach him, the need of speech charged his stare with explosive urgency. . . . Nothing remains of him: he bears witness through these words of mine. (as quoted in Agamben 1999, 37–38)

Figure 3.3. The silent witness (*Dita Saxová*).

Dita Saxová starts with a three-minute-long close-up of the face—and the "live" eyes—of such a voiceless nobody, a Hurbinek figure. It is a young girl, skinny, mute, and staring into the camera. Her face fills the screen as the opening credits roll on the melancholic musical soundtrack by Luboš Fišer. Her gaze conveys innocence and maybe the same desire to speak as Levi's character, or a call on the survivor to speak in her name.

Agamben quotes extensively from Levi's reference to Hurbinek in order to emphasize not only the representative role played by the testifying survivor—who speaks in the name of those who cannot—but also of the intertwinement of language and non-language in testimony. This means, Agamben argues, that testimony is the disjunction between two impossibilities of bearing witness. It means that, in order to bear witness, language—written or cinematic—must give way to manifestations of non-language, to indistinguishable noise: stammer, dumbness, or pure silence (which, in turn, reveals the impossibility of bearing witness). The face in the prologue does not reappear in the film, only two avatars of it, embodying the dumbness and the silence of the ultimate victim. One is the young Dita from before the Nazi persecution, who is silent and who appears in two flashbacks presenting her with her family.[33] The other is Tonička, whose physical resemblance to the girl in the prologue is obvious (similar bodies, eyes, and light hair and innocent demeanor—as opposed to Dita's darker complexion and seductive appearance), and who is not silent, has language, but, like the Muselmann, lacks the prowess to use it, and who is introduced to the viewer through the words of another girl from the shelter, "dumb as a mummy." Tonička is a character without a statement and without a future, who dies of tuberculosis before having the chance to live a post-camp life. Dita takes her under her protection, spends significant screen time with her, bonding in what seems to be a mother-daughter relation. When asked by the doctor who is closest to her, Dita indicates Tonička. After Tonička's death, the film discreetly suggests, Dita's precarious inner balance is disturbed, and soon after that she commits suicide.

Unaware that she is dying, Tonička speaks mostly about marriage. Her words represent exactly that noise, that radical foreignness, specific to, as Agamben argues, the complete witness, who can no longer bear witness because he or she is no longer able to understand his or her condition (1999, 38). Her words gesture toward the lacuna in the cinematic text, and, in a way, the ultimate use of irony as a narrative trope. Paul de Man calls irony "the trope of zero" (1996, 61), a reference to the radical heterogeneity upon which linguistic enunciation is built and of the dependency of enunciation on silence.[34] In the case of the Holocaust testimony, it can be called "the trope of Hurbinek," as Tonička's chatter gestures towards the unrepresentability of the camp experience.

Dita's suicide cannot be reduced to a reaction to the death of Tonička. Not even to her understanding that full testimony is incomplete and paradoxical (language betraying the ultimate truth). Dita kills herself because, as the film brilliantly shows, she has another revelation, which Agamben does not take into account when talking about testimony: the fact that there is another lacuna, as important as the one referred to by the trope of Hurbinek, which does not rest with having or not having language, but with having an audience. Dita's suicide, her self-privation of language, becomes thus the ultimate effort to make herself heard through a testimony made with her own body. It is a mute statement, but at the same time the only way to make herself heard and to return to the truth. It makes the chilling argument that, as long as the postwar world does not listen and understand the testimony of camp survivors, the Holocaust continues. It also revisits ironically the dialogue Dita had with Dr. Fitz and that, indeed, the survivor has to go over (her) dead body in order to "make a push."[35]

* * *

In both *Somewhere in Europe* and *Story of a Young Couple,* orphans enter the postwar world as strangers, but, as these films end, the destinies of their protagonists become tied to their communities. They have been socialized, integrated. A 1960s film, like *Dita Saxová,* no longer shares this denouement. Integration becomes tantamount to disciplining and silencing. In Balázs and Radványi's film, a child dies, killed by the remnant forces of the Old Order, but his death is invested with a cathartic function. The deaths in *Dita Saxová* have no ritualistic goal; they mark only the failure of a subject to regain itself. The world according to *Dita Saxová* already starts to have postmodern shapes, one of them being that its teleology becomes hazy and catharsis is no longer possible.

The question that lingers after watching the film is, why is Dita, the Holocaust orphan, sentenced to death in a 1960s narrative about the postwar world? The answers to the question reveal again the intellectual potency of the trope of the orphan. The Holocaust orphan must die because the postwar world needs to be made responsible for devising strategies of rejecting the experience produced by the orphan's bodily link to the violent event. But the orphan also dies in Moskalyk's film because she is a reactive subject that refuses to integrate into the New Order. Is it only Dita's fault? the film seems to ask. Obviously not. As a testimony of its times, *Dita Saxová* speaks also about the melancholic subjects of 1968, and thus could not have articulated an apology for conformism. The fact that the film avoids psychologizing and constructing Dita as a traumatic subject suggests that, if there is an explanation for her death, it is not individual and personal. When showing Dita giggling ironically at Professor Munk's praise of socialism and optimism, the film hints at the cause of the problem. Radical modern political dreams produce not only the liberation of individuals, but also, as history has shown, huge numbers of victims, and even piles of corpses. Dita Saxová the orphan and *Dita Saxová* the film stand to bear testimony, even disjointedly, for these victims, for the many deaths of those who could not integrate, or for whom refusal to integrate became an essential existential gesture.

4 Children of the Revolution
The Rebirth of the Subject in Revisionist Discourse

The Eastern European Auteur

This chapter focuses on Krzysztof Kieślowski's *Camera Buff* (*Amator*, Poland, 1979). So far, I have discussed the work of directors whom history has not included among the major cinematic innovators of the Eastern Bloc. After *Somewhere in Europe*, Radványi participated in uninteresting projects (*Women without Names*, 1950) or in politically problematic ones (*The Doctor from Stalingrad*, 1958). In spite of his long and successful career with DEFA, Maetzig never became a director whose personal style would be remembered,[1] while Moskalyk, who made a bold step towards auteur cinema with *Dita Saxová*, continued his career in the less prestigious medium of television in the conservative, post-1968 Czechoslovak climate of "normalization."[2] In contrast, Kieślowski's work was nominated and won some of the industry's most desired international awards[3] and became the object of book-length studies. He is nowadays remembered as "one of the most acclaimed Polish film-makers" (Iordanova 2003, 109), representing a generation that gained artistic prominence in the 1970s, when, one can speculate, intellectual, aesthetic, industrial, and to a certain extent political conditions were more conducive to art cinema than in the 1950 or early 1960s.

In order to better understand Kieślowski's work and canonization, some clarification of the political functions of authorship in the Poland and Eastern Europe of the 1970s is necessary. First of all, critics and the public regarded authorship differently in the 1970s than in previous decades: 1950s—socialist realism, 1960s—New Waves. The 1970s were inclined to link cinematic style with political activism (a usually oblique contestation of Communist Party policies), and to put more emphasis on art as a medium of expressing individual moral consciousness. The 1970s auteur was expected to reflect independently (or as independently as possible) on contemporary issues and articulate social and political judgments. His or her work became almost synonymous with oppositional activity (Iordanova 2003, 108).

This statement is best confirmed by Polish cinema. Through films such as Andrzej Wajda's *Man of Marble* (1976) and Krzystof Zanussi's *Camouflage* (1977)—both of which had a strong influence on *Camera Buff*—the Polish cinema of the 1970s stabilized the common representation and valuation of the Eastern European filmmaker as an artist resisting the bureaucratized communist power of the post-1968 Brezhnev Doctrine era. Spurred also by Poland's signature (and those of other Eastern European countries) on the 1975 Helsinki Accords, with their provisions for freedom of thought and expression, the cinema became a locus of the public sphere where various public issues were debated both onscreen and in various more or less overt forms of post-screening dialogue.[4] And it is not a coincidence that this socially and politically engaged cinema occurred in Poland. According to a report by the American Commission for Human Rights, Hungary and Poland were the Eastern European countries that implemented most thoroughly the provisions of the Helsinki Final Act, with Romania "a poor third" (Czechoslovakia, the country of the vanished New Wave, came in last).[5]

Hungary of the late 1970s and early 1980s also produced films that questioned the way in which socialism treated its subjects; one of them, Márta Mészáros's *Diary for My Children*, will be analyzed in the next chapter. Film history remembers Kieślowski and Márta Mészáros as inquisitive, truth-seeking, political directors, with a solid upbringing in documentary filmmaking and an unwavering moral backbone. Regarding Kieślowski, historians single out his interest in realistic reconstructions of present-day situations. He is presented as a director who scrutinizes characters and situations closely, from a leftist revisionist position, in order to start a debate on a certain issue of social and political relevance:

> Kieślowski's starting point was the same as that of all cineastes in the socialist countries: the conspicuous gap between the drab social reality and the optimistic, bright image which pervaded the heavily censored official media. The first reaction to the fact that, in Poland, social reality was "unrepresented," as Kieślowski put it, was, of course, the move towards a more adequate representation of real life in all its drabness and ambiguity—in short, an authentic documentary approach. (Žižek 2001, 80)

This envisioning of the auteur differed from that of socialist realism and the New Waves of the 1960s. Socialist realism was a cinema that was supposed to have no authors. As workers' art, it regarded auteurship as a by-product of bourgeois art and of its concern with form and commercial branding. As heir of the interwar avant-garde, it defied the canonizing function of the auteur. It scorned the institution of film history and the museum (see chapter 2) and questioned their role as horizons of artistic activity. Socialist-realist art was made by auteur-mediums, who did not transpose their individual Weltanschauung into their work, but reflected the driving forces of history and the vision of the proletariat—as expressed by the policies of the Communist Party.

The 1970s vision of the auteur also differed from that of the 1960s, whose talented filmmakers were regarded first and foremost as experimenters and formal alchemists: think of the Czechoslovak New Wave or the Yugoslav Black Wave, of Milos Forman, Věra Chytilová, and Dušan Makavejev.[6] What migrated from the 1960s to the 1970s, however, was the role of the filmmaker as deconstructor and opponent of the institution of art promoted by socialist realism. Unlike Western European film history, which imagined its auteurs battling cinema's commercialization and depoliticization, Eastern European cultural historians envisioned authorship in the context of liberating art from politics, aesthetic formulas, ritualism, and falsification of history. They also expected auteurs to save film from bad taste (a function Eastern European auteurism shared with its Western counterpart) and bring more sophistication to the screen for a more segmented (that is, more educated) audience, rebuffing the steamrolling of the 1950s imperative of art for the masses.[7]

The fact that Kieślowski gained the status of auteur reflects, however, not only his unquestioned artistic merits, but also his adamant opposition to the interpellation of the filmmaker as a public relations agent for the achievements of socialism, specifically of socialist-realist art. His work exemplifies why 1970s auteurism, in part paradoxically, went often hand in hand with calls for realism in representation. Not surprisingly, auteurs of the 1970s, such as Kieślowski, found poetic inspiration in theoretical texts that called for depicting life "as it is" and rediscovering that which had been left out or suppressed in presentations of social truth informed by hegemonic artistic formats of representation (the "unrepresented" Žižek refers to in the quote above). Thus a collection of essays symptomatically titled *The Unrepresented World*, written by the Polish poets Julian Kornhauser and Adam Zagajewski, fueled the cinematic and artistic impulses of the 1970s.[8]

The return of the auteur in the post-socialist-realist era, and consequently of some of the values associated with auteurism were echoed already by 1956 and post-1956 political and intellectual calls for a return to Europe (imagined as the legitimate bearer of the cultural and artistic heritage of the prewar era) (Kemp-Welch 2008, 128). No surprise then that a "return" in aesthetic vocabulary also took place. Since artists reclaimed the social function of representers of reality and rejected the way socialist realism regarded them as producers (or spin doctors) of it, filmmakers and their commentators reintroduced concepts specific to the bourgeois institution of art in the valuation of their work. Sometimes cautiously, sometimes brazenly, they resuscitated earlier debates on artistic representation. They understood their films as *depictions* of *life*, and promoted concepts such as *truthfulness* and *personal perspective*.

Each of these concepts was heavily loaded with anti-proletarian subtext. "Depiction" harked back to bourgeois realism and challenged the constructionist discourse of socialist-realist aesthetics. The "depictor" opposed the author-builder of reality. His or her art sought to represent reality "as it is" vs. "reality as it should look" and expressed the freethinking and feeling sensibility of a bourgeois humanist discourse. "Life" was also a heavy concept. Unlike "reality," which, for socialist realism, was human- or proletarian-made, it referred to an essence that escaped political control and that developed naturally towards plurality, as the dissident and human rights activist Vaclav Havel would later theorize (see chapter 5). The ranking of these observational depictions of life as more truthful than those informed by the science of dialectical materialism was also subversive. It suggested that the cinematic apparatus could be transparent and generate an output that was liberated from ideological bias (in contrast to proletarian militant art). Moreover, this output would be *personal*. It meant that it expressed the insights of a free subject unbarred by ideological dogmas or stylistic formulas.

A Film of Moral Distrust

Kieślowski's feature films of the late 1970s confirmed these aesthetic expectations. History signaled his "directness and raw edge realism" (Taylor et al. 2000, 130) and called him, even in his own time, an "artist" who believes not in the image, but in reality (Wach 2000, 10–11).[9] Like other landmark Polish auteurs of the 1970s, Kieślowski was regarded by historians not only as a moral screener of society, but also as a distrustful one. *Camera Buff* articulated its social commentary within a broader trend in Polish cinema that bore the name "cinema of distrust" (or "cinema of moral concern," "cinema of moral unrest," or "cinema of moral anxiety").[10] Kieślowski recalls:

> There were about six years of this Cinema of Moral Anxiety, from 1974 to 1980. . . . I became friends with Krzysztof Zanussi, and then with Edek Zebrowski and Agnieszka Holland. And for some time, with Andrzej Wajda, too. We were all, as it were, in a group which shared the feeling that we could do something together, that we positively had to do something together, and that in such a group we'd have some sort of power. (1998, 41)

By the late 1970s and the beginning of the 1980s, Kieślowski became one of its emblematic representatives (Haltof 2007, 29; Taylor et al. 2000, 130). Film historians identified the Polish cinema of distrust as representative of the "autumn years of state socialism" (Iordanova 2003, 108). As suggested in the previous discussion on auteurship, the cinema of distrust called for expressions of individual will and strong moral subjects, and, in the spirit of anti-state socialism, "examined the massive gap between the 'progressive' postulates [of socialism] and their implementation" (Haltof 2003, 147). It focused on "contemporary issues" (Haltof 2007, 29), was concerned with the destinies of "small people" (Iordanova 2003, 108), reacted "to the absence of life 'as it is' from the Polish screen" (Haltof 2003, 147), and targeted conformism, manipulation, corruption, "and other social and political effects of the Communist system" (Haltof 2007, 29–30). This critique was articulated—and this is an aspect of Polish film and civil society that is often overlooked—from a socialist (Marxist) revisionist perspective. It resonated with the student and worker protests that upset Poland in October 1956, continued into the 1970s, and anticipated the better-known Solidarity movements of the early 1980s.

According to Iordanova, *Camera Buff* also addresses "the leading themes of the 'moral concern' strand such as conformity and compromise" (2003, 110). It is a moral and political fable whose protagonist, Filip (Jerzy Stuhr), is an orphan born and raised in socialism. He embodies the "small person," the average and "innocuous" product of the new order (Iordanova 2003, 110). He is not a war orphan; he was born around 1948. He is about thirty, an utter product of communism, fully socialized by the New Order. The screenplay emphasizes that he has grown up in an orphanage (Haltof 2004, 42), and Filip makes reference to it too. This is the reason why, he explains, he likes to eat plain bread. He picked up the habit, which characterizes him as a simpleton, in the orphanage.

The film shows how the orphan of socialism has thrived in the order that produced him. He benefited from a successful social integration that reared him to live the peaceful and honest life of a family man. He received the professional training necessary to attain a white-collar job, some degree of wealth, an apartment, a happy household (his first child is about to be born in the first scenes of the film), and a reliable circle of friends.[11] In other words, he was socialized to live a contented small-town, petty bourgeois provincial life, typical of the stagnating years of the Brezhnev era in Eastern Europe and of the pragmatism of the Gierek administration in Poland, when the system no longer demanded revolutionary dedication from its citizens, but only silent and self-centered conformism.[12]

The purchase of an 8 mm camera changes the dynamics of Filip's mellow existence as a citizen of socialism. Initially bought to document the growing up of his newborn daughter, the camera, with its intrinsic power to historicize, propels Filip into the public sphere and changes his perception of life and himself. The change starts with a demand from his boss to make a short film about the twenty-fifth anniversary of the factory he works in. He accepts the assignment and enjoys capturing the celebration—and here his transformation begins. The virus of filmmaking infects him. Driven by his passion, by the recognition shown to his work at an amateur film festival, but also by the support of his employer and the system he lives in (with its aim to enlighten working men and women), Filip engages in telling more stories about the world around him.

He makes more films and becomes a witness and a "chronicler" (Haltof 2004, 12) of life in small-town Poland of the late 1970s, shooting documentaries about it and the people in his factory. He uses the camera to explore (for himself) and to represent (for an audience) a universe outside his familiar realm. Filmmaking brings him power and increases his social consciousness. If in the initial sequences of *Camera Buff* Filip seems to be depicted as the dummy subject of socialism, towards the end he has become a citizen proper, engaged in the improvement of his life and of his community. From an amateur he has turned into a skilled professional; from a small-town simpleton into a reflexive and concerned individual; from an obedient employee into a shrewd negotiator with the powerful.

It is important to notice that Filip's transformation is neither controlled nor inspired by party-orchestrated socialist discourse. In fact, the new Filip develops by challenging that discourse. If Plato's epigraph at the beginning of this book referred to the second birth of the subject once he or she is reared by the institutions of the state (which Filip, the child of the orphanage, has experienced), *Camera Buff* documents a third. As we shall see, this third birth is not in contradiction with socialist principles—or, at least, not with some interpretations of Marxist-Leninist dialectical materialism. This third birth which marks Filip's transition from a devoted subject of socialism to a reflexive (autonomous) one is substantiated not only by the dialectics at the core of Marxist thought (which in fact left historical room for an infinity of rebirths and redefinitions), but also, and more importantly, by the post-1968 departure from the doctrine of the dictatorship of the proletariat. Once socialism reached a certain stage of development and the material conditions and the relationships of production specific to capitalism were dismantled, subjects could develop free and autonomous thought because it would be articulated within and informed by appropriate revolutionized economic and social structures.

This rationale would underpin the reformist movement in Poland and Eastern Europe in the late 1970s and even find its expression in Gorbachev's policies of glasnost and perestroika. If the repression of 1968 showed that the party could no longer be trusted to change the world (and its people), the reformist movement argued that, in the spirit of materialist dialectics, the emancipated people who grew up entirely under socialism, men and women of Filip's generation, could be now trusted to change the world (and the party). In the post-Helsinki conference context, all these emancipated socialist subjects needed were the rights to express these thoughts freely and to associate in order to discuss them and increase their relevance and their social basis. These were some of the major demands that would spur the Solidarity protests, just a few years after the release of *Camera Buff*.[13]

The Uncertainty Principle

The passion for representing reality spurs Filip's desire to understand it. He wants to improve his observational skills. In order to make better films, he looks for teachers, helpers, companions, and inspiration. But his quest for self-improvement does not follow the institutionalized path. According to the principles of political resistance of late 1970s Poland, an artist seeking to improve his skills needs to build his artistic and civic self outside of the institutions of the state. He must be self-taught—as *Amator*, the Polish title of *Camera Buff*, suggests—or tutored by alternative figures, whose views diverge or directly oppose officially sanctioned ones. And he must find venues to express himself freely, without censorship, and cultivate his autonomy.

Filip's mentors include leading figures of Polish alternative film discourse. The most important are film historian Andrzej Jurga and the internationally better known film director Krzysztof Zanussi. Jurga was a filmmaker and a professor at the Katowice film school (Haltof 2003, 154). He organized a film group that advocated realism in representation and was politically associated with the Catholic Church.[14] Both Jurga and Zanussi appear in cameo roles in *Camera Buff*. Jurga plays a television producer and director of a festival jury. The latter presents his 1977 *Camouflage*, the archetypical film of the cinema of moral distrust (an allegory of the corruption and conformism of Polish society [Haltof 2003, 148]), within a screening organized by Filip's film club.

Filip's education as a filmmaker suggests that in 1970s Poland (and Eastern Europe) a true political consciousness could develop only by participating in informal and under-the-radar networks, with their growing samizdat literature, invisible universities, and underground artistic events. Being an amateur in political thought and public performance becomes equivalent to becoming an orphan in relation to the discursive patronage of the Communist Party. For Filip, this means rejecting his own socialization as a child raised in the institutions of the system. The party's mobilizing and mentoring role is to be called into question in favor of discovering self-government and self-organization, two concepts developed by one of the leading figures of Polish resistance, Jacek Kuron. This political position was also cultivated by groups connected to the Catholic Church and especially by KOR (Workers' Defense Committee, which included Kuron among its founding members).

One of Kuron's seminal samizdat essays was "Notes on Self-Government." It argued that the self-governed thinker of the Brezhnev era was expected to cultivate his autonomy and spontaneity, be part of and respond to civic grassroots impulses that created moral, political, and aesthetic oases necessary for one's individual fulfillment. The times, historians suggest, were not yet ready for more tightly articulated counter-discourses:

[It] was not yet that a more independent culture and society could one day develop into an effective political opposition. Rather, the development of autonomous groups, unofficial initiatives and eventually social movements can in themselves constitute an opposition. Participants would actively enjoy the benefits of self-organization and freedom of expression, across an increasing range of social activities. (Kemp-Welch 2008, 204)

In *Camera Buff*, Zanussi teaches Filip not only how to improve and distribute his films, but also the social importance of the independent artist. *Camera Buff* shows Zanussi presenting *Camouflage* in workers' clubs and other alternative exhibition spaces, vividly dialoguing with his audience. The message he aims to convey is that political film is neither socialist-realist *Bildung* (mobilizing art) nor entertainment, a product that is supposed to be silently consumed in one's spare time. The political film of his time addresses issues of civic interest and functions first and foremost as a discussion starter, rendering the Q&A as important as the cinematic experience. Consequently, a film club, such as Filip's, can represent an environment in which, as mentioned above, groups of men and women could produce autonomous thinking and a place where progressive knowledge is articulated.

In such a dynamic Q&A session, Zanussi expresses his point of view on artistic "self-government." He articulates it shrewdly, anticipating possible attacks from those who speak within the hegemonic discourses on art of his time, the defenders of socialist political correctness. One of his interventions cautiously starts by depicting what he believes to be the epistemological landscape of his time: the artist of the 1970s perceives the intellectual and the political space as deprived of grand narratives. His argument, which harks back to Vaclav Havel's concept of post-totalitarian society, discussed the latter's seminal essay "The Power of the Powerless." For Zanussi, the Gierek-Brezhnev era witnesses the arrival of a postmodern sensibility, coinciding in some Eastern European regions with the party's politics of "normalization." In this context, Zanussi argues, artists must understand that they "are no longer alchemists of the soul capable of changing the world," as the communist revolution (and socialist realism) demanded of them. "Criteria are relative," he continues; "there are no hard and clear rules" of modeling reality and outlining how social progress is to unfold. The universe is unstable, there is a fundamental limit to the possibilities of science to describe it, and when it is made, this description is fundamentally influenced by the standpoint and techniques of the observer.

Zanussi employs concepts taken from post-Newtonian physics. He has expertise in this field since, as he tells Filip, he studied physics before becoming a filmmaker. He argues that the late 1970s live in a climate of limited determinism. This climate is beneficial to filmmakers because art, as he perceives it, is creative ambiguity and a subjective (read "personal") rendering (read "depiction") of social truth. If the epistemological underpinnings of political metanarratives have been challenged, so has been the task of the artist. "We are no longer capable of changing the world," Zanussi argues, hinting at the fact that, in the official discourse, artists are still expected, at least in theory, to perform the functions of the 1950s and Marx's call on intellectuals (and artists) not to describe the world, but to change it. Zanussi claims that the post-deterministic intellectual context of the 1970s calls for contributions from filmmakers who are auteurs. "The uncertainty of the world has become our [the self-governed artists'] strength." Cinema should no longer be preoccupied with metanarratives, searching for the ultimate formula to bring history to an end. It should just strive to be truthful, first of all in relation to the artists' consciousness. It should no longer be a confirmation of the communist worldview, but the expression of an independent and self-governed eye. Consequently, the product of the auteur's labor will not claim to deliver a universal truth, but, as Zanussi puts it, it will fire shots in the dark or spark temporary illuminations, whose social role and political effects are not immediately discernible, but still serve human enlightenment.

Zanussi shrewdly builds the case for a defense of artistic freedom. The hypothesis that the political effect of an artistic product is no longer easily measurable calls into question the logic of political censorship and preempts attacks along ideological lines. He also clarifies why he made a film about a ruthless careerist (*Camouflage*), indirectly arguing why another important theme of the cinema of moral distrust, the "ideology of success," is central to his film (this theme will be discussed in more detail in the epilogue). He tells his audience that he addressed careerism because he believed that in his time honest people succeeded with difficulty. Since the Gierek era envisioned itself as one of re-democratization of Polish society, Zanussi touches a sensitive point. He argues quite overtly that socialism has not brought the social justice its science has predicted. Privileged social groups, elites, still exist in classless Poland. These elites strive to preserve their hegemonic position and are no longer interested in democratizing society and in introducing a meritocracy predicated on proletarian ethics.

Zanussi's views on the role of the artist in society—in particular, his emphasis on the descriptive task of the artist who reflects on a world where change cannot be controlled—hark back to the fundamental tenets of the bourgeois institution of art and its construction of the auteur discussed earlier in the chapter. Zanussi's position contradicts not only socialist conceptions of art, but also the worldview of scientific socialism and its reliance on economic and social determinism. For scientific socialism, economic and social laws exist and become the laws of history. By employing the uncertainty logic of post-Einsteinian (Heisenbergian) physics, Zanussi uses arguments from the hard sciences to relativize socialist discourse, which also regarded itself as scientific. No surprise, then, that the communist state leadership disliked *Camouflage* and the epistemological and intellectual unrest it suggested.

Viewed from the point of view of the Communist Party, what makes Zanussi's hypothesis even more problematic is that it seems to be informed by the existential, economic, social, moral, and political instability of capitalism and its grounding in the unsteadiness of the free market (which socialism's scientific economic approach aimed to stabilize). What is of interest here is the fact that Zanussi could publicly articulate such a point that could reflect a capitalist perception—and that Kieślowski could quote him in his film. It confirms what was argued earlier in this chapter that, in comparison to other Eastern European states such as Czechoslovakia and the GDR, Poland of the late 1970s was more tolerant of self-organized thinking (Lepak 1988, 167). The social criticism expressed in the Polish films *Camera Buff, Camouflage,* and *Man of Marble* would have been unimaginable in other Eastern European countries of the time (for example, Romania). The freedom people benefited from in that period (relative to the controlling society they were living in) and the fact that the state only partially blocked revisionist information reveals that independent thinking in socialism and the regime's tolerance of it conditioned and influenced each other. Spurred by this mutual conditioning, the Polish public sphere developed, like glasnost ten years later in the Soviet Union, due to both civic resistance and the flexibility of the regime. For a while, the regime allowed more dissent not only because it was pressured internationally by the Helsinki Accords, but also because it sought social reconciliation, popularity, and stability, and it wanted to distance itself from the more rigid practices of previous administrations. For a short period of time, the Polish regime borrowed the stance of Hungary of the 1970s, defined at an international meeting in Sofia of the central committee secretaries of all Eastern European countries in charge of international affairs in March 1977. Here the Hungarian representative argued that

> our propaganda will be most effective if we tell the whole truth about socialism, if we show its weak side as well as its strength; if we disclose the dynamism and the contradictions of its development alike; if we point out that socialism . . . is still a young and developing social organism in which there are still [to] be seen many traces of the past. (8)[15]

What remains unanswered is how much of such statements was just liberal posturing and how much of it was truly meant. One thing was certain: in Poland it happened in parallel with arrests of dissidents and ended in 1981.

The Independent Eye

Through the positions of Zanussi and Jurga, Kieślowski smuggles into his film many KOR ideas. KOR represented the quest of leftist revisionist intellectuals to reconnect with the working class. The reawakening of class consciousness and the re-empowering of the worker, both along Marxist lines, were the main goals of KOR's agitation against the system. In order to locate itself in the landscape of the Left, KOR restored the lineage of Polish communism all the way back to Rosa Luxemburg, arguing that she had been a Polish, not a German, activist, and like other revisionist groups in both Eastern and Western Europe, it reclaimed tenets of the interwar radical socialist Left as its guidelines (Lepak 1988, 173). It cultivated the figure of the "independent worker," and its mouthpiece *Robotnik* argued that deviance from the hegemonic rules of political thinking was the key practice of understanding oneself and the problems of socialist society (170, 171). Following Leszek Kołakowski's thesis that (authoritarian) state socialism was the regime of non-choice (Satterwhite 1992, 43), the goal of KOR, pursued through its tactic of civil disobedience, became the production of a free space in which the (liberated) subject of socialism could perceive life or reality allegedly unwarped by ideology.

Camera Buff presents the 8mm camera as the tool that can produce perceptions of life that deviate from hegemonic representations of it. The source of this deviation is the raw, uncensored, and symbolically unprocessed flow of images and sounds it can engender. The camera becomes the social device that mediates and enables Filip's access to public reason. It has a defamiliarizing and depersonalizing role, and is instrumental in distancing him from internalized ideological discourses. It not only captures a visual truth (against "ideology"), but also reveals to the "man with the movie camera," to borrow from Dziga Vertov, how the subject is disciplined to see and understand the world and himself. Slavoj Žižek summarizes the ultimate critical task of the camera articulated in *Camera Buff*:

> If our social reality itself is sustained by a symbolic fiction or fantasy, then the ultimate achievement of film art is not to recreate reality within the narrative fiction, to seduce us into (mis)taking a fiction for reality, but, on the contrary, to make us discern the fictional aspect of reality itself, to experience reality itself as a fiction. . . . We are shown what "really happened," and suddenly, we perceive this reality in all its fragility, as one of the contingent outcomes, forever haunted by its shadowy doubles. (Žižek 2001, 80)[16]

The camera brings reality back into Filip's life, and awakens him from a certain social dream he might have been living in. It makes him determined to see beyond his private interest and notice that which goes unnoticed and/or is declared contingent within the ideological shaping of the world of his time. The camera also empowers him. It renders his gaze public. What he sees through its lens can be viewed by anybody who watches his films. His sight performs a testimony. And since Filip's perspective is that of a worker and, as an orphan, of a subject socialized by the institutions of state socialism, his testimony gains extra political weight. Thus the story of Filip's apprenticeship in filmmaking becomes the story of a gaze preparing to become public and assuming its representative function. This is why Filip instructs himself not only in observing reality—that is, in film technique—but also, intellectually, in understanding it better. He learns not only how to handle the camera and splice film, but also how to absorb the cultural trends and political ideas of his time. He teaches himself how to keep the pro-filmic object in focus and at the same time is reading journals such as *Politika, Kultura,* and *Film.* As the film progresses, he acquires improved film-making equipment, experiments with style, and enjoys the recognition brought by the broadcasting of his documentaries. But he also becomes bolder in choosing his topics, and his films pay tribute more manifestly to the "moral distrust" of his time.

His passion for film is so sweeping that he neglects his private life. He has become a public person. He travels to the capital city, his films are shown on national television stations, and new ones are commissioned. He has gained a certain visibility in his plant; he leads its film club, and his activity is monitored by the general manager of the plant himself. But his professional success is not matched by private life bliss. In response to the changes in Filip's life, his wife, Irka, leaves him. The film does not provide a convincing psychological argument for why she does it, and maybe *Camera Buff* leaves her reasons not fully clarified in order to avoid stereotyping women as guardians of the private. In this context, however, which has been denounced in most of the scholarly literature on *Camera Buff* (Haltof 2004, 49), one can construe that Irka leaves her husband because his passion for filmmaking has corrupted the rosy dream of the quiet life she has envisioned.

But one can also argue that it is not petty bourgeois bliss that motivates her to leave her husband, but the apprehension that Filip's public activity will bring persecution upon him and his family. Irka's logic was not alien to those who remembered the Stalinist period and the state's reaction to the various revolts and protests that marked the experience of socialism in Poland in the post-Stalinist era. After all, in Poland, every bold manifestation against the regime was met with police brutality and subsequent waves of arrests and marginalizations. The post-1965 life of KOR leaders such as Jacek Kuron and Adam Michnik was a constant commute between prison, house arrest, and liberation, while other regime opponents such as Jerzy Popiełuszko even ended up beaten to death by the secret police.

Her worries do not influence Filip. He is so taken with his filmmaking that he hardly reacts to her protest, and does little to stop her from leaving. He is much too much concerned with his other life, the public one. The change in his priorities is illustrated by a scene depicting the domestic fight that leads to the couple's separation. As they argue, Filip no longer perceives their confrontation

Figure 4.1. Filip, witness of one's own life (*Camera Buff*).

only from a personal point of view. *Camera Buff* astutely shows how he looks at it also from a third-person perspective. He both participates in it and observes it unaffected emotionally. When there is nothing more to say, Irka exits the room and reaches for her luggage. Sitting on the sofa Filip watches her walking away, not with the teary eyes of an abandoned husband, but through a frame made with his fingers that resembles the view through a viewfinder. His gaze has literally become defamiliarized.[17]

Camera Buff gives another example of such a "defamiliarized gaze" when, later in the film, after Irka's departure, Filip edits footage of his baby daughter, Irenka, playing in the crib. His assistant Witek sits behind him, learning the trade of editing. In this sequence, *Camera Buff* intercuts between Filip's and Witek's faces and the screen of the editing machine. Filip talks about his child as if she is just an image on the footage: "Look, there she is in a long shot," he explains to Witek. Then he shows Irenka in close-up and informs his assistant that he had to slightly doctor the take in order to respect the rules of continuity and spatial orientation. When Witek switches to the personal register and tells Filip that he has a pretty girl, Filip has a moment of relapse. His eyes blur as they could have blurred in the separation scene. But he rapidly suppresses his emotions and continues with the lesson. His daughter becomes again an element of the mise-en-scène, a character. "When you edit this," he instructs Witek, "remember that when a long shot is followed by a close-up the subject must look the same way."

The Ideological Bliss of the Private

The growing depersonalization of Filip's perception of his private life gestures toward another strategy of political resistance in Poland and Eastern Europe of the 1970s. Socialism is often and legitimately accused of politicizing the private lives of its subjects. But, at the same time, post-1968 socialism also aimed to depoliticize the lives of its subjects and, in particular, of its workers. Too much political mobilization has led, since 1954, to various resurgences of class consciousness, public protests, demands for free trade unions, strikes, and even street riots. To prevent future political agitation, post-1968 leaderships all over Eastern Europe, the Gierek regime among them, aimed to create spectacles of social dialogue and political participation whose main goals were not only social progress, but also to control and eventually minimize the say workers had in the way their country was governed.

In Poland, the Gierek regime proceeded to set up a bogus campaign to reproletarianize the Communist Party. However, its goal was not to remobilize the workers and empower them, because at the same time the policies of the Gierek regime continued to be exclusively top-down. The campaign served the pragmatic goals of, on the one hand, countering the growing popularity of KOR and, on the other, of containing the public participation of the workers. Their apparent return to political life was designed to domesticate them even more, because it was a "co-optation of people into the party who were value-neutral or even hostile to the ideology—but who were induced to join because of the material and career advantages it promised" (Lepak 1988, 177). This successful co-opting sealed a silent truce (a social bargain—which will be discussed in detail in the epilogue) of complicity between workers and power. The communist leadership bought the workers' passivity with support for private life conditions, which included increased access to consumer goods and entertainment and promotion of the traditional family.[18]

Filip, I argue, does not neglect his marriage because he is simply overtaken by a careerist hubris, which is the argument of many commentators on *Camera Buff*, including Kickasola, who talks about the separation as marking Filip's moral collapse (2004, 118). My reading surmises that Filip represents the socialist subject who instinctively understands that resisting domestication is a crucial act of political resistance. He must ignore his private life to a certain extent, because of its ideological effects. He needs to achieve self-government. As another ideologue of the Polish revisionist resistance, Leszek Kołakowski, argued, morality and public reason can be achieved only in such a situation, which he calls freedom (Satterwhite 1992, 42). When Irka goes out the door, Filip is surprised. He has just experienced a taste of self-government, which has increased the quality of his life. "Why now?!" he shouts at her, frustrated that she is not on the same page as he is. Why would she leave when, after practicing independent thinking, Filip can say of himself "I'm beginning to understand what this shitty life is all about"?

One thing Filip understands is that the privatization of the subject's perception (his or her use of private reason) becomes the ultimate barrier blocking him from noticing the "fragility" of reality referred to by Žižek in the long quote above. In its last scene, *Camera Buff* details the virtues of deprivatization. In order to be moral and political, Filip needs to be alone with his camera because this is the predicament necessary for him to discover morality and become, as KOR urged the worker, an independent thinker. In this last scene, Filip turns the camera on himself, but not to "shoot" himself with it, as other commentators have interpreted[19]—that is, as an artistic and political "suicide." When he turns the camera on himself, Filip does it to tell a story. He retells the plot of *Camera Buff*, which the viewer has just watched. But he tells it differently. The main difference is that Filip is no longer an "escapist" subject—another important category for Kołakowski, referring to the subject who has turned his back to public reasoning (Satterwhite 1992, 42). When he retells his story, Filip is liberated from petty bourgeois bliss. He has changed. He can see, judge, and decide in the framework of public reason. He reconsiders his story positioned within a situation of freedom, from which he is able to make moral choices. Alone but transformed, Filip turns the camera away from the street, directs it to himself, and provides the plot of *Camera Buff* with a voiceover. He is no longer just a character in this retold plot, but also, like in the domestic fight episode, its narrator.

Camera Buff approaches the complexity of the issue of domestication of the subject of the Brezhnev-Gierek era by including sequences from a documentary Filip makes about Wawrzyniec, a dwarf worker from his factory (an episode that uses recycled footage from a documentary made by Kieślowski himself).[20] Not accidentally titled *Worker*, the film, as we shall see, encodes the battle for the loyalties of the working class between the ruling Communist Party (with its reproletarianization tactic) and KOR. Aired on national television with the help of Jurga and Zanussi, Filip's film is a humane and respectful treatment of the everyday life of an honest and hardworking subject of socialism who has a physical handicap. In it, socialism comes through as integrative, giving equal opportunities to people with disabilities. Even if he has to face more challenges than the average person, the protagonist of Filip's film can make a decent living, earn the respect of others, and even build a happy and content family life.

Camera Buff tracks the development of Filip's project at all its levels. It shows him shooting and editing it, getting his first professional feedback on it (from Zanussi), pitching it to the national television station (to Jurga), celebrating its

You've done it beautifully, Filip

Figure 4.2. Wawrzyniec—the paradox of dignity (*Camera Buff*).

acceptance, and nervously watching it with his film club mates in the home of Wawrzyniec. While the positive impression on Zanussi helps Filip sell his film to national television, the positive feedback he receives from Wawrzyniec and his wife is what impresses the audience. Wawrzyniec is in tears. He is overwhelmed by the way the film recognizes his hardworking life and his effort to find happiness and make his existence meaningful in the extraordinary and limiting condition he is in. "You've done it beautifully . . . I was so moved," he tells Filip.

But Halski, the manager of the factory and patron of the film club, is not so moved by Filip's film. He regards it disapprovingly.

HALSKI: "Couldn't it be someone else? Why him?"

FILIP: "Perhaps because it is harder for him to work well."

HALSKI: "Making a cripple as a subject? You are using him to make fun of him."

The manager's advice, which Filip disobeys, is harsh: "You will never show this to any film festival." Filip is as surprised as he was when his wife left him. "Why?" is again the question on his lips, which he does not dare to ask, but to which he will receive an answer during a later encounter with the manager. He thinks his representation of the "cripple" has been respectful, showing that socialism accommodates difference and equally appreciates their contribution to the building of the New Order.

After his initial puzzlement, Filip understands that Halski's critique refers to something else. The manager sees other things in *Worker* that have nothing to do with making fun of Wawrzyniec's predicament. For most film historians, the reason Halski blocks the film is that it can be interpreted as gesturing toward the "dwarfed"—that is, oppressed—condition of the working class in Poland (Wach 2000, 181). While this interpretation is convincing, I argue, things are slightly more complicated. Halski's reaction also throws light on the paradoxical political game of re- and depoliticization of the working class in late-1970s Poland and Eastern Europe.

We know from interviews that one of the reasons Kieślowski abandoned documentary filmmaking was a certain guilt he experienced with regard to his subjects. He felt he was using and sometimes abusing their life stories in order to make a directorial career for himself. Apparently Halski embodies Kieślowski's admonishing inner voice. Kieślowski thought that by bringing their lives to public view his films affected his subjects, sometimes negatively (Haltof 2004, 48), reproducing also Irka's logic that becoming public renders one a target of sometimes inexplicable and definitely paranoid persecution. Alongside his growing distrust in the capacity of documentary filmmaking to show "unrepresented reality" (Haltof 2004, 48)—for example, the "small" existence of "small" workers of "small" towns such as that of Wawrzyniec—this feeling of guilt was one of the main reasons that Kieślowski switched to fiction cinema in 1976 and, more importantly, why he considered it to be superior to documentary filmmaking (Žižek 2001, 80).[21]

In *Camera Buff*, Halski's main role is, however, not to voice Kieślowski's scruples on the ethics of representation, and only partially is it about the political consequences of rendering issues or people public. Halski's critique voices deeper concerns than just the fact that "the film does not conform to the expected portrayal of socialist work and workers" (Haltof 2004, 46), that the dwarf might be "used" in order to articulate an ironic statement on 1950s Stakhanovism, or that his crippled predicament can allude to the violent (and crippling) reaction of authorities to the workers' protests of 1970–1971 and 1976 (when, as Kuron declared, "Polish workers had paid in blood for the mistakes of those in power [Kemp-Welch 2008, 211]).[22] The manager's worries are the outcome of the complicated hermeneutic process of decoding the intricate play of policy and ideology in state socialism and of the way it produces reality.

Surprisingly, Halski responds to the documentary in a similar way to Jurga, a figure of the opposition. After seeing it and deciding to broadcast it, Jurga exclaims: "It's not just about the plant. It's a broader issue." Even if they stand on opposing sides of the struggle for power in Polish society, for both the issue is indeed not that workers with disabilities are disrespectfully represented onscreen. They both have in mind the disability of the Polish working class under socialism. The story of Wawrzyniec becomes thus a fable addressing the condition of workers in all Eastern European proletarian states of the 1970s. They have become a crippled political class and their political agency a simulacrum. In the Polish context, the most problematic aspect of this critical message was the fact that it seemed to have been taken from the revisionist catechism of KOR, an organization which, of course, Jurga indirectly represents and Halski opposes.

If the handicapped body of the protagonist of Filip's documentary reflects the incapacitated predicament of the working class, its representation also explains one of the tools used by the Gierek regime to keep the Polish working class in a crippled condition. This device was domestication. The means of achieving it were the social minimum of the welfare state, "linked to high wages, cheap food, and social recognition" (Eley 2002, 432). When asked what he does in his spare time, Wawrzyniec answers: "We stay at home; my wife cooks dinner, we play rummy, sometimes go to the cinema, or to a café on Sundays.... One way or another we pass the time."

For Haltof (2004, 46), Wawrzyniec invokes here "the small 'communist luxuries'" of a life in a regime where services and consumer goods are scarce. The issue is, however, more complex. The predicament of Poland's and Eastern Europe's workers is not to be regarded only from a consumptionist (i.e., capitalist) perspective. The worker is crippled and his life rendered "small" not only because he or she cannot own and consume more, or enjoy superior services, but also because he or she is alienated.

The counter-alienation stance was central to Polish (and Eastern European) revisionist Marxism. In a different key, *Camera Buff* revisits Kołakowski's assumption that the political emancipation of the proletariat has not eliminated alienation. The worker is alienated again in a socialist society that has given up its revolutionary mobilization (Satterwhite 1992, 40), and Wawrzyniec's predicament shows how power discourse aims to discreetly persuade the worker to find true happiness and fulfillment in the realm of the private and of the family. In the public realm there is only the spectacle of participation. As Wawrzyniec himself puts it, the primary political concern of the domesticated worker of the late 1970s is to maintain a good relationship with authorities. The film about him shows that public smallness can, allegedly, condition private delight. "My relations with the management are good. . . . They seem to value me," Wawrzyniec confesses. Good relations with "the management" guarantee that he can enjoy his coffee and movie.

Amateurs, Auteurs, and Censorship

Filip, who becomes a public figure, can no longer enjoy such good relations with the management. With every film he makes, the tension between him and the management increases. Moreover, as we have seen, he is confronted with opposition on the domestic front too. Irka is also a Wawrzyniec figure, desiring a "small" life. When she leaves her husband, she tells him that she does it because he has betrayed their initial dream. Filip inquires what that dream was. "I wanted a little peace and quiet, that's all," she replies, aware of the implications of her words. She understands her false consciousness, but, she believes, alienation and domestication are a price she is willing to pay. What she miscalculates is the degree of her false consciousness. The choice of life in domestic bliss is the ultimate dream of an alienated consciousness (and not only of socialism, but also of modernity), which KOR and Vaclav Havel battled passionately.

Filip is Kieślowski's cinematic response to KOR and revisionist socialism's call for struggle against alienation and for developing independent eyes and minds to reflect, and reflect on, the realities of Eastern European socialism. To better understand Kieślowski's position, one needs to return to the issue of realism, but approach it differently. Of interest are not the power, the limits, and the truthfulness of representation, but the subject and observer producing it. *Amator*, the Polish title of *Camera Buff*, indicates the line of inquiry one must follow. But this hint seems, at first glance, paradoxical. How can one become an auteur and remain an amateur? How can Filip be both socially concerned and an unsophisticated observer?

Kieślowski imagines himself as filmmaker on a similar pattern. In interviews, he introduces himself as an expert-amateur and rejects his status as auteur, even if film critics and audiences address him as one. "I am not an artist; I am an artisan," he replies. "Artists have answers." Artisans don't (Kieślowski 1998, 106). Artisans have skills. "They used to call me [the] 'engineer'" (Stock 1993, 40). "I know a lot about lenses, about the editing room. I know what the different buttons on the camera are for. I know more or less how to use a microphone. I know all that, but that's not real knowledge" (Kieślowski 1998, 106). Artisans know how to craft movies, how to represent reality authentically, and, if they develop a consciousness, how to pose questions. But he declares that interpretation of reality, voice, style, projection of one's self in their work—all marks of the auteur—do not interest him.

Kieślowski knows, however, that artisans and their cameras are not transparent media. They choose characters, locations, concepts, lenses, and angles. Their choices prove they have a certain sense of reality—how it looks and develops—and of what is relevant about it (why certain aspects of it are more worth recording than others). This is what Filip learns throughout his *Bildung* in *Camera Buff*. From Halski's feedback he understands that apparently strictly technical choices—including the mere commitment to represent life "as is"—are deeply political once his films become public. Such a commitment was central to Kieślowski's activity during the 1976–1980 period and to the directors of the cinema of moral distrust. They sought the real, "to see what was happening in the world, how people were living, and why they weren't living as well as they could" (Stock 1993, 37).

These words could also describe Filip's drive for filmmaking. Besides *Worker* (the Wawrzyniec film), he makes shorts about the superficially improved housing conditions in his town, about a street in his neighborhood that has not been fixed, and about an abandoned brick factory. His public commitment transforms Filip into more than an amateur. He understands it, and, in the end of the film, turns the camera on himself to find out who he has become. He is caught, as Kieślowski puts it, in a "trap." He has made films with "good intentions"—that is, with no intentions in particular. He has not aimed to interpret reality; he has striven only toward artisanship. But it seems that his work is not perceived as descriptively as he wants it to be. Audiences articulate the ultimate meaning of his films.

This is what happens with *Worker*. The manager reads it differently than Filip, his colleagues, and Wawrzyniec. Filip realizes that, regardless of how much they try, directors do not have control over the public signification and the social consequences of their work. Artisans in particular. The broadcast of *Worker* on national television makes waves. Filip's next film about the renovation of apartment buildings in his town leads to investigations of local finances and to the firing of the factory's cultural officer, Josuch, a father figure for Filip, who has supported him in all his projects (and who represents the old, authentic, illegalist, pre-Stalin, and pre-Brezhnev-era communism that the KOR discourse drew on).

In the last scene, the camera is turned toward the filmmaker because, whether he wants it or not, Filip the artisan is becoming Filip the auteur. It expresses a major concern Kieślowski had about his own work: the awareness of its multiple ramifications.

> If you don't understand your own life, then I don't think you can understand the lives of the characters in your stories, you cannot understand the lives of other people. Philosophers know this. Social workers know this. But artists ought to know this too, at least those who tell stories. (Kieślowski 1998, 35)

Camera Buff suggests that the transition from amateur to auteur (or artist) starts with gaining self-consciousness. It is not interest in formal experimentation that makes one an artist. Wondering and understanding how one's work will be interpreted is the most important aspect of authorship and by extrapolation of socialist citizenship. In fact, as filmmaker and auteur of the 1970s with roots in documentary filmmaking, Kieślowski criticizes experimenters. He surmises that increased concern with style—once chastised as formalism—has become, in the 1970s, in the years of oppositional cinematic realism, a tool of socialist censorship. Formalism is escapism and immaturity, he argues—schizophrenia. He even surmises that, at one point, the communist regime has supported formalist experimental filmmaking in order to distract directors from social engagement:

The authorities vested their interest in people who claimed to make artistic films. [The authorities argued:] "There's no point in filming people and their living conditions. We're artists, we have to make artistic films. Experimental films preferably." (Stock 1993, 37)

Kieślowski articulates his critique of experimentalism cinematically too. *Camera Buff* includes a caricature of one such filmmaker. Filip encounters him twice. The first time is at the film festival, where—nonconformist in clothing and attitude—he voices disdain for all the films in the competition, the jury, and the festival system itself. The second encounter takes place in the office of a television producer while Filip pitches his new film.[23] The producer calls for an assistant to give Filip some film stock. The door opens and Filip meets the former festival rebel again. This time, however, he looks and behaves differently. Eager to please his boss, he no longer displays avant-garde arrogance and artistic radicalism. A job in the system seems to have tamed his revolt. The ex-rebel recognizes Filip and greets him amicably. After he leaves the office, the producer asks Filip if he knows him. When Filip nods his head, the producer comments ironically: "Maybe you'd like to be an artist too?" Filip shakes his head vehemently: "No, God forbid!" he replies, conveying Kieślowski's ironic view on the moral and political backbone of the experimentalists of the 1970s.

But Kieślowski understands that self-consciousness is a double-edged sword. And this is why he sticks to artisanship. Filmmaking that is too heavy on political engagement also bothers him, and Filip's "God forbid!" might refer to this aspect of filmmaking too. Kieślowski's amateur becomes also a commentary on the work of filmmakers such as Andrzej Wajda and his *Man of Marble*. "Twice in my life I tried my hand at politics and twice I came out very badly," Kieślowski recalls (Stock 1993, 38). The first time he had been active in the student-intellectual rebellions of 1968. The second time, he took a leading position in the "moral distrust" movement between 1976 and 1980 (alongside Wajda in an association of filmmakers)—that is, during the time he made *Camera Buff*. He recalls this latter experience as an "unpleasant and painful trap," a word we have heard before describing Filip's predicament (38).

> [It] was only politics on a small scale. But it was politics. . . . We thought we were very important and then it turned out that we were completely insignificant. . . . When Solidarity came along, I simply asked the Association to dismiss me—I wasn't cut out for such revolutionary times. (39)

The irony in his last sentence should not go unnoticed. The complicated and challenging constellation of filmmaking, politics, commitment to realism, and artistry of the 1970s, which Kieślowski faced, is reflected not only in Filip's gesture to turn the camera on himself, but also in his decision to destroy the negative of his latest film. In the causal chain of *Camera Buff*, the destruction of the film and the turning of the camera on oneself follow another key scene, the one which presents the discussion between Filip and Halski about the consequences of the broadcast of his films, including *Worker*. If the sequence showing Filip visiting the TV station included several references to Andrzej Wajda's *Man of Marble*, the peripatetic encounter between Filip and Halski (they go for a walk out of town) pastiches the sequence from *Camouflage* that is included in *Camera Buff*. In both, a socially superior character enlightens the hero about career pragmatics. The manager initiates Filip into his hermeneutic process, what Filip's films and their airing on TV mean to him.

In another interview, Kieślowski describes the role of Halski in *Camera Buff* as being similar to the one of the censor. But not any sort of censor. The manager "isn't merely a representative of dull-witted bureaucrats who cut scenes out of films," as Eastern European artists and intellectuals often tend to portray them. The encounter with Filip attempts to show how an enlightened—and enlightening—censor operates: "Through *Camera Buff*, I wanted to observe him and find out what lies behind his actions" (Kieślowski 1998, 66). In his dialogue with Filip, Halski formulates persuasive arguments as to why any public statement, be it through film or otherwise, has to be made with care, mindful of all the implications and consequences it can produce.

The other edge of authorship comes to the fore here. The process of becoming auteur, of developing an awareness of the implications of one's work, is also an effect of censorship. And the two scenes that follow the dialogue—the destruction of the film and the turning of the camera on himself—show that censorship is working and confirming Kieślowski's post-factum realization that, in those times, "essentially, censorship lay in ourselves—the writers, directors, and dramatists" (1998, 48–49). The story of Filip, which ends with the destruction of one film and the careful retelling of another, presents also the process of internalizing the gaze of the censor. Hence one can notice a fourth birth of the socialist subject: after gaining and expressing autonomy, Filip destroys his work and starts refilming the new Filip, the one that has gained self-consciousness in his encounter with a socialist power that has itself transformed.

Becoming auteur and developing an artistic consciousness seem thus to be unpleasantly linked to panoptic technologies of power. The turning of the camera on oneself means that from now on every artistic statement Filip produces will involve a double act of filming. He will record not only what stands in front of the camera, but also scrutinize what is thought behind it, in the mind of the artist. If indeed this is the meaning of the last scene, and *Camera Buff* is after all a film about the insidious practices of censorship, then Filip's future as an ethical filmmaker and as an agent of progressive social and political transformation is challenged. He has become part of the game of cultural struggle in socialism, a player in a complicated ballet of power and resistance, which draws now also on the "uncertainty principle" of the times. Censorship and subject production adapt also to the fall of grand narratives and tend to prefer—more and more—the negotiation table, as we shall see in the epilogue.

This predicament also explains why the management does not reprimand Filip for his films, but instead targets his superior. Filip's initiation into being an auteur with answers in socialism has only begun. He can still be persuaded, co-opted, maybe even corrupted, and his art integrated into the simulacrum of civic agency produced by the Gierek regime. In fact, after shooting *Worker*, Halski, in apparent contradiction to his opinions on the film, buys Filip a more professional camera. The ban falls on Josuch because he is a lost cause, an old leftist, who tells Filip not to listen to the deceptive words of the manager. If Filip feels he is telling the truth, he should not stop saying it. In the game of telling the truth, there will always be someone hurt and someone rewarded. Filip should not internalize Halski's message. He should remain "self-governed." "You must follow your instincts," Josuch instructs him. "Something good has awakened in you." Filip should develop it. Josuch assures Filip that he does not speak only in his name, but in the name of a community that stands behind his camera and feels represented by it. "We all come to believe in you" is his exit line.

Realism and Revisionism

The dialectic of amateurism and auteurship, of intellectual freedom and self-censorship, is also one of instinct and reflection. The amateur and the artisan follow their instincts. The auteur is self-reflexive. Self-consciousness can make one's work more complex, but it can also trigger self-censorship. Josuch's emphasis on instincts is the key to the question posed earlier about the compatibility between being an auteur and being an amateur. The independent eye of the anti-state-socialist resistance needs consciousness and artistic skills in order to produce compelling and insightful representations of reality. But instinct remains as important because, as long as it is not perverted, it can become the most reliable faculty that grants one escape from self-censorship and other forms of rationalizing one's social intervention. Filip needs to remain a Candide of socialism, like Voltaire's character:[24] a self-taught artist, the naïve boy from the orphanage, the "passionate neophyte," the "simpleton" (Haltof 2004, 46, 47), and the "rather comical, sheepish, yet inquisitive fellow" (Kickasola 2004, 115) who eats plain bread and hiccups when nervous. His limited education in filmmaking, his more relaxed relationship with himself as auteur, and his less standardized work practices put him in a better position to "follow his instincts," as Josuch puts it: look askew, notice difference, and make his camera record the "unrepresented world."

The amateur's alternative practices are subversive because they are liminal. They articulate the view of an outsider. "Amateur cine[ma] is neither cinema nor art, and it is precisely this which makes amateurism a radical alternative" (Reekie

2007, 112). According to Reekie, the amateur movement questions "the ideology of professionalism and quality," that is, a certain smoothness of the filmic artifact that renders its maker invisible and helps representation pass as reality (108). At a fundamental level amateur filmmaking "was an experimental culture since every amateur maker was engaged in a personal, playful, and inquisitive exploration of the medium" (115). The amateur points to the suture of the institution of cinema, to cinema's closing upon itself. There is thus an involuntary and immanent self-reflexivity of the amateur artifact, which keeps it linked to its maker and shows that the real is made and remakable (109, 113).

Instincts, looking askew and capturing the unrepresented, are thematized early in *Camera Buff*. While shooting his first film, the one about the factory's twenty-fifth anniversary, Filip also records two pigeons eating bread on a windowsill. He has no explicit reason for doing it. They drew his attention. He just followed an instinct. His instinct also drives him to record how industry bosses exit a meeting for a smoking break or for a visit to the toilet, and the moment when the musicians who played for the anniversary are being paid. His intuition also tells him to include these shots in the final version of his film, a decision which, predictably, irritates Halski, who calls for their removal. When asked why he filmed the pigeons or, later, why he made a film about a "cripple," Filip shrugs his shoulders. The pigeons were recorded because they attracted his attention and he liked to play with the camera. He is an amateur, a camera buff. He films, as the etymology of "amateur" suggests, out of love, love for the camera, love for life, and passion for reality.

For Halski, these shots have nothing to do with the narrative rendering of an anniversary. A professional rendering of an event must stay on topic and document the moments that are considered important. Filip's film needs trimming. But when he submits it for the amateur film festival, with the more general title *The Anniversary*, documenting thus not only a particular event, but a type of event, he includes the unwanted shots. Since the president of the jury is Jurga, the voice of the Polish revisionist resistance, it is exactly these shots that draw the jury's interest and bring Filip an award as a promising talent. Not only because they represent the unrepresented (as Kornhauser and Zagajewski's manifesto called for), but because they expose the way power operates to control representation. What is to be shown and presented as real and relevant is controlled by power via canons, standards, and rituals of visual presentation, and, especially, by downplaying artistic instinct.

At the festival, the first prize is not awarded. The president of the jury (Jurga) explains why: the main deficiency of the competing films is their conformism. Filmmakers show reality in the same way as television programs and newsreels do. They have internalized what Reekie calls the "the ideology of professionalism and quality" and can no longer articulate difference. Jurga makes use of the same argument as Reekie:

JURGA: "The 8 PM news show what they must show. An amateur does not have these obligations. He can do what he wants, when he wants. That's where you must find your strength."

The amateur is the subject of socialism as he should be. The amateur scene is not pressured by the same demands about content and form as the professional one, which has undergone the next birth of gaining self-consciousness. Hence amateur activity should not be a mere replication, of lower quality, of professional film-making—which is what the authorities of 1970s Poland wanted. It should produce difference and not be a tool to control the leisure time of the Polish worker. From less conventional filmmakers Jurga demands less conventional filmmaking. He expects personal observation and ingenuous representation. Filip's shots of pigeons seem to be exactly that. And the fact that the management recommended their cutting boosts their relevance. They bring in a different reality, intruding upon and decentering the one produced by power. Kieślowski himself confesses to being driven by this quest for difference: "There was a necessity, a need—which was very exciting for us—to describe the world. The Communist world had described how it should be and not how it really was" (as quoted in Žižek 2001, 76).

Jurga expresses one of the grand hypotheses of Kieślowski's generation of visual auteurs: the real—the truth about the world they live in—is to be found in that which is left out, censored, ignored, or not integrated. Disguised as an amateur, the cinematic auteur of the moral distrust era is expected to produce testimonies about unrepresented reminders of the socialist world, deliver ideologically unperverted representations, and initiate the public into perceiving it.[25] Filip's instinctual curiosity makes him a radical realist.[26] The revolutionary power of realist representation rests in its denial of transcendence. It challenges discourses of state socialism because it undermines their function of producing a political religion and questions their messianic grip on the meaning of history. Consequently, in his conversation with Filip, Halski aims to reinsert some "transcendence" into his views. He explains to Filip why showing things as they are creates disruption. According to Halski, mid-1970s Poland is not prepared or not willing to see things as they are. In order to function as a political community, it needs injections of transcendence. Filmmakers and power will negotiate the dose, and Filip must learn to participate in this bargaining.

* * *

The intriguing aspect of Filip's cinematic ingenuity is the fact that he is a Candide of socialism and that he embodies a yearning of immanentism reminiscent of the socialist discourse of film discussed in the first chapter, *Somewhere in Europe*. But we are dealing here with a different kind of immanence. Filip is an orphan raised within and integrated by the institutions of socialism. He is infused with socialist optimism, and identifies with socialism's political narratives. He maybe even believes he lives in the best of all possible worlds and, with his filmmaking, engages in good faith in the perfection of this world. But it is important to notice that, unlike the orphans of World War II of *Somewhere in Europe* or *Story of Young Couple*, he is not a political tabula rasa, a de-ideologized subject. Filip's ingenuity and political legitimacy rest in the fact that he can cast an uncorrupted (state-)*socialist* gaze at life. He is a tabula rasa only in the sense of being untouched by the compromises and deviations from socialism that the pragmatics of the Gierek regime triggered.

Filip's quality of being a pure subject of socialism, one that takes its narratives at their word, is the main point of entry used by revisionists in order to start a dialogue with Eastern European regimes. Filip and all naïve figures like him are revisionism's Trojan horses designed to attack the way in which state socialism departed from the original impulses of communist discourse (for example, from Marxism) and produced, as we have seen earlier, alienation. KOR, the main intellectuals' resistance movement of 1970s Poland, also adopted this position, and suggested a return to some of the basic questions regarding the condition of the worker in the name of which the regime can be held accountable. Realism in representation can, in this context, become a useful tool for such a return. The true Candide of the time, with his unperverted realist and socialist gaze, can best notice the alienation of the working class, its domestication and manipulation.

5 The Family of Victims

Stalinism Revisited in the 1980s

Returning Exiles

Márta Mészáros's 1982 *Diary for My Children* (*Napló gyermekeimnek*) is a story of a failed adoption, both personal and political. The film starts with the arrival of its orphan protagonist to her future home and adoptive mother and ends with her departure. Juli, the film's heroine, is in her teenage years and is brought to Budapest by an elderly couple whom she calls her grandparents. It is the year 1947. She comes from "somewhere" in the Soviet Union. She has grown up in its countryside (Kyrgyzstan), but is of Hungarian origin, from a communist family that fled Hungary before World War II to avoid political persecution. Magda, the foster mother, is a friend of Juli's dead parents and the younger sister of her adoptive grandfather, Dezső. She is single, occupies a high position in the postwar Hungarian Communist Party (HCP), and works for the Soviet authorities and the Red Army. She has arranged Juli and her grandparents' return from exile and hosts them in her spacious and elegant apartment, offering Juli a room of her own, plenty of food, access to a good school, security, warm clothing, and several extras, such as books to read, a free movie pass, and access to Budapest's postwar cultural life.

But Juli's integration into her new environment doesn't run as smoothly as planned, foregrounding the main theme of the film. To a certain point, it is similar to that of *Dita Saxová*: in spite of the good conditions offered to them and a firm narrative of social integration, the protagonists of both films refuse to play along. Uncontrollable psychological factors disrupt the process, and are linked to the loss of natural parents. Dita's perished in the Nazi death camps. Juli's died during Stalin's Great Terror (1934–1939), sharing the destiny of many leftist political exiles from Central and Eastern Europe who sought protection in the Soviet Union. They fled anticommunist persecution in their own countries only to face it again, suspected of revisionism or conspiracy, in the place where communism was the doctrine of power. Juli's father, a sculptor, disappears in 1936. Her mother, a painter, perishes soon afterwards in a rural hospital.

The adoptive grandparents, who take care of Juli after the death of her mother, are also exiled Hungarian communists, of a different generation than Juli's parents, yet not less exposed to purges. Dezső, the grandfather, left Hungary earlier, escaping the 1919–1920 White Terror that followed the defeat of the Hungarian Soviet Republic led by Béla Kun (who also sought refuge and ended up executed in the USSR).[1] The grandmother's biography is not detailed, but it seems she has also been active, like her husband, in the (communist) movement, witnessing, as an old-school illegalist of the Second International, communism's various theoretical metamorphoses and the attempts, both radical and eventually violent, to turn utopia into reality.[2] The Hungarian Soviet Republic lasted only from March to August 1919 and was one among several failed European attempts to profit from the post–World War I turmoil and install a communist regime in their countries. They followed the Soviet model, but lacked Soviet support, which came, in the case of Hungary, only thirty years later, in the wake of World War II, and helped the rise to power and the forty-year rule of the communist regime.

Unlike Juli's father and Kun, the grandparents survive the Great Terror of the 1930s, and their return to Budapest allows them to witness another such attempt, still inspired by Stalinist political practices, to revolutionize the political space. Their repatriation and the protection of Magda signals the initial impulse of the New Order in the making to concentrate under a single banner—and thus take control of—various experiences of communism that preceded it. All forces of the Left are called to participate in the reconstruction of Hungary. Géza Radványi and Béla Balázs's *Somewhere in Europe* testifies to this call. As emphasized in chapter 1, this initial ecumenical impulse will soon be abandoned. After 1948, when the communist regime comes to power in Hungary, it will be replaced by doctrinaire approaches, purges, imprisonments, and executions.

Diary for My Children suggests that Magda's drive to adopt Juli combines this centralizing impulse with a certain sense of political duty to raise an orphan child. She responds to the call to show solidarity with comrades who perished during illegalism (regardless of at whose hands) and to a more personal desire to rebuild a family—something that exile, war, and imprisonment have destroyed. But Juli, who also happens to be in her teenage years, cannot appreciate Magda's commendable intentions. Magda's efforts to befriend her, such as taking her to movies or to fashion shows, bringing her presents, talking cordially with her, tolerating her teenage whims and difficulties to adapt to her new school, prove to be insufficient. She resists Magda's overtures, and, affected by the political developments of post-1948 Hungary, antagonizes her. Towards the end of the film, Juli asks to be sent to an orphanage. Her demand is, however, too radical and unwise to be supported even by her advocates. Yet soon afterwards she leaves Magda's house and moves into a home she finds more suited to her.

Negotiating the Past

The first part of the film takes place before 1948, that is, before the HCP and the Soviet administration take power. The second part unfolds in 1949, as the New (Stalinist) Order starts its radical and violent practices of controlling the political space. In this interval, not only Juli but also Magda change. The latter becomes more intransigent, more consumed by her work and perhaps less interested in family life and rearing her protégée. In spite of her brother's vehement protests, Magda becomes associated with some of the most condemnable practices of the Stalinist regime. Her thinking and attitude grow more rigid and dictatorial; she seeks less Juli's love and respect and more her obedience. Magda's change culminates in her acceptance of a position as warden of a penitentiary in which political detainees are kept, interrogated, and, it is suggested, beaten, tortured, and assassinated.

Juli changes too. She cannot accept what she is expected to do: to distance herself, emotionally and politically, from her parents. On the contrary, she starts asking questions about their disappearance. Her teenage whims give way to a more mature perception of life. She becomes more political, and aims to understand and react to the radical changes she lives through. She builds a network of friends around her, all of whom, in one way or another, raise objections to Magda's choices—both parental and political. This network becomes not only one of personal support for Juli, but also one of resistance against Magda's political beliefs and actions. The network includes her grandparents; János, a Western communist; András, his educated son; and Tomi, Juli's teenage boyfriend, who belongs to a family of class enemies.

Juli's feelings toward Magda also transform. Earlier in the film, she tells her grandfather that even if she cannot love Magda (as she loves her parents or him), she will do her best to respect her. Later she admits she has lost even that. Dezső criticizes her, vehemently, because under Magda's protection, Juli is not only sheltered from persecution, but can live a privileged life. But it becomes clear that revolt against Magda and her practices constitute an important feature of Juli's identity. When Magda asks Juli why she hates her so much, Juli looks at her with a bold gaze and tells her that it is not hatred she feels for her but pity. For Juli, the strong Magda, who once earned her esteem, has been broken. The prison warden who stands in front of her is a woman who cannot or dares not talk candidly. She has grown opaque and dictatorial; she lives in fear. Like many others, communist or not, the times she lives in have crushed her. The only difference is that she plays, for the time being, for the winning team.

The most important bone of contention between the foster mother and her protégée is the memory of the latter's parents. She not only wants to find out the

Figure 5.1. Juli asks János whether she can be sent to an orphanage (*Diary for My Children*).

truth about them, but also seeks an acknowledgment from Magda that they perished in times that are similar to those Hungary is experiencing in the present. The turn from respect to confrontation in their relationship takes place also in connection with the memory of Juli's parents. Juli fills out a form from her school requiring biographical data. When it asks her to disclose information about her father, Juli refuses to fill it out the way Magda demands. A sharp exchange follows. Juli accuses her guardian of lying and of not having the courage to speak up and tell the truth about what happened to her father. Magda tries to present her point of view. She is a soldier fighting the Cold War. Historical necessity sometimes trumps the truth, she argues. They live in dangerous times, and winning the battle (and the war) is more imperative than responding to "impulses," as Magda puts it, toward individual justice. More vital are party discipline, loyalty to the Third International, intransigence, and pragmatism. If silence and deceit serve the cause of building socialism and defending it, then one has to be silent and deceitful.

Magda's arguments cannot persuade Juli. The latter's position, shared by reformers and revisionists of the post-Stalin era, is that every individual counts, and no one is killable for a superior purpose.[3] Magda's appeal to historical necessity in support of the brutal political practices of 1949–1954 is seen by Juli as a sign of cowardice or, even worse, opportunism. This is why she tells Magda she has been broken. Magda admits that filling in "disappeared in 1936" on the form is a misrepresentation, but that explaining why her version works better for Juli will be useless. She will not understand anyway. History is too complicated for a teenager to understand, or, even worse, practice-oriented communists like Magda have become so devoted to changing the world that they have lost the skills, the patience, or the will to explain their deeds.

Juli "struggles to preserve the familiar identity she is urged to forget, clinging to her own feelings and the memories that enable her to resist attempts to suppress her personal history" (Portuges 2004, 198). She fights back against Magda's silence and argues that Magda refrains from explaining her reasons because her arguments do not stand the test of reason, common sense, and elementary ethics. Juli's position thus puts an interesting twist on Marx's famous claim that intellectuals have to change the world and not talk about it. The secretive and brutal practices of a Stalinism that no longer considers it necessary to explain itself seem to be the nightmarish realization of Marx's words. Magda's attitude suggests she doesn't believe they live in times of dialogue. She tells Juli that filling out the form as "she dictates" is an order. If Juli refuses, she will do it herself.

Stalinist Rearing

The form episode is important because it reveals how Stalinist subject production practices are remembered in the 1980s. Identities and personal histories can be changed and rewritten according to "historical necessity." Destinies can be made and unmade, as the focus of government falls on the economic, social, and political output, and not on the individual as a goal in and of himself or herself. The world of Stalinism is not one of humans, but one of collective achievements such as those defined by the five-year plan. And this is the point of intervention sought by *Diary for My Children*. Juli's character brings to the fore the idea that subject production is not to be perceived differently. The productionist perspective of the 1950s is insufficient. Humans are not as malleable as they are expected to be. Not even orphans. And the film's humanist discourse aims to emphasize exactly that the essence of the human is exactly the excess that makes a subject resistant to radical transformation—not because he or she is traumatized by the war and the death camp, Dita Saxová's message, but exactly because resistance lies at the core of human life.

The fact that Magda's pedagogy does not work on Juli is reinforced by János. János is Juli's main ally and the character whose ideological adoption Juli seeks. He is of Magda's generation, but a "Western" communist—a Hungarian illegalist who spent his exile in France and not in the Soviet Union like Magda. His political opinions diverge from the Stalinist line of the era, though he never overtly opposes it. He plays along but refuses a spot in the front row. He argues that getting the economy going is more important than party politics.[4] Regarding Juli, he tells Magda that she is too impatient with the girl. Like the Stalinists, she "wants an overnight change: of the world and the people." He believes change happens more slowly, and the effort to accelerate history may stand behind many of the "errors" and "abuses" of the time, as Khrushchev will call them later in his 1956 speech against Stalinism.

Such an abuse, against which János himself intervenes, takes place soon after his conversation with Magda. In order to punish Juli for trying to run away from home to her parents' relatives, Magda asks István, a friend who also happens to be a high-ranking party official, to spank Juli and thus persuade her to be more obedient. As Juli gets her first hits, János breaks into the room, frees her, and engages in a fistfight with István.

The fight between the two men is not only over Juli and methods of disciplining rebels or deviant thought. Tension between them has built ever since István had criticized János's refusal to show more interest in politics. He insinuated that people in the party leadership might wonder about his activity during his stay in the West, out of contact with Moscow and the Comintern. They might suspect that foreign espionage agencies had recruited him, which was the typical line of denunciation of Western communists of the time and which led to long prison terms and death sentences.[5]

The spanking episode reveals that, in Juli's eyes, Magda has lost her credibility. She can control Juli only through fear and corporeal violence and no longer through arguments. *Diary* visualizes Juli's thoughts and feelings by inserting a domestic violence scene Juli sees in one of her visits to the movie theater. The insert is from a foreign film and shows a mother sadistically beating her daughter and locking her away in a pantry that looks like a basement prison cell. It operates a division in Juli's perception of the world of grown-ups, which also describes postwar politics. On one side are those who are willing to use violence to meet their interests; on the other are those who do not, who prefer gentler means of persuasion and who are always willing to discuss their decisions. Magda's figure rules over one camp, János's over the other.

The grandfather is the character who stands in between, who embodies the contradictions of these positions. On the one hand, as a survivor of Stalin's Great Terror, he opposes the political violence practiced by the HCP in the new Hungary. On the other, he is still the product of his generation, which found it normal to use violence in order to get things done. Moreover, unlike János, he is afraid to speak up, to argue and debate. He admits several times—once during a nervous breakdown—that he belongs to a frightened generation, hunted, imprisoned, show-trialed, and murdered by both noncommunists and communists alike; by both Horthy and Stalin, and perhaps, without Magda's protection, by Rákosi too.[6] Thus, in spite of his apparent gentle demeanor, he cannot keep himself from slapping Juli when she once talks brazenly back to him and is even close to slapping the powerful Magda herself (as older brother and patriarch) during a dispute they have about her accepting the position of prison warden.

When he later apologizes to Juli for losing his temper and hitting her, he explains the mindset of his generation. He tells her that even if he is against it now, violence is ingrained in his mindset. His father had beaten him heavily when he was a child. It was normal for those days. Through beating, his father won a son's respect. It was condemnable but it worked, at least in those days, and the son reproduced in part the behavior of his father. For Dezső, during the Budapest 1919 Revolution, it felt normal to chase, shoot at, and imprison anticommunists. In those days, he believed that violent takeovers were necessary to change the world. His life experiences have altered his perceptions. He has witnessed the ugliest consequences of violence. Since the Budapest revolution, another world war has unfolded, genocides, Stalin's Great Terror, and now the bloody Hungarian Stalinist takeover. He understands what life in fear means. He has grown old, has become doubtful about revolutions, and knows he might be sent to prison even now, were he not Magda's brother. He questions his earlier beliefs, and at the same time acknowledges that maybe the only reason he does it is because he is old, ill, and useless.

Magda and the Grandfather

In spite of rising tensions over political allegiances, János and the grandfather have many words of praise for Magda. This makes Mészáros's film stand out. Mészáros does not demonize Magda. She adds an extra dimension to her character in order to reveal, like Andrzej Wajda in *Man of Marble,* that the issue of Stalinism is more complicated than the memory of the Cold War has it. Magda protects her brother; maybe even János, and her advice to Juli about how she should fill out the form is not necessarily the result of fear, but a demonstration of practical wisdom, something that an intransigent teenager might indeed not be able to understand. She knows that it is not in Juli's best interest to disclose full information about her purged father. Revealing that he was arrested during the Great Terror might make school officials regard Juli as the daughter of a "class enemy"—a label that would lead to persecution. She might be thrown out of the good school she is in—something that happens once Juli flees Magda's home.

Both the grandfather and János offer Juli biographical details about her foster mother. The grandfather praises Magda for being tough, for making things happen, for fighting fascism, for resisting imprisonment and torture. And so does János, who even admits he considered marrying her. For him, Magda of the 1920s and 1930s was the embodiment of the modern woman: strong, smart, and vital. Opposing her, his praise suggests, means more than just showing contempt to an opportunist, a brutal henchperson, or a power-thirsty apparatchik. She is not István, but an experienced activist, who has made the political choice to follow the Stalinist line, a choice shared by many intellectuals of those times from both Eastern and Western Europe—the most illustrious Hungarian example being the literary scholar and theorist Georg Lukács.[7]

This assumption about Magda does not exclude the possibility, as Juli apprehends, that the times might have also broken her. But János insists that Juli regard Magda as a person with clear and thoughtful deliberations behind her decisions. He is on Juli's side and disagrees with the line Magda has adopted. Also like Juli, and unlike many other characters in the film (for example, the grandparents), he is not afraid of her. In the name of their long friendship, he tries to understand Magda, and understand the practical Marxist vision beyond her decisions. Unfortunately it is only a one-way understanding. Stalinism is not about understanding, but about discipline. For people in uniform like Magda, János looks more and more like a interwar bohemian communist, who, like the grandfather, can no longer keep up with the toughness of the times they live in.

The grandfather's comments about Magda reveal he feels inferior to her. Unlike him, she was able to live the Marxist intellectual's dream of not only describing the world, but also changing it. His time of turning theory into praxis during the 1919 Soviet Republic lasted for a short period of time and failed. Forty years later, his insights and know-how are no longer in demand. *Diary* presents him as old and ill. The only thing left for him is to return to becoming an old-school intellectual of the Left, moreover one whose range of influence is limited. Since the public voicing of his suspicions regarding Stalinism might become his ticket to the penitentiary, he is in a way again in illegality, but also in a position to become a caricature of the fighter he was (see his slapping of women). Defeated, he is protected by his sister, that is, by the regime itself. While Juli moves out of Magda's house and thus makes her opposition to Magda public, Dezső admits he has lost the energy and perhaps the courage to do so. He protests only via domestic ironies—for example, comparing Magda's affluent life in her spacious and elegant apartment with that of the bourgeois aristocracy communism struggled to depose and whose properties it nationalized.

Grandfather's main gesture of protest is the secret writing of his memoirs. But, like his living room ironies, they remain private. Catherine Portuges emphasizes that Mészáros's films often depict weak and defeated men. Behind this depiction lies Mészáros's reproach. The history of the Stalinist takeover of Eastern Europe has been written mostly as a history of an implacable conquest by the Soviet Union and as a betrayal by the West (at Yalta). The history of Hungary's Stalinization has been articulated similarly, as a history of victims, in the same way as the history of Central Europe has been written for the last two centuries as a history of small and defenseless nations in between superpowers.[8] Mészáros's reproach seems to suggest that Stalinism was made possible also because communists of Dezső's generation have not resisted it properly, as younger Hungarians will do in 1956. She suggests that the manuscript Dezső hands Juli on his deathbed—with the hope she will read it, make it public one day, and reveal what he believes are some relevant truths about the history of the movement—is a text written in the same melancholic language of disappointed leftist intellectuals (of the 1950s through the 1980s), blaming history for their own personal and collective shortcomings.

The dialogue between Juli and her grandfather underscores this muted reproach articulated by Mészáros. Juli tells him she is just like him. They share political ideas and oppose what Magda represents. The difference is that Juli is not afraid to speak up and to overtly resist Magda. The new generation that grows during Stalinism shares the ideas of the older one that precedes it. The younger ones, however, might have more resolve to oppose it. The 1956 rebellion is the proof. Juli's determination is documented in the epilogue of *Diary for My Children*. It is set in 1953, the year of Stalin's death, which announces a new era, a "thaw" in Hungarian leftist politics that would lead to the 1956 declaration of independence from Moscow and to the articulation of a Hungarian road to socialism (which will be repressed by a Soviet invasion). Juli embodies the student generation that will spark the 1956 rebellion. In 1953 she is completely politicized and a resister of Stalinism. She might have even been inspired by her grandfather's manuscript.

Juli's development in the post-1953 era, as a daughter of her grandfather and János, is detailed in the two sequels Mészáros made to her film, *Diary for My Loved Ones*[9] (*Napló szerelmeimnek*, 1987) and *Diary for My Father and Mother* (*Napló apámnok es anyámnok*, 1990), and a prequel, *Little Vilma: The Last Diary* (*Kisvilma—az utolsó napló*, 1999).[10] The sequels tell the story of a Juli confronting, more publicly, Stalinism. *Diary for My Loved Ones* is set in both Moscow and Budapest between 1953 and 1956. It shows Juli's professional growth as a filmmaker and the development of her political consciousness by revisiting, in Moscow, the roots of Soviet communism (and cinema). *Diary for My Father and Mother* documents the 1956 revolt, with Juli not only participating in it, but also attentively observing the way in which the event is perceived in various political circles. *Little Vilma: The Last Diary* presents a return to 1930s Kyrgyzstan to investigate, based on recently declassified KGB documents, the arrest and subsequent murder of Juli's father.

History, Memory, Resistance

Among the films discussed in this book, *Diary* is the most historicizing. The distance between the time of narration and the time of the plot is the longest. Consequently, it is also the most reflexive, in the sense that its representation of the past is articulated with an assumed method. The method Mészáros employs is suggested in the title of the film. Diaries are fragmentary writings and open structures. They don't bear the burden of telling an impersonal truth. Their narrative focuses on the transformation of a consciousness in response to political changes. They testify to a lived history, and the discursive rendering of these experiences is the result of an effort to work through them: an "evolution of a young woman facing the major historical moments of the twentieth century

[and] passionate yet critical studies of personal development and political awakening" (Portuges 2004, 192).

Because they are fragmentary, they do not have to obey the rhetoric of historical writing, whose closed structures might create the illusion that the truth about a certain time and place has been completely reflected in its representation. The diary format makes the statement that the partial and personal truth it relates is open to discussion. It assumes a methodological incompleteness, which gestures not only to the subject's limited understanding of the times she lives in, but especially to the fact that, as briefly suggested before, the immediate postwar era in Eastern Europe is one of the most complex moments of modernity and thus needs extensive consideration.

The fact that the diary format is an assumed method of representing the past is reinforced by the second part of the title of the film. The auteur tells the story of an account made *for* a specific and concrete audience, "my children" (or "for my loved ones" and "for my father and mother"—the sequels to this film). It is articulated as if Mészáros was communicating with people who are close to her: family members, companions, friends. The diary is a gift to them. Its audience is not the imagined and abstract, de-individualized and de-corporealized public of the major formats of historical writing. It constitutes a tangible (face-to-face) community of memory, of people who know each other, can bond with each other, and thus experience a sense of shared destiny. Moreover, their reactions to her reminiscences continue the writing of the story, which the specific form of the diary leaves open.

The purposive nature of the diary and its interest in creating an active community of remembering also reveals Mészáros's militant understanding of memory (and history). The diary format, as a minor genre of historical representation, better fits the militant mission of challenging more official accounts. Juli is a young revisionist. She emplots events differently than the winners of history (Magda) or the defeated (Dezső), and from a woman's perspective. By bearing testimony she aims not only to fight forgetting, but also show that history is plural, multivocal, and multilayered. Moreover, there is also a particular interest in her account. She aims to show how history repeats itself, how practices of power are reiterated at different moments in time and ideological contexts, and how that abuse and oppression do not have a specific political color.

Mészáros's method may have been inspired by Marx's famous insight that history returns at least once as farce.[11] Though never ironic—that is, not interested in looking for replications as farces—the narrative of *Diary for My Children* centers on a series of ominous recurrences. Consequently, the film's storytelling avoids being linear; it seeks to stage a dialogue between the present and the past, on the one hand, and between the actual and the spectral on the other. It presents moments when the lived, the remembered, and the fictional mirror each other; it marks coincidences, draws parallels, and shows how places, characters, and situations replicate each other in different temporal or ontological settings. The political importance of testimony comes to the fore here. It unravels and fights the perpetuation of such repetitions:

> JULI: "I don't want to forget my mother and father. And that's what Magda wants. She acts as if they never existed. And I can't forget them."

The episode in which Juli confronts Magda about filling out the form shows not only how power aims to rewrite individual and collective history and how it regards the subject, but also how it prepares the terrain for possible repetitions of oppressive practices. The arrest of Juli's father in the 1930s needs to be erased and forgotten because similar arrests are made in the present, and because Magda, the formerly imprisoned, beaten, and tortured, repeats history (almost as farce here), as she has become the one who makes men and women face the same ordeals she did for their political beliefs in the present. Power needs forgetting in order to suggest that political abuse is an extraordinary intervention, a state of exception, and consequently that it is temporarily necessary and acceptable.

The Community of Memory

This is why remembering becomes an act of resistance. Resistance to unjust power practices and its abuses is rooted in the understanding that they are not historically conditioned. Remembering and gesturing toward repetitions brings to the fore that oppression, terror, and unjust appropriation of privileges are practices that transcend time and political doctrines. No surprise, then, that the chroniclers of history's repetitions are often its sufferers. Juli is surrounded by such a community of victims and witnesses of the déjà vus of history. Her story intertwines with those of many others. They are her helpers and counselors. Besides her grandfather and grandmother, her boyfriend, Tomi, is also one. His father has disappeared during the war, and his mother is arrested toward the end of the film. So is János, who will spend his next five years incarcerated, victim of the internal HCP purges. Juli bonds with his crippled son, András, who is, like her, an indirect victim of his father's arrest and of the war and a half orphan.[12]

The community of victims is completed by characters with spectral presences, who either haunt the present (another reference to the idea of repetition) or suggest escapes from it. Such specters are "flashbacks, childhood memories, fantasies and reveries," or they emerge from Juli's "surreptitious and obsessive love for the cinema" (Portuges 1993, 89).[13] The scene Juli watches in the movie theater in which the mother abuses her daughter is one such example which enables her to bond with all those who endure similar treatment in the present. Another important film-viewing episode shows Juli watching a sequence from the Hungarian 1940s classic, István Szőts's *People from the Mountains*. While the domestic violence clip presents a specter of Magda, the excerpt from Szőts's film recalls Juli's parents and, moreover, injects a reminiscence of them she does not have.

The sequence presents a ritualistic dedication of a newborn child to nature. A mother and a father carry their baby through the forest and present it to a tall tree, the tree of life. The scene is filmed form a sharp low angle suggesting, on the one hand, the perspective of the child (Juli) and, on the other, the overwhelming greatness of nature. The individual existence of the baby will be bonded to the tall tree. The parents call on nature to protect the newborn. "Let no one raise his hand against you," the father declaims against an impressionist musical background reminiscent of Claude Debussy's *Prelude to the Afternoon of a Faun* (an important musical commentary because it clears the film of suspicions of fascistoid patriarchalism). He continues ominously, his words clearly referring to the times of political radicalism Juli and those close to her live through: "May your days not end before the appointed time."

This scene also plays an important role in sacralizing family bonds, placing them beyond history. The scene presents the natural order of the world as being good, harmonious, and peaceful. The child should have no fear of it. "The forest loves you," the father concludes, implicitly suggesting that injustice and violence are products of modern human behavior. The family is the social outcome of this good, natural, antimodern order. As hinted in the title of *Diary for My Children* (and of the other films of the series), bonds to one's children, parents, and loved ones are critical to one's identity and thus have a politically subversive dimension. This might be regarded as a conservative point of view, in the line of Ferdinand Mount's 1998 anti-Engelsian argument that family bonds subvert authority; resist social conditioning, propaganda, and political calls to violence; and provide the subject with an unalterable sense of identity (Mount 1998, 1–4).

Replications of the Past

The main interface bringing the specters of the past onscreen are Juli's flashbacks, mostly presenting episodes related to her parents. As the film progresses and her conflict with Magda sharpens and becomes more politically loaded, the flashbacks grow longer and more factual. They spur Juli's resistance, contextualize her present condition, slow down the pace of the storytelling, and invite the viewer not only to take history in, but also to reflect on it. There are two kinds of flashbacks in *Diary*. Some have a lyrical, others a narrative function. The former show serene moments of Juli's childhood, the latter recall the death of her parents. The former are either set in nature, mostly family idylls in sunny fields and forest clearings, or present, in a gray and abstract setting—such as that of a marble quarry—Juli's father sculpting. They reveal Juli's feelings for them, her nostalgia, and suggest that they spur her resistance through remembering. The reminiscences of Juli's father are accompanied by the sounds of hammer and chisel, over ominous synthesizer music.

While the idyllic outdoor recollections express yearning for loved ones and past times (similar to the short flashbacks of *Dita Saxová*) and are coupled with the voice of a happy child calling her parents, the flashbacks related to her father suggest a more reflexive way of remembering with reference to the so-called coincidences and déjà vus of history. Like the dedication sequence in *People from the Mountains*, the reminiscences set in nature participate in articulating the myth of the private. Their role is to create a contrast between past and present, and to highlight what Juli has lost: the protection and love of her parents and the apparent stability of her childhood in the Soviet countryside. In contrast, the flashbacks documenting the death of her parents aim to show similarities between past and present, more exactly the repetitions of history. The grand repetition *Diary for My Children* addresses is that of the Stalinist terror. The Great Terror that took place in the Soviet Union in the 1930s and that killed her father and mother (and hundreds of thousands of others) returns, perhaps as a caricature of communism, to Hungary of the late 1940s and early 1950s, but with similar devastating effects.

The film employs a series of narrative devices to emphasize these replications, but before analyzing them, let us notice the context in which the narrative flashbacks appear in the film. Unlike the lyrical ones, which show impressions in Juli's mind, the narrative ones, recalling the deaths of her parents, are connected to a situation of communication in the present. They visualize a verbal interaction, a confession, a testimony. In this respect, they hark back to the only flashback scene included in a much more present- and future-oriented film such as *Somewhere in Europe*, discussed in chapter 1. In Béla Balázs and Géza Radványi's film, a Jewish girl revisits, like Juli, her traumatic experiences. The act of remembering takes place in a moment of comfort, when she feels protected and listened to, in the company of a trusted friend.

Similarly, Juli tells her story to her boyfriend and most trusted companion, Tomi, in a private moment. They spend a quiet afternoon at his house. But perhaps because she recalls not only an event that affected her private life, but also one that stands proof for violent practices of power repeating themselves, her account becomes also a testimony. It must be conveyed and remembered collectively. It is, in fact, Juli's message to the present, or, as the titles of the series put it, to those who are close to her: her children, parents, loved ones. The more repressed the memory, the more imperative the duty to find the proper context and the courage to recall it and turn it into a testimony.

One of the devices employed by Mészáros to unravel the repetitions of history is the casting of Jan Nowicki in both the role of Juli's father and that of János.[14] While there is a striking difference between Juli's natural mother and her foster one, the image of her perished father overlaps with that of János—the only physical difference between the two, one that mainly serves the narrative purpose of distinguishing between the two characters, is that János wears a beard.[15] While Magda has a "stern appearance," a "severe coiffure, tall leather boots, and tailored uniform," she "contrasts sharply with Juli's sensual, rapturous recollections of

Figure 5.2. Juli remembering the arrest of her father (*Diary for My Children*).

her biological mother" (Portuges 2004, 195). János, however, seems to function not only as a substitute for Juli's father, but also as a character in a "what if" story: what if her father had survived the Great Terror as János survived the air raid that killed his family and crippled his son? What would her father have said about the present? What would the present say about him? Would he be purged again?

As the embodiment of the returning father, János's role is to answer these questions. Through him the biological father reemerges to guide his orphan daughter. As replica, János tells Juli what the vanished father in the flashbacks was not able to say to a Juli too young to understand. But as in Shakespeare's *Hamlet*, ghosts return to question the political state of the present. In *Diary for My Children* the ghost inquires about the development of the communist movement and its practices. The replication of the perished father becomes even more conspicuous when Juli, toward the end of the film, moves in with János and his son and becomes, at least symbolically, his adoptive daughter, closing the period of orphanhood in her personal life (but only for a short while, because János's arrest can be regarded as her second orphaning). Throughout the film, János counsels Juli, protects and shares his life experiences with her. No surprise, then, that she sees a returning father in him.

Arrests

With the characters of the past, its situations also return. When Juli moves into János's house, she puts herself in the situation of witnessing a reiteration in the present of her father's arrest twelve or thirteen years earlier. This is another important narrative device Mészáros employs to warn her viewers against the repetitions of history. The arrest of János and a prison visit a few years later mark the end of *Diary for My Children*, suggesting that Juli's orphanhood continues. In the prison visit, which is the final sequence of the film, a shaved János looks exactly like Juli's arrested father and seems to speak from somewhere beyond life. This effect is enhanced by the fact that two rows of net-wired fence separate the visitors from the visited, blurring their faces. On a lane between these two fences, emphasizing their separation, a prison guard paces slowly from one end of the room to another. János asks Juli what is happening in the other world. She gives him a brief account. She works, takes care of András, meets with Tomi, reads, goes to the movies, and both she and András do what the survivors of stormy political times do: they wait. They wait for better times, for the father to return and for a life in a world with no early morning arrests.[16]

Political arrest scenes are frequent in films that depict violent regimes. They have a specific set of characters (the victim, his or her spouse and children, the policemen), settings (the family's home in the early morning hours), and movements (the storming of the private, the search, the summary packing, the confrontation with the arrogant policeman, the farewell from the family). One of their functions is to construct the victim as martyr, especially by highlighting the dignity with which the victim exits the scene. Searches serve to reveal the overwhelming nature of power in the police state and its brutal invasion of the private. The reaction to this invasion is the emphasis on the family bonding that the imminent separation engenders, the loyalties expressed, and the transfer of responsibilities from the arrested to his successor, such as a spouse or an older son.

One way or another, the two arrests in Mészáros's film follow this pattern. They are both short scenes, similar in their unfolding, and loaded with muted tension. Both take place in the early morning hours. The state breaks into the realm of the family in moments of intimacy and vulnerability, when the family is asleep. The victims follow their henchmen subdued, with dignity. The main difference between the scene in the past and that in the present is that Juli has grown up and is old enough to understand what is happening. In fact, the second arrest is anticipated. János is fired from the plant. At home, he prepares for his departure, puts his belongings in order, and destroys possibly incriminating documents.

What is specific to Mészáros's film is that the perspective on the two arrests belongs to Juli and not to the seized person. The narrative purpose of the two scenes is to show a moment of change in the life of the witness, not of the arrested. The first arrest marks Juli mostly psychologically. It causes a brutal separation from her father. The second arrest, taking place more than ten years later, affects her not only psychologically but also intellectually and politically. When she visits János in prison, she has become a young woman, and the arrest seems to have contributed to her maturation. During the arrest scene, János's farewell

Figure 5.3. The spectral János from behind the prison fence (*Diary for My Children*).

words call on Juli not to cry. If she cries he will feel ashamed of her. He expects something else. He expects her to behave like an adult: to survive, testify to the abuses she has witnessed, and fight against their return.

A Film of the 1970s

Diary appeared in 1984 but is, both in style and in theme, a film of the 1970s in the vein of Andrzej Wajda's 1977 *Man of Marble*. It addresses boldly and directly the Stalinist era, reenacts it, and tackles some of the key issues of its remembrance with a high degree of sophistication and not from an anticommunist (not even an entirely anti-Stalinist) position. Like Wajda, Mészáros started her project in the early 1970s, but the industry blocked it at various stages in its preproduction (Portuges 2004, 194).[17] Moreover, even after its completion in the 1980s, the film was shelved for more than a year and released only with two scenes cut out (Portuges 1993, 200).

If one excludes from consideration Yugoslavia, a country that, since the 1940s Tito-Stalin dispute, had antagonized the Soviet Union, the first bold cinematic investigations of Stalinism are the products of the late 1960s.[18] *Diary for My Children* expresses this artistic but also intellectual drive that began in Czechoslovakia and culminated in the 1968 Prague Spring. Films of the Czechoslovak New Wave such as *All My Good Countrymen* (dir. Vojtech Jasný, 1968), *The Joke* (dir. Jaromil Jires, 1969), and *Larks on a String* (dir. Jiri Menzel, produced in 1968–1969, but not released until 1990 due to the Soviet invasion) thematized the radicalism, the violence, and the paranoia of the times.[19] Hungary was maybe the first to follow suit, but more timidly (taking the post-1956 normalization into account). The best-known films on this topic are *Love* (dir. Karoly Makk, 1970); *Angi Vera* (dir. Pal Gabor, 1976), though it articulated only a veiled critical engagement with the period;[20] and, later, *Whooping Cough* (dir. Peter Gardos, 1986). The film historian Balázs Varga has drawn to my attention that these films are only the tip of an iceberg.[21] They were part of a trend in the Hungarian cinema of the 1960s that addressed "the near past," and was concerned with the continuity between present and past (the mid-1960s, the era of the consolidation period of the Kádár regime, and the 1950s).[22]

With the exception of the 1977 *Man of Marble*, Polish cinema, like most other cinemas of Eastern Europe, did not address Stalinism until the 1980s. The other notable Polish films on this topic emerged in 1982, during the Solidarity period, and were both banned and properly released only after 1989: Ryszard Bugajski's *Interrogation* and Janusz Zaorski's *Mother of Kings* (Haltof 2007, xxvii). In Romania veiled references to Stalinism surfaced in Mircea Daneliuc's *Fox Hunt* (1980) and in Alexandru Tatos's *Sequences* from 1982, while Bulgaria and East Germany, for different reasons, did not overtly address the issue until after 1989, a period in which a fidgety and strictly incriminating revisitation of Stalinism (and socialism) began all over Eastern Europe.[23]

This summary inventory of Eastern European productions thematizing Stalinism confirms David Robinson's argument that Hungarian cinema was in the avant-garde of politically challenging films that conflicted with censorship (2004, 173). The other explanation of why *Diary for My Children* could be released only in the 1980s is given by János Rainer in a study of the historiography of Stalinism in Hungary. He shows that the 1980s context was more permissive to historical research on Stalinism, at least because it could stand as a substitute for the major taboo in Hungarian history writing: the 1956 rebellion (239). Also a comparison between *Diary for My Children* and *Love*, an earlier film about Stalinism and the most complex before Meszaros's, explains insightfully why Mészáros's project was so many years in the making.

Love addresses Stalinism vicariously, emotionally, and never truly sets out to analyze it. It tells the story of the wife and the mother of an arrested political prisoner of the Rákosi purges, waiting for his return. The wife knows he has been arrested, but the dying mother doesn't. The daughter does not want to sadden her mother-in-law with the news of her son's imprisonment, so she invents an alternative reality, a procedure employed thirty years later by one of the most popular films about the Eastern European socialist experience, *Good Bye, Lenin!* (Germany 2003).[24] She makes up the story about the world they live in order to create the illusion that political change has not taken place. She tells the dying mother that the missing son has left Hungary and is thriving in the United States, from which he frequently sends them letters.

Like *Love* and *Angi Vera* and even like *Man of Marble*, Mészáros's project filters history through a female character, and one can speculate that, for the more patriarchal context of socialist gender dynamics, the choice of a female protagonist might serve to soften the polemical tone of the argument against Stalinism. *Love* reflects the prevalent position of the Kádár era,[25] replicating Khrushchev's 1956 denunciation of Stalinism, whose critical approach was that "some errors and exaggerations took place." In *Love*, a man is abusively arrested—the error—and his arrest causes suffering for him and his family. In contrast, *Diary* looks at Stalinism as not just the product of mistakes and too much revolutionary zeal. It filters its approach by linking terror and the repetitions of history with the red oligarchy that Soviet communism produced,[26] a position that was already articulated by Imre Nagy, the leader of the Hungarian 1956 revolt, under the term "minority dictatorship" (Rainer 2009, 232).[27]

If the 1956 critique of Stalinism focused on Stalinism's authoritarian and dogmatic approach to politics, its socially homogenizing effects and the loss of contact with grassroots organizations such as workers' councils (Rainer 2009, 235), Mészáros's project speaks more about the fear and terror that the apparent incertitude of the Cold War context and the effort to accelerate history engendered in those days. The cause of the terror or its ultimate agent remains obscure, being somehow inscribed in the times themselves. Like Wajda's *Man of Marble*, *Diary for My Children* is, first of all, interested in understanding the historical period, with both its pluses and minuses, and in revealing its spirit, how it felt to live in those years. Condemning it is not explicitly on the film's agenda—regardless of whether censorship did or did not have anything to do with it.

Because of 1956 and 1968 and because Soviet tanks were stationed in Hungary until the end of the Cold War (the last troops left in 1991), a bolder approach that would view Stalinism as a form of Soviet colonization was impossible. But it is possible that such an approach didn't interest Mészáros. The sequels to *Diary*, all made after 1989, in which she could have stated this argument explicitly, prove that her approach to Stalinism did not involve identifying it as Soviet occupation. Her film does not voice the typical statement of the late 1980s anti-Soviet propaganda that communism leads to dictatorship and to Stalinism. It presents Stalinism as a political choice, a mistaken one, but still a historically embedded and understandable response to turbulent political times.

Her more analytical approach is even noticeable in the film's visual texture. The cinematography and the lighting underscore a double incertitude: one in the present, belonging to an observer who tries to stay open-minded; the other in the past, presenting the ambiguities of the immediate postwar era. The diffuse lighting reduces sharp contrasts of blacks and whites, suggesting that individuals who lived through those times (and those who reflect on them from the present) did not benefit from clear landmarks and worldviews to orient themselves and their political choices (in contrast to the Manichaeism that informed the political discourse of the times of Stalinism). *Diary for My Children* depicts the era as an eternal winter, with cold weather, cloudy skies, shriveling bodies, subdued faces, hibernating nature, and, outside of Magda's circle, scarce resources.

Mészáros's position is more in line with the revisionism of the 1970s which led to the Solidarity movement and is detectable in the narratives of the Polish cinema of distrust (discussed in chapter 4). On the other hand, there is one aspect that *Diary for My Children* shares with 1980s views of Stalinism. The 1980s historiography became sensitive to the concept of totalitarianism even if it could not articulate it overtly until after 1989. Developed by Hannah Arendt, picked up by anticommunist discourse and then employed in notorious historians' debates to find common ground between communist and fascist regimes, totalitarianism played into structuralist approaches to history and addressed Stalinism more as a consequence of modernization in the twentieth century, and less as a historical period contingent on the world wars and on the development of capitalism, as Marxist historians such as Eric Hobsbawm have it (2011, 383).[28]

Diary for My Children shares with the totalitarianist approach of the 1980s the emphasis on the conflict between power and family and the fact that the latter can produce an essential identity, a point of anchorage and protective network against ideology. It aims to show, as Dina Iordanova emphasizes, that Stalinism aimed to disrupt the sacred relation of the family, especially the bond between mother and child (2003, 127). The positive message of the film is that these bonds endure even if there are no blood relations between the oppressed. Juli takes care of her adoptive grandfather's manuscript and promises to continue his legacy. Similarly, she will wait for the return of her adoptive father, János, and take care of his son, her adoptive brother.

* * *

The family becomes the locus of resisting violent governance. Orphans seek families because only in this context can they have a sense of self, articulate an identity. Stalinism produces thus a new form of family kinship, a social one, whose ties take the form of alliances of the oppressed, and, more importantly, a new subject. The true subject of the Stalin era, *Diary for My Children* argues, is not the Stakhanovite worker, but resilient and feminized resisters produced within the extended family of the oppressed. This vision of the subject is in stark contrast to the new man depicted in the films of the 1950s, contemporary with the period which *Diary for My Children* is presenting. Juli's resistant stoicism is meant to show the reverse side of the optimism that had become, as Mira and Antonin Liehm argue, a duty and a staple of the Hungarian cinema of the Rákosi era, whose poster films were *Singing Makes Life Beautiful* (1950), about a politically committed factory choral group; *Full Steam Ahead* (1951), about "the victorious efforts of railroad workers to fulfill their production plan"; and *Honesty and Glory* (1951), a happy-ending melodrama (Liehm and Liehm 1977, 152).[29] *Diary for My Children* even shows Juli watching the first film in the movie theater.

In contrast to a Stalinist film like *Story of a Young Couple* (analyzed in chapter 2), Mészáros's orphan, like Moskalyk's character Dita Saxová (discussed in chapter 3), shows that Stalinism produced not only a subject that was fully motivated to forget its past and uncritically embrace the New Order and identify with the passion of its construction, but also one that held on to her memories as one of the key aspects of her identity. As the sequels to *Diary* show, the Rákosi era also brought to life the anti-Stalinist fighter. They were the young men and women, workers and students, who took the streets of Budapest in 1956 and demanded a break with Moscow. These were identities created in the civic school of resistance against Stalinism, some even employing national belonging as a key element of their self-understanding.

Epilogue

The Abandoned Offspring of Late Socialism

THE MOST ILLUSTRATIVE social and political predicament for writing a coda to a study on subject production in socialist Eastern Europe is that of Romania of the 1980s. A dictatorship, almost as bombastic and as leader-centered as that of the Stalin era, emerges here in the last decade of socialism. Social revolution, increased nationalism, Stakhanovist industrial expectations, grand biopolitical and urban projects, and the production of a new subject are again high topics on the regime's agenda. The population is more intensely mobilized and exposed to propaganda, its private lives more attentively scrutinized, its links with the rest of Europe more limited, and the pressure of social conformism more suffocating.

But Romania's late socialist period, also known as the Ceauşescu era, was no Stalinism. It was an example of history repeating itself not as caricature, but as simulacrum. It lacked some of Stalinism's basic ingredients. First of all, the timing: during Romania's late socialism, international tensions had been loosened, state borders had been at least tacitly recognized, and the two-system cohabitation in Europe accepted. Europe was neither in ruins nor at a crossroads which could open toward a revolutionary road. The traditional bourgeois opposition had been silenced and the country's economic structure transformed. The government talked insistently about human rights, and political violence was dampened. It was no longer articulated in a climate of reconstruction and hope, and most importantly it was no longer conceived as geared toward changing the world, but toward saving socialism and its elites.

For Ceauşescu and his regime, this simulacrum of Stalinism became a mode of government aimed at countering the growing dissolution not only of the communist dream, but also of the social fabric that legitimized the articulation of grand narratives such as the communist one.[1] The Ceauşescu regime retained Stalinism's grand promises and threats, but they were no longer backed by the drive to achieve or enforce them. Romania of the 1980s was spared the witch-hunts, show trials, deportations, and executions of the 1950s. The regime felt less challenged and undermined from abroad—as its main enemy was probably the American-sponsored anticommunist propaganda broadcaster Radio Free Europe. Internally, the challenges were even less dangerous. If it existed, the "class enemy," as we shall see, expressed itself rather biopolitically than politically. The regime governed a passive, undereducated, and politically corrupt population, which, unlike Poland, did not have the practical and intellectual know-how (or maybe the historical chance) to articulate a coherent political resistance.

The discourse on the production of revolutionary subjects also simulated Stalinism. Party officials repeatedly addressed the issue of the socialist new human (*omul de tip nou,* in Romanian) who will lay the concluding bricks on the communist edifice, but the actual transformation unfolded differently than the generous scenario of socialist humanism envisioned. In official discourses, commitment to the revolution was the key factor. Preschool children were already expected to take responsibility for building socialism. Organizations such as the Falcons of the Fatherland (*Şoimii Patriei*), which included pre- and elementary school children, pledged allegiance to the revolution and the party. Similarly, sometimes in mass ritualistic gatherings, the Pioneers Organization (for elementary and middle school children), the Union of Communist Youth (for high school students and young workers), and the Communist Student Union (for college students) expressed total dedication to the socialist cause.

The main goal of such organizations was "the cultivation of love for the fatherland, the Party, and communist ideals among children," and "the planting in the children's consciousness of the seeds of the duty to prepare to become future builders of communism."[2] The socialist press—not only the Romanian one—of the 1970s and the 1980s featured titles such as "Pioneerhood, Years of Revolutionary Apprenticeship." The Falcons of the Fatherland (a Romanian invention of 1977) was defined as "an organization fostering revolutionary and patriotic spirit among children."[3] Likewise, the identity of the communist youth was presented as one articulated in the concepts of Marxism-Leninism and marked by its adoption of the ethics of the working class. On each May 2, Youth Day, the Communist Youth Union addressed telegrams to the beloved comrade Nicolae Ceauşescu expressing the "ardent revolutionary engagement of the young generation to actively participate in the realization of the Party Program of raising the country to new heights of civilization and progress."[4]

The examples above present a political landscape of intensive effort to forge revolutionary subjects. One of the mantras of the time was "revolutionary romanticism," indicating the desired emotional context in which the new human of the socialist order was to develop. Another mantra was "education through work and for work." As an article touting the party program emphasizes, "the preparation of the youth for the production of material goods" is one of the main priorities of socialist organizations, and the "cult of work" must be advanced as a key feature of their identity from their early days in school, through productive activities and various patriotic initiatives and on the "construction sites of youth" (alleged voluntary work environments),[5] but also via cultural, educational, recreational, and sports activities.[6] The press of the time abounds in titles such as "Youth—an Active Presence in the Harvesting, Transportation, and Depositing of the Crop"[7] and "Give the Children a Piece of Land and Reliable Tools."[8] Work serves as the main socializing and disciplining practice of the young generation, which, another article argues, is defined as "the generation of work." "The cult of work becomes . . . ," the article continues, "an inexhaustible well that feeds their essential energies, the spirit of sacrifice, and the faculty of revolutionary thought."[9]

But in spite of the bombastic rhetoric, the enforcement of the actual political and biopolitical practices needed to live up to its claims was done halfheartedly and had a limited effect on the population. In spite of the strong emphasis that the 1980s put on youth's freedom, multilateral development, respect for human rights, and unprecedented opportunities for learning and self-edification, the reality was different. Youth, "the mirror in which a country views its future,"[10] was neglected or, at most, feared for its potential for rebellion. The mobilization that started at an early age aimed exactly to discipline this aspect of life and immunize youth against the pop culture and individualism coming from the West. This is why, along with the calls for revolutionary dedication, youth was also exposed to a critique of Western attitudes, especially to the West's concept of freedom—which was depicted as leading to social passivity, professional self-neglect, moral decay, drug consumption, promiscuity, crime, and recruitment into fascist organizations.

Youth in Romanian Cinema

In reality, the ultimate goal of Romanian late state-socialist mobilization was demobilization. The subject of late socialism grew more politically passive and pessimistic, reoriented its efforts toward achieving individual gains, and, socially, practiced schizophrenia. It regarded the state as nothing but a corrupt oppressor, in the hands of a steadfast elite, which, as time went by, even took the form of a ruling clan. A review of the cinema of the times shows that, in fact, the Communist Party understood this predicament of the youth and the way in which the youth perceived it. Thus it reached out to cinema for help—not to mobilize but to compensate for the limits of its policies and promises, to simulate interest in the problems of the youth, and to make the youth believe that their issues were being taken into consideration and debated onscreen.[11]

An article published in the mouthpiece of the Romanian Communist Party, the newspaper *Scînteia*, marks this change in Romanian youth films.[12] It praises youth films not only for presenting positive heroes with no concerns other than building socialism, but also for realistically tackling topical issues and exploring "the destinies of some alienated characters" of socialism (Cernat 1980, 6). The article quotes the supreme leader of the country himself in order to support its praise for the emergence of these new youth films in the 1979–1980 season. It praises in particular *Microphone Test* (*Probă de microfon*, dir. Mircea Daneliuc), *The House between the Fields* (*Casa dintre cîmpuri*, dir. Alexandru Tatos), *The Bride in the Train* (*Mireasa din tren*, dir. Lucian Bratu), *Opening Middlefield Player* (*Mijlocaş la deschidere*, dir. Dinu Tănase), and *Snapshot around the Family Table* (*Stop cadru la masă*, dir. Ada Pistiner).

The article argues that these films "contributed to the modeling of the personalities" of the country's young men and women. They showed them that moral autonomy was acceptable, and that it represented an important precondition of political participation. Romania respected human rights and allowed its young citizens to freely decide which way they want to go, professionally and existentially. The films taught them that socialist society could not produce flawless subjects on an assembly line and that the imperative revolutionary duty of the youth was to perfect themselves. The films persuaded them to learn from the mistakes of their predecessors, but their stories also conveyed the positive message that self-improvement was possible (as long as one stuck to the right socialist principles) and easily achievable within the optimistic and supportive community of the socialist state.

The article credits "the 1970s Generation" with returning the Romanian screen to realism and topicality. Among the promising talents of this cohort was the director Dan Piţa, whose 1975 *Filip the Kind* (*Filip cel bun*) was, according to the critic, exemplary of this trend. The article calls on film producers (and implicitly on the state) to give "gifted" directors such as Piţa more chances to produce topical youth films. Their activity has shown that they have the "courage," the "depth," and the "responsibility" to do it. They will raise "the prestige of Romanian film," their work will have a growing "impact on audiences," and they will foster the "feeling of dignity and revolutionary humanism among the young men and women of the country," thus contributing in their own way to the building of socialism (Cernat 1980, 6).

The Films of Dan Piţa

History shows that the Romanian film industry listened to the critic's suggestions. Three films the Romanian director Dan Piţa made in the 1980s explore the condition of the young men and women of late socialism, with their growing dilemmas, contradictions, and alienation. It also shows that the trend started in the 1970s tried to be in sync with the moral and intellectual impulse of the Polish cinema of distrust of the 1970s, even though Romania lacked the opposition groups such as KOR and Solidarity that Poland had. Like the Polish films of the late 1970s, *Sand Dunes* (*Faleze de nisip*, 1983), *Contest* (*Concurs*, 1984), and *Two-Step* (*Pas în doi*, 1986) present the subject of socialism's developing double consciousness, the ideology of success; put onscreen the aspects of life ignored or omitted by the official visions socialism produced of itself; and even suggest resistance strategies.[13]

But Piţa's three films take the critique of state socialism one step further than those of 1979–1980 mentioned by Cernat. Piţa's reflect, in bleaker tones, on the failure of socialism to fight social alienation and to create social justice, and on the pressure toward conformism it exerted on its subjects. The optimism and positive message referred to above are more difficult to distinguish. The learning experience of the hero is no longer discernible. His or her mistakes are no longer presented as obvious mistakes, and the plots of the films narrate generational and class conflicts, and structure-superstructure tensions, in which young working-class men are shown opposing those who try to discipline them: the socially settled, middle-aged people in white-collar jobs who have internalized the compromises that come with their ascent on the social ladder.

In contrast to the Polish cinema of the late 1970s, Piţa's films feel bleaker. Passive and taciturn recluses, more representative of the social pessimism of the 1980s, replace the inquisitive heroes of *Camera Buff* and *Man of Marble*. Piţa's films bring peaceful rebels onscreen and recommend them as counter-models to the schizophrenic and corrupt personality produced by socialism. These rebels, however, have lost their sense of community and show much more concern with keeping their own backyard clean. They refuse to play along with the social and political game of socialism, without trying to publicly articulate the reasons for their resistance (and even less to reach out to their compatriots for organizing collective opposition). In Piţa's cinematic vision, they are lean young men with dark complexions in an alternative dress code, usually without a name and with an uncertain family background (in *Contest* and *Sand Dunes* they are generically addressed as "Kiddo.")[14] What is essential to them, however, is that they perceive themselves as abandoned by power, as political orphans, and they evince symptoms of Western influence and individualism.

And they want to stay this way. Consequently, the political adoption narrative—the second birth of the orphan referred to in the epigraph of this book's introduction—is blurred or totally dropped. Piţa's protagonists don't believe in social dialogue anymore, and like the 1968ers all over Europe, they distrust anyone over thirty, suspecting them of being already corrupted by power. But unlike the 1968ers, Piţa's heroes don't confront the system; instead they show more concern with their individual salvation, as they try to rediscover themselves in the blind spots of power. In Piţa's vision, the socialist world—in stark contrast to its propaganda—has turned its caring eye away from them and scrutinizes them only with its disciplining one, which is prone to abuse. Consequently, his protagonists barricade themselves in the realm of the private, defend their values and lifestyles, and follow the tenet of existing in an honest relation with themselves. The only thing they seem to expect from power is to leave them alone: "I don't need anything [from you]" and "Let me live my life the way I want to!" they say.

The pessimism of the 1980s informs the endings of Pița's stories. Unlike the Polish films from the previous decade, Pița's conclude more ambiguously or plainly unhappily. In order to remain true to themselves, their heroes have to endure more persecution and humiliation than Zanussi's or Kieślowski's. In *Sand Dunes*, the protagonist is forced to confess to a crime he never committed and serve a prison sentence. In *Contest*, the hero must accept being bossed around and treated like a servant though the only thing he wanted was to be helpful. In *Two-Step*, the main character might even lose his life for trying to defy the misogynistic and paternalist prejudice of his co-workers. Violence lurks around the corner. It is incidental to the plot, but suggestive for the mood of the film. In *Sand Dunes*, a child is killed; in *Contest*, a woman is gang-raped; in *Two-Step*, a boxer character is always on the verge of settling issues with his fists.

The ideas of the Charter 77 movement, the economic crisis starting in the mid-1970s, and especially the violent repression of the 1980–1981 Solidarity strikes affect the translation of the poetics and politics of the cinema of moral distrust into the 1980s. Even if critical, the Polish films of the mid-1970s mentioned above still conveyed a certain hope that dialogue between civil society and the government was possible. So do the Romanian films. Filip from *Camera Buff* trusts that his documentaries can have a social impact and influence power's decisions—and even Pița's Filip from *Filip the Kind* develops in a more redemptive context. In contrast, Polish films made in the next decade abandon this confidence in the political process. *A Woman Alone*, directed by Agnieszka Holland and released in 1981, presents some of the bleakest images ever made about socialism. Its plot excludes any sort of redemption or optimism and develops coldheartedly toward absurd situations and the dissolution of human values.

Pița's narratives amplify bleakness by including haunting surreal and even grotesque episodes. Moreover, these sequences also distance Pița's films from the commitment to realism of the cinema of moral distrust of the 1970s. Long and slow tracking and crane shots through dimly lit hallways, desert-like landscapes, misty forest roads, and wintry seashores gesture toward the existence of a different reality—oneiric, unconscious, repressed—that questions the stability of the one represented in realistic mode. Bizarre dream sequences, clouds of chicken feathers floating in the middle of the forest, beautiful women emerging like sirens from the sea, and a brass band sinking in a narrow swimming pool trigger similar effects. Ominous synthesizer musical scores accompany these scenes, enhancing the overall sense of unrest and catastrophe.

Figure 6.1. Kiddo interrogated (*Sand Dunes*).

Sand Dunes

A neighbor believes that Kiddo, the protagonist of *Sand Dunes*, is cursed. Ever since he was a child, the neighbor recalls, destiny has been cruel to him. He was fated to be persecuted. He had to flee his home and find shelter in an aunt's house. He grew up with the fishermen, abandoned, having to take care of himself. His parents gave him up when he was a child. His mother left with another man and never returned. His alcoholic father beat him sadistically with no other reason than the desire to break his spirit. "Like a tyrant," Kiddo recalls. "Permanently telling me: 'You must obey! You must obey!'"

The plot of *Sand Dunes* is concerned with documenting another persecution this abandoned child is subjected to and with outlining its causes. As the title might suggest, the story is set in a "desert" area of the socialist universe, on the eastern outskirts of the Romanian political space. It is a world apparently overlooked by socialist modernization, stuck in a different order, which, one can infer, is conducive to abuse. The locals are mostly fishermen, but they are surrounded by a plethora of exotic characters: peddlers, beggars, dumpster diggers, Gypsies, exotic beauties, and thieves, all creatures indifferent to or even in conflict with socialism. The only apparatus of power that still makes itself known in this remote village by the Black Sea is the police. Its strong arm, it is suggested, might be the only way to govern a political community that is no longer sufficiently organized (and mobilized).

Well-to-do people from the capital city spend their vacations in the area. Their belongings are stolen from the beach. None of them has seen the thief close up, but the next day, when Kiddo passes them by, they "recognize" him. They contain him and take him to the police. An investigation is initiated, which includes reenactments, searches, and long and stressful interrogation sessions. The revelation that, on the run, the thief accidentally collided with a child complicates the situation. The child fell, hit his head on a rock, and died. Consequently, the accusation against Kiddo becomes heavier. It includes not only theft but also involuntarily manslaughter.

But there is no hard evidence against him. Whether he is guilty or not boils down to the tourists' testimony against his. Most of the stolen goods belong to Dr. Cristea, a ruthless, self-absorbed, and career-oriented physician. He embodies the "the ideology of success," thematized by the Polish cinema of distrust in films such as Zanussi's *Camouflage.* Cristea is the member of the group who most vehemently claims to have seen Kiddo stealing. Flashbacks show Cristea chasing the thief through the dunes, suggesting, however, that he has also never been able to clearly see the culprit's face. But Cristea is convinced Kiddo did it and, with the help of the police, invests all his energy into obtaining a confession of guilt from him.

To Cristea's frustration, the confession never comes. Kiddo's refusal to admit his guilt reshuffles the priorities of the investigation. As the film progresses, the questioning serves less and less the purpose of finding out the truth. It turns into a power game. Cristea himself declares that the recovery of the stolen goods does not interest him, nor even does the punishment of the thief. He is only after Kiddo's admission of guilt, which will establish the power relations between them, that is, the latter's subalternity. "It is just your vanity," Cristea's girlfriend comments, pointing out what truly spurs Cristea's ambition to make Kiddo confess: "A nobody refuses to let you crush him," and Cristea, as he himself confesses, cannot stand defeat.

Thus, the true reason why Kiddo goes to prison is not theft, but disobedience. He is reprimanded because he refuses to admit guilt and accept the power relations imposed upon him. He will spend years in prison because the hegemonic class of socialist Romania of the 1980s cannot tolerate defiance, or, better put, is afraid of it. From this point of view Kiddo embodies certain aspects of the younger generation that several newspaper articles of the time try to incriminate as antirevolutionary with terms such as parasitism, social irresponsibility, superficiality, non-conformism, egotism, individualism, and adventurism, and tougher labels such as hooliganism. These disobedient young men and women are depicted as overly concerned with looks and clothes, as wearing longer hair and jeans (like Kiddo), as smart talkers, pub goers, and slackers.

But *Sand Dunes* aims to be more than a parable of class stratification in late socialism. It aims to reflect on the disciplining practices of the system, the origins of abuse, and the lack of legitimacy of power. It makes the clear statement that the marginal community on the Black Sea represents in fact Romania of the late Ceaușescu era. Moreover, it suggests that is not marginal or desert-like in itself, but has been purposively produced as such; that is, it is not marginal, but marginalized, not desert-like but desertified. The Ceaușescu regime has created an abusable body politic in order to make its rule more comfortable and less democratic. Unlike Stalinism, which used the political and economic project of accelerated modernization to spread fear and rule its subjects with an iron hand, the Ceaușescu regime has chosen to turn back the clock of modernization and political emancipation and to rebarbarize its population in order to legitimize its elitist authoritarianism.

Let's Talk!

But *Sand Dunes* also gestures toward the vulnerability of this type of governance, and perhaps this is the main reason why it was banned a few days after its release. It shows that the insistent quest to impose rigorous power relations has counter-effects. Excessive concern with control not only produces strictly striated political spaces but also delegitimizes and self-destructs. Cristea's cross-examinations do not confirm his hegemony; they suggest the opposite: his craving for confirmation, his insecurity. And so are his efforts to intimidate and even to bargain with Kiddo. His obsessive visits to the crime scene and his effort to piece together every step of the robbery affect his life as well. He becomes more vehement, aggressive, suspicious, and intolerant—not only with Kiddo but also with his friends and his lover. He compromises their seaside vacation and falls prey even more to the ideology of success. The self-destructive outcome of excessive concern with control is underscored by the ending of the film. Cristea's preoccupation with making Kiddo confess will eventually cause his own death.

The last part of the film depicts this lethal denouement. Cristea seeks Kiddo after the latter has served his years in prison. In the meantime, in the capital city and in the center of power, Cristea has climbed the professional ladder all the way to the top, becoming the manager of a hospital (choosing, as his best friend notices, an administrative position, one that controls and coerces life, over that of a healer, which liberates it). In contrast, on the outskirts of the political space, Kiddo has sunk into an even more isolated existence. He has lost his skilled job and his girlfriend; he works for the fishermen, mending boats. Cristea revisits the village ostensibly to make up with Kiddo and help him start a post-prison life. He brings money, but also the same self-righteous attitude he displayed before. As he talks to Kiddo, it becomes obvious that it is not remorse that has brought him back, but his ambition to win an unsettled conflict.

Since *Sand Dunes* is a film that praises life in truth and resistance to compromise, Cristea does not acquire what he came for. Not even the money he pulls out of his wallet can buy Kiddo's confession. The latter intractably refuses to admit guilt and, as he did a few years earlier, asks the doctor to leave him alone. Confronted again with Kiddo's intransigence, the powerless Cristea loses his temper. He can't believe that the "nobody" will not obey. As happens in such situations with illegitimate power, Cristea turns violent. But as he attacks Kiddo, an accident takes place—another in the life of Kiddo, which will again get him into trouble. More or less by chance, a sharp tool in Kiddo's hand pierces the doctor's chest. The doctor stares in stupefaction at his opponent and his blood-stained shirt. How can this happen to an invulnerable person like him.

The next shot shows Kiddo running away. In denial of the mortal wound inflicted upon him, the obstinate doctor follows him. But he can't keep up, and Kiddo disappears in the distance. To his last breath, however, the dying Cristea doesn't give up his quest. He chases Kiddo along the gray and gloomy seashore and calls on him to stop and confess. His last words, before he collapses, defeated, humiliated, with his face in the sand, are "Wait, let's talk! Admit you have stolen my things." But no one hears him anymore. With his death, the issue of Kiddo's guilt, one of purely personal ambition and quest for power, has become irrelevant.

"Let's talk" is used several times in the film when addressing the young protagonist. It is the phrase that frames the interrogation. But it is not an invitation to real dialogue, only to a simulacrum of one. Kiddo's reaction suggests he apprehends the abuse behind the phrase. This is why he repeatedly asks to be left alone. He doesn't want to participate in such a dialogue because he is aware that power does not seek exchange, but only obedience. "Talking" becomes a public ritual in which only one actor speaks and neither listens. Its purpose is to produce a spectacle of dialogue. Since it interacts with a politically marginalized population, late socialist power no longer seeks persuasion. It no longer employs discourse to access the minds and thoughts (and maybe even hearts) of those it governs. It just wants to control the ears, eyes, and bodies of its subjects. Its act of disciplining is limited to making its subjects respond to the invitation and pretend to participate in the exchange.

Though apparently useless and schizophrenic, since no actual exchange takes place, this pretended predicament of communication is nevertheless instrumental in the political relegitimizing of power. By seeing and hearing it speak, its subjects acknowledge their subaltern relation to it. This is why outcasts like Kiddo, who try not to participate in the simulacrum of public life—and thus reveal its forged nature—become targets of harassment. They need to be coerced back into the ritual of "talking" to power, because their gazes and hearing have strayed away. They might have turned to themselves, to inner beliefs, values, and thoughts, preoccupations that might undermine the smooth functioning of the rituals that produce the legitimacy of power. Such non-participation might prompt them to ask themselves whether there is coherence between their private and their public lives, their inner and their outer selves. It might trigger "moral distrust" and the pursuit, as in Poland, of more organized forms of questioning the order they live in.

In order to prevent this from happening, power has to put drifters like Kiddo in certain situations that compromise their quest for self-coherence. *Sand Dunes* presents exactly such an act of framing of a consciousness that seeks autonomy. Power accuses the protagonist of a crime he has not committed in order to force him to resume "talking," and to draw him back into the social game. Since Kiddo does not respond to the call to confess, power apprehends him physically. The tourists bring him to the police headquarters, where he is detained and questioned. By force he is thrown into a dialogue situation. Kiddo wanted to render his social presence invisible. By being brought to the police, photographed, fingerprinted, identified, and coerced to speak, he is taught that he cannot choose the limits of political participation. Power has indeed turned the population into a multitude of irrelevant political subjects, but irrelevance is not synonymous with lack of supervision.

The questioning sessions are thus only apparently aimed at finding out the truth. Their main function is to awaken an estranged subject from his dialogic passivity, and reteach him to respond and talk to power. They become a crash-course in late socialist public participation, which Kiddo, however, stubbornly resists. Consequently, power changes its persuasion tactic. If intimidation doesn't work, it starts bargaining, as many socialist governments did in the post-Stalinist era.[15] In his seminal essay *The Power of the Powerless*, Vaclav Havel regards this quest for a political bargain as specific to "post-totalitarian" socialism, a political order that no longer seeks revolution and subject reeducation but complicity instead. It aims to negotiate a secret truce with each of its subjects; agree on a deal of non-aggression and pretended mutual interest, but practice in fact reciprocal ignorance. To paraphrase Jean-Jacques Rousseau, this truce can be called *the social bargain*. The citizen's main duty for his or her community is the participation not in political dialogue, but in its lip-syncing.

Whether Kiddo is or not guilty of theft does not matter. What matters is that he is guilty of not playing by the rules of the post-totalitarian social truce. The investigation seeks to negotiate a confession, because the confession will provide the basis of the bargain. Power offers to pardon him and "leave him alone" as he repeatedly asks, if he agrees to talk to it and, by entering the dialogue, accept its domination. "We know you have not stolen the things," the policemen seem to tell Kiddo. "But we nevertheless want you to confess you did." "Accept you have stolen the things and I'll set you free," Cristea declares. Kiddo has to acknowledge that power has the leverage to accuse him of crimes he might not even have committed—that he is, like the character of Franz Kafka's *The Trial*, eternally guilty or can be rendered as such. In exchange, the regime will never make use of its right to abuse him.

Kiddo understands the three main consequences of the bargain. First, it will make him internalize that there is no such thing as living outside power's reach. Second, that regardless of where he is located, alternative lifestyles will be tolerated only as long as he limits them to the realm of the private and constantly participates in a ritual of confessing his guilt for seeking autonomy. Third, the bargain will compromise his inner coherence. Power wants him to confess because, as he puts it, "You want to make me question myself, lose my self-confidence and then make me say what you want me to say."[16] His confession will function as an oath of eternal complicity, guaranteeing his long-term participation in the bargain. It will lock him into a subaltern relation to power and teach him that the only way to be left alone is to play along with the social game of pretending to obey.

Drifters, Petty Crime, and Socialist Education

In addition to being a brilliant parable of the way in which power plays with its subjects the game of exclusion and inclusion in order to assert its sovereignty,[17] *Sand Dunes* makes an ironic comment on socialism's conception of youth education and on its approach to the delinquency of young men and women. As mentioned above, the Romanian socialist press continually printed articles that tried to define the causes of unsocial behavior and petty crime, especially because the crime rate was on the rise in the early 1980s.[18] *Sand Dunes* engages in a dialogue with such press coverage. But by emphasizing that Kiddo did not steal from the beach and that the entire case against him is false, it turns the arguments of the state's discourse on juvenile disobedience upside down, revealing first and foremost the demagogic and self-comforting thinking that underpins it.

The description of most of these petty criminals whose cases are presented in the press starts by disclosing their names, ages, and the places they are from. According to the standard of socialist crime reporting, the next piece of information about them would have been their occupation, but the protagonists of most of these articles are unemployed. Consequently, the articles label them as such, "without occupation."[19] In the logic of the basic tenets of socialism regarding education through work and for work, the "without occupation" label construes unemployment as a cause of criminal behavior. Another predicament the articles present as a cause of delinquency is the family situation of their protagonists. Most of the young men and women come from dysfunctional environments; they have been neglected or abused, like Kiddo. The nefarious influence of others—such as gang members—and the lack of vigilance shown by co-workers and communist organizations are also listed among the social causes of delinquent conduct (the latter more rarely than the former).

Sand Dunes's critical comment on socialism's rationalization of the social causes of criminal behavior starts with the presentation of Kiddo as employed and as a hardworking young man. He is employed even after prison, when Cristea returns to "talk" to him. Moreover, when the police visit the little factory that has hired Kiddo in order to inspect his locker and inquire about his background, his superior has only good words to say about him. His aunt and the fishermen also praise him. From this point of view, Kiddo is a model subject of socialism. Through hard work, he has elevated himself from family abuse and abandonment. After serving his term in prison, he tries to follow the same path, but it is society that rejects him, as he is not able to obtain the skilled position he had before and must work as a helper for the fishermen.

In this context, the question *Sand Dunes* asks is why the police or Cristea aren't animated by the same logic of socialist education: why do they suspect an honest and hardworking young man of theft? The answer is obvious: the system no longer believes in its own statements. The film takes a similar approach on the second cause of youth criminality. At first glance, Kiddo's disrupted family situation seems to fit the profile, but again only to a certain extent, because his abandonment is representative of the whole community he lives in. The state does not practice revolutionary work in the region because, as mentioned earlier, it prefers to rule over desert-like political spaces, populated by disenfranchised subjects. Thus, if abandonment and marginalization are factors, then the actual policies of socialism, with their interest in depoliticizing the population, make the Communist Party an accomplice to Kiddo's alleged crime.

Moreover, the family argument contradicts socialist views on subject production. Even if it has been empirically proven that children from disrupted families are more likely to commit crimes, accepting family dysfunction as a cause throws a dubious light on communist revolutionary theory and its views on education, which favor the social and the political over the private. True socialist consciousness is forged in "the factory, the school of work, and communist life." Nicolae Ceaușescu himself emphasizes that "each economic and social unit must become a big family of working people, a citadel in which life will be led according to socialist norms and principles [in order to generate] an exemplary behavior on behalf of all working people" (Georgian and Mureșan 1981, 1).

Things become more revealing of the way in which socialism regards its youth when one reads an op-ed from *Scînteia tineretului* titled "The Sad Anonymity of Some Slackers" ("Trista anonimitate a unor pierde-vară").[20] The article does not deal with criminals, but with young men who choose, like Kiddo, to drop out, and is part of a rubric that bears the suggestive title: "Let's talk"—and in a different font—"about Youth, Education, Responsibilities," which harks back to the rituals of coercion exercised by power through the invitation to participate in the social bargain.[21] The article is written in pretentious professional language and presents itself as an anthropological exploration of the causes "that interrupt" the normal development of the lives of young men and women. It aims to find out "what disruption occurred in the system that a young person establishes with the world and its values, with the written and unwritten laws of existence" (Ghinea 1979, 1).

As we have seen, for *Sand Dunes*, this "disruption" is the exclusion-inclusion process that sets the stage for the social bargain. A close reading of the article shows that power cannot and is not even interested in understanding the dilemmas of its youth. As expected, the official press cannot acknowledge such a practice, but one can see it at work in the article too. The official version of why young men and women drop out is, as the title of the editorial suggests, the drive to escape anonymity, to stand out and be recognized by peers. This is, of course, not the case with Kiddo, who seeks the opposite, anonymity—that is, life in the blind spots of power. The accusation that they are trying to cut corners to fame—by wearing long hair and jeans rather than by dedicating themselves to the five-year-plan—marks their exclusion. This happens in *Sand Dunes* too, only the accusation is of burglary. It is then followed by the process of inclusion into socialist normality. Like Kiddo, the protagonists of the article are invited to the dialogue table to explain themselves and their deeds. (In the article, the dialogue does not take place in the police headquarters, but in the meeting room of the Union of Communist Youth.)

The exclusion process consists of the publication of pictures of its protagonists—which is in fact the true escape from anonymity into the realm of discipline and "normalization." It is perhaps not a surprising coincidence that one of them physically resembles Kiddo and that, like Kiddo, he is also from the seaside, from the margins of the Romanian socialist universe. He has the same longer black hair and, like Kiddo, wears jeans. The inclusion dialogue with the young drifters is presented as difficult. The author of the article tries to participate in it and *talk* to these Kiddos. He approaches one of them, who "looks more intelligent." The author asks the staple why-questions, trying to find out why his interlocutor is not animated by revolutionary impulses. He receives the same answer the policemen and Cristea receive in *Sand Dunes*. "I have done nothing wrong," the young man replies. I am not a criminal, and I can benefit from "the freedom of the individual to do what he wants" (Ghinea 1979, 3).

Western Influences

The main difference between the young man whose photo is shown in the newspaper and Kiddo is the caption under the photo of the former, which reads "What's the use of starting work?" The caption makes an ironic comment on the predicament of Kiddo, because, unlike the protagonist of the article, Kiddo tries to play by the rules of the game and improve his condition through work, save money, get married, and so on. Seen from a different perspective, the socialist discourse of the time might agree that, indeed, hard productive activity is not enough to forge a reliable socialist subject, and that, in theory, the state demands more from its citizens than just being dedicated economic actors. The Communist Party expects its subjects to be politically more active, more engaged in the building of socialism.

This is what makes Kiddo suspicious, but as emphasized before, not because the party, in its actual governance, expects real political involvement. It demands only its simulation though the participation in the social bargain. Dedication to the cause of building socialism, official discourse trumpeted, must be (or be presented as being) a core element of the identity of any young man or woman of the time. It is political education and participation that inspires the creative thinking of the new man of socialism, "acting dynamically upon his lively, innovative spirit, engaged in the struggle against everything that is old, supportive of the vigorous affirmation of the new, and creating a bold and confident way of looking at the future" (Sîrbu 1981, 3).

The article commenting on the results of a survey conducted by the Research Center on Youth Problems accepts, even under the pressure of ideological censorship, that more political education needs to be done because commitment to building socialism does not rank among the highest life goals of Romania's youth. The main concerns of the country's young men and women are unfortunately framed in an individualistic perception of life. According to the report on the survey, the country's youth place "achievement of personal fame" as their first priority and, as their second, their personal development. The more politically correct causes stand lower on the list and are mixed with such not specifically socialist demands as "professional success," "personal happiness" (quite low on the priority list), and material well-being.[22]

Kiddo's behavior plays into socialist debates on the concept of freedom. According to the socialist perspective, Kiddo's lack of political involvement and his desire to be left alone and do what he wants in his private sphere are symptoms of a mistaken understanding of freedom, which Romanian (and socialist) youth might have picked up from the West. In the wake of the 1975 Helsinki conference and the debates on human rights and freedoms it triggered for the next fifteen years, party intellectuals launched a campaign against the illusion of "absolute freedom" that images of Western lifestyles might generate. Two of these arguments are relevant for Kiddo's story: one, the political passivity that "absolute freedom" generates; and two, the abuse and existential disorientation it causes.

The socialist press abounds in presentations of the degenerate behavior of Western youth. Articles bearing titles such as "Youth without Hope in a World without Future" present pictures of punks and skinheads with captions reading "Grotesque and shocking appearances—expressions of an anarchic drive of young men and women to escape the anonymity to which their society condemns them."[23] An op-ed published in *Scînteia* by one of the most famous playwrights of Romanian socialism, Paul Everac, theorizes the link between absolute freedom, excessive behavior, existential disorientation, and political passivity. Everac tells the story of a generic young man from the West, who, like Kiddo of *Sand*

Dunes, works hard from nine to five, makes good money, and then, according to the West's understanding of freedom, can do "what he wants" in his free time (of course within the limits of the law). He has the right to listen to the music of his choice, lie in bed for hours, shave his head, dress like a hippie, consume pornography, party hard, or join a neo-fascist organization. Western individualism has devised the ruse of absolute freedom in order to let its subjects neglect themselves and become morally and intellectually corrupt, egotistic, alienated, and politically manipulable, a predicament that socialism finds problematic and preempts with its mobilization strategies and emphasis on the collective.

This is why political participation is the most efficient way of liberating the subject, combined with a collectively understood perception of freedom. Political participation cures alienation and offers an alternative to the path to self-neglect and the exposure to manipulation that the Western-style illusion of autonomy and absolute freedom could engender. Such reasoning recalls the arguments of Stalinism discussed in chapter 2. Socialism functions as an aid, as a *Leitkultur* (guiding culture) that takes into account the social dimensions of human life and realization. It productively limits the freedom of individuals to express themselves as they want in order to guide them to connect their lives to the "great aspirations" of the community they live in (Everac 1977, 5). And this is why the state and the collective have the right to intervene in the personal life of the subject. Socialist conceptions of freedom legitimize the call to talk addressed to Kiddo, even if, in reality, the reasons for the conversation and the negotiation between state and individual have changed.[24]

The Power of the Powerless

By the time Piţa made his films, in Poland the cinema of moral distrust was already history. But Western-based anticommunist lines of communication spread the message of the 1970s throughout Eastern Europe. When *Sand Dunes* began production, even the more inert and more prone-to-compromise Romanian public space was already intensely exposed to anticommunist discourse. Through media such as Radio Free Europe, the opponents of state socialism had made their voices heard in Romania. Their calls to live in dignity (Leszek Kołakowski, Poland), no longer live in lies (Alexandr Solzhenitsyn, the Soviet Union), defend the truth (Cardinal Wyszyński, Poland), and, of course, the most famous dictum, to *live in truth,* theorized by Vaclav Havel (Czechoslovakia) in his 1978 essay "The Power of the Powerless," were influencing Romania's and the entire Eastern Bloc's intellectual life (Falk 2003, 173–174).[25]

All these calls, expressed by prominent figures of anti-state-socialist resistance, prescribed strategies of subverting the legitimacy of the communist power elite. Piţa's hero embodies them. Even if he is an advocate of a passive protest (withdrawal into the private sphere), *Sand Dunes* envisions Kiddo as a figure of resistance, an example of Havel's life in truth in the context of 1980s Romania.

Just as Havel prescribes it, Kiddo refuses to participate in the social bargain. He understands that it calls for the "abdication of one's reason and conscience to a higher authority" (Havel 2009, 130). He understands how the bargain "conceals [from the one that has accepted the bargain] the low foundations of his obedience" by internalizing the message "I am obedient and therefore I have the right to be left in peace" (133). He questions its promise of social peace because he realizes that it turns the subject into an eternal accomplice and even perpetrator of socialist disciplining (133). The most basic gesture of disobedience that Kiddo embodies (which refers to Havel's well-known parable of the greengrocer) is the refusal to participate in the simulacrum of public life stipulated in the bargain, that is, to pretend that he pretends to believe in the political order of his times.

The potential resistance inscribed in Kiddo's silent political strike gestures toward a different approach to identifying and understanding ideology in the late socialist era. Ideology becomes less and less understandable as the product of communist doctrine, but more understandable as an independent apparatus of social control, that is, "a multiplicity of interlocking governmentalities, regimes, institutions, and processes" loosely and mostly pro forma linked to a political theory, such as communism (Tormey 2005, 75). Understood as the symbolic horizon instrumental in producing social and political control, the ideology of late socialism (and maybe not only of this era) is more easily grasped, as Havel suggests, as a repertoire of excuses for conformism (134). Ideology is the effect of the rationalization of one's alienated predicament, the interface facilitating the absorption of individuality into the ritual of political non-participative participation (Havel 2009, 139).

Consequently, Kiddo's asceticism, his refusal to partake in the rationalizing of his condition and his effort to extricate himself from the ideological automatisms that produce the subject (Havel 2009, 146), proposes a credible practice of resistance. For Havel, however, it is not enough. He expects more from dissenters. Life in truth calls for more courage. It means more than self-coherence in a niche—that which many survivors of socialism recall as the social practice that made life bearable (Maier 1997, 46).[26] Truthfulness needs to be externalized, and one's public participation must also bring to light the rules of the political game (ideology) late socialist power expects its subjects to play (Havel 2009, 147).

Havel argues that initially resistance is hidden, passive, at the "human level of consciousness and conscience, the existential level" (149). But there is a second stage of dissent which is vocal, and this is where Pița's film can no longer keep up with Havel's demands. Life in truth, "humanity's revolt against an imposed position" (153), demands public expression of disobedience: the signing of petitions, writing of essays, participation in demonstrations, hunger strikes, and so on (149), actions that the cinema of late socialist Romania (and its citizens) had no leverage to present—the most vocal exception being the writer Paul Goma, who signed Havel's Charter 77 petition and expressed his dissent publicly—with minimal support from his more cautious literary and intellectual peers.

In the context of the ideological censorship of the 1948–1989 period, very few Eastern European films were able to tell stories of characters who publicly protested against the regime, the most noticeable exception being Andrzej Wajda's *Man of Iron* of 1981, which documents the Solidarity strikes. The model of resistance presented in *Sand Dunes* articulates only an invitation to boycott the bargain, assuming that this refusal will lead to the implosion of the system. For the political context of Romania of the early 1980s, *Sand Dunes* was articulating a daring statement. Even *Contest*, the film Pița directed afterwards, was more understated, as were all Pița's films after *Sand Dunes*.[27]

The New End of the World

Even if limited, one of the interesting aspects of Kiddo's resistance is that it does not oppose socialist discourse per se. Kiddo's main antagonist is Cristea, the ambitious doctor from the capital city, who is neither a communist activist nor a worker hero, but a representative of a new social elite that wields power because it has best internalized the social bargain and the ideology of success. Kiddo's silent provocation reveals something important about power. Its internal functioning in late socialism is less informed by the quest for a social justice rooted in proletarian ethics, than driven, on the one hand, by elite interests and their strategies to produce hegemony and, on the other, and even more problematic, by a cynical social Darwinism echoing the ideology of success (and capitalism) and not socialist competition, with its roots in the economy of the gift to the common.

Subject production is influenced by this transformation of the dynamics of power in socialism. When power invites Kiddo to "talk" and sign the bargain, it no longer intends to forge a good communist, but to persuade him to participate in a political game of complicity and subalternity that no longer has anything to do with socialism and its fight to relieve the world from alienation. This teleology of power reveals how much socialism has changed since the reconstruction era of the mid-1940s, when films like *Somewhere in Europe* were presenting radical decentralized images of governance, and even since Stalinism, which, as indoctrinating as it was, still regarded power as a means and not as an end in itself and aimed to craft revolutionary subjects, as *Story of a Young Couple* shows.

The merit of *Sand Dunes* is its emphasis on the consequences of signing the social bargain. It shows how this agreement is instrumental in a subject production that betrays the tenets of socialism. Kiddo's calls to be left alone are articulated with a goal similar to that of the Polish KOR (even if more limited) to foster self-government. They also seek, however, to achieve something else: Kiddo's withdrawal into the private expresses an eschatological sensibility. It is the result of a social and political fatigue that can prove lethal to any regime, a consequence reinforced by the death of Cristea. Loss of hope and belief in the social macronarrative of socialist progress produces, among other things, an apocalyptical political subject, who looks for hiding places in which to morally survive the end of the socialist world and await its collapse.

Pița also thematizes this apocalyptic sensibility in his next film. Titled *Contest* (a telling title about the social Darwinism of late socialism), it is, like *Sand Dunes*, a film about power and its practices. In both films, this apocalyptic sensibility is hinted at by a specter of gloominess and violence that haunts representation. In *Sand Dunes*, Pița anticipates the accident that leads to the death of Cristea with a dynamic montage sequence that includes images of conveyor belts, puffing engines, noisy grinding mallets, and wheels turning faster and faster, all intercut with snapshots of brutality against Kiddo. The montage creates a sense of imminent restlessness and tension that foretells the approaching violence. In *Contest*, the forest (read "jungle") in which the film takes place (it tells the story of a scavenger hunt) is also presented as mysterious and chancy. The hero, also called Kiddo, discovers a gang-raped woman in a clearing. Emergency vehicle sirens, helicopters, walkie-talkie exchanges, and bullhorn announcements create the aural background announcing a major mining intervention that will blow up the area.

* * *

One can interpret the reference to the coming explosion as anticipating the popular outbursts of 1989, which wiped away the state-socialist governments from Eastern Europe—the Romanian uprising being the most tumultuous. With 1989, the story of socialist subject production this book presents also comes to an end. To trace its continuation in the post-1989 era—the new agents and apparatuses employed in the process, their structures, aims, and practices—is as interesting and can become the topic of a second study that, among other things, will surely reveal the persistence of socialist socialization dynamics and content.

Several films featuring orphans have been made in post-socialism. Some insightful ones are *King of Thieves* (Ivan Fila, Czech Republic, 2004), *Lady Zee* (Georgi Djulgerov, Bulgaria, 2005), and *Beyond the Hills* (Cristian Mungiu, Romania, 2012). They present a new kind of political orphanhood, a post-utopian one. They are no longer regarded, as the postwar orphans were, as builders of a New Order, but only as citizens of a collapsed one, and perhaps even as witnesses of the disintegration of the European social and political order as we have known it since World War II on *both* sides of the Iron Curtain. Not only must the post-socialist subject deny his or her own socialist past, which has been relegated to the trashcan of history, but he or she must also learn to live the life of the victim of the new (dis)order of the region, as it tries to come to terms with the challenges of global capitalism.

Like the immediate postwar films, the post-1989 ones again associate orphanhood with nomadism, circulation of bodies, and quest for a home. A New

Figure 6.2. The orphans of post-socialism (*Beyond the Hills*).

Order is in the making, but the orphans are no longer its builders. The films mentioned above show how new agencies, which are no longer state ones, come to take control of the abandoned offspring of the region and circulate them through Europe. They tell stories of existential disorientation and abuse, and of their protagonists' unfulfilled longing for dependable human bonding and settled existential projects. As Nikolai Ekk's *Road to Life* (a film discussed in chapter 1) anticipated, some are criminal organizations, interested in rendering the orphans as objects of sex trafficking, international adoptions, transborder crime, and labor migration. *Beyond the Hills* shows that even the Orthodox Church, an apparent solid and trusted adopter of those who are materially and existentially in need, can become a locus of abuse. The general message conveyed by the destinies of the orphans of these films is that of frustration with the dynamics of the capitalist order.

It would be, however, a limited interpretation to view how, in post-socialism, the orphan becomes a key figure of the nostalgia for a stronger and more caring state, ironically one not totally alien from the socialist one. The orphans of the films mentioned above are, after all, the only ones who can show the true face of socialist subject production—envisioned beyond censorship, and also beyond anticommunist propaganda. They have experienced socialism to its very end and become its living witnesses in the present. They can help us see beyond the rise-and-fall story of socialist subject production, or as the modern became post-modern and the political post-political, beyond the story of its turning into its own caricature.

The most predictable insight in the rise-and-fall story of socialist development reveals how an order that put so much emphasis on scientific government became schizophrenic and oligarchic. With regard to subject production, it shows how accelerated development created, in the long run, underdevelopment.

This is another important message carried by the orphans of the post-1989 films. Eastern European socialism has not been able to produce strong, ethical, and especially intellectually emancipated subjects, but only second-class citizens of the world, ironically properly prepared to be exploited by capitalism. This is the most disturbing disappointment of socialism, not its economic failure; not even, I argue, the gulag. The post-socialist landscape is populated by subjects perverted by authoritarianism and the corruption of the system, by weak personalities in quest of strong community ties.

In addition to the confirmation of Marx's saying about the repetitions of history, there are also important lessons to be learned from the story of Eastern European socialist subject production turning into its own caricature. Without engaging here in a full assessment of socialism, I would emphasize two. On the positive side, socialism's critique of the alienation of the subject in capitalism still stands, especially as it is experienced in the second-world environment of the former Eastern Bloc. Political activism and participation in a development project to free the world from alienation and exploitation made or could have made (and could make again) the lives of the subjects of socialism more meaningful, more passionate, and happier.

Márta Mészáros's *Diary for My Children* emphasizes one of the negative aspects of accelerated development. On the one hand, her film presents a world that is out of control, in which even the ones who are in power are as unsure about their tomorrow as are history's pawns. Soviet-style fast-tracked subject production has engendered violence and terror. Somewhere along the way, socialist revolutionary education has traded enlightenment for abuse—and I don't refer here to the gulag. It ended up regarding subjects as too malleable, and their revolutionary consciousness as forged by their interaction with institutions and individuals that were no longer in history, but somehow above it. These were the party elites or sometimes just a chosen individual, the leader of the party, who was entrusted with the unquestioned knowledge and wisdom about how this molding of the "new human" was supposed to be done.

Violence was exercised when discourses (and practices) in charge of subject transformation collided with the immanent resistance of minds and bodies to change. And if the nature and the technologies of this abusive intervention morphed over time, violence remained a constant, even when the discourse of subject production became only pro forma in late socialism. Even if the word "revolution" implies violence, and revolutionizing consciousness might require transcendent intervention and radical self-engineering, the main lesson that leftist discourse needs to learn from Eastern European socialism is, on the positive side, to produce hope and meaningful life, and on the negative one, to keep violence under control, which still remains the main task of government—not only because violence causes suffering, but also because it produces passive political subjects—that is, caricatures of the revolutionary personality.

Notes

Introduction

The research for this book was funded through a Marie Curie Grant as part of a larger project, EASTFILM: Rethinking Eastern European Cinema in a Post–Cold War Ideological Framework. I am also grateful to the OSA Archivum Budapest and the Romanian Film Archive for supporting my research and to all the people who provided me with insightful feedback.

1. Yugoslavia and Albania also, but following a different scenario.

2. One could regard Eastern Europe similarly to the European Union, as a collective political actor and as a community of states with a shared past (and traumas) and common political goals. The Eastern European experience describes a locus of an incidence between a revolutionary project and the hard ground of history, with its traditions, inherited turmoil, social networks, inertia, resistance, and predispositions to error and abuse.

3. Also pejoratively called "homo sovieticus."

4. In capitalist-informed narratives, this vision of the orphan also animated U.S. narrative modernism and postmodernism (Friedman 2002, 706).

5. It is the title of the third volume of Michel Foucault's *The History of Sexuality* (1988).

6. "The Foreigner carries and puts the fearful question, he sees or foresees himself, he knows he is already put into question by the paternal and reasonable authority of the *logos*. ... The question *of* the Foreigner only seems to contest in order then to remind people of what ought to be obvious to the blind!" (Derrida 2000, 11). "The foreigner—precisely like the philosopher at work—does not give the same weight to origins as common sense does" (Kristeva 1994, 29).

7. Eastern Europe produced several other films with orphan protagonists that discuss, one way or another, subject production. Some of these films are *Mitrea Cocor* (Romania,1952, directed by Marietta Sadova and Victor Iliu), documenting the production of the proletarian subject in rural areas in parallel with the collectivization of agriculture—another radical decision of development; *Destinies of Women* (GDR, 1952, directed by Slatan Dudow), introducing gender and, as many films located in Berlin, East-West competition in the discussion of subject production; *Five from Barska Street* (Poland, 1954, directed by Alexander Ford) and *Berlin—Ecke Schönhauser* (GDR, 1957, directed by Gerhard Klein), both of which depict how revolutionary subject production disciplines juvenile delinquency, with the latter also introducing the generational conflict with fascism; *Father* (Hungary, 1966, directed by István Szabó), showing how imagined paternity produces historical destiny; *Adoption* (Hungary, 1975, directed by Márta Mészáros), presenting the fully institutionalized subject of socialism, who, similar to the protagonist of *Camera Buff,* is puzzled by some of the unrevolutionary aspects of the world outside the institution; *A Hungarian Fairy Tale* (Hungary, 1987, directed by Gyula Gazdag), revealing how socialist identity is shaped by dreams of escape into a different political realm; and *Time of the Gypsies* (Yugoslavia, 1988, directed by Emir Kusturica),

revealing the ultimate form of political abandonment, the ghettos of socialism, the fact that socialism, like capitalism, also produces a precariat.

8. http://www.youtube.com/watch?v=9zty9nJYCtQ. Accessed September 12, 2013.

9. It is a key concept of her book *Gender Trouble* (New York: Routledge, 1990).

10. There are several other Eastern European political films, not discussed here, that received international recognition. Many films of the Czechoslovak New Wave scored well abroad (such as those directed by Milos Forman, Jiří Menzel, and Jan Němec), but also the films of Miklós Jancsó (Hungary), Andrej Wajda (Poland), and Emir Kusturica (Yugoslavia).

11. This argument is confirmed by Milos Forman in his *Turnaround: A Memoir* (New York: Villard, 1994).

12. They were expressed in her polemic book *The Russian Revolution*. https://www.marxists.org/archive/luxemburg/1918/russian-revolution/ch01.htm (accessed April 5, 2014).

13. See for example, Slavoj Žižek's "Jacques Lacan's Four Discourses": http://www.lacan.com/zizfour.htm (accessed on April 5, 2014).

14. With regard to the family, the discourse of the church changed in time as Christianity turned more into a state religion and became more interested in power. Unlike the church, communism did not attack the family in terms of sin and fornication, but along the line of Engels's writings, as a locus of exploitation. Romanian state socialism intervened in family life by means of its natality politics, banning, like the church, abortion and limiting contraception.

1. Creatures of the Event

An earlier and shorter version of this chapter was published as "The Continent in Ruins and Its Redeeming Orphans: Géza Radvany and Béla Balázs's *Somewhere in Europe* and the Rebuilding of the Post-war Polis," in *Central Europe* 10, no.1 (May 2012).

1. The film is also known under the English title *It Happened in Europe*.

2. The date of the premiere unwittingly revealed how fleeting the chance was to advance alternative visions of socialism in Eastern Europe. Only three months after the film's premiere, the Hungarian film industry was nationalized and Hungary's and Eastern Europe's cinematic and political discourses had to follow directions from Moscow.

3. Released just before the formal establishment of the Zhdanov Doctrine and its assumption of a world divided into two hostile camps, *Somewhere in Europe* envisions Europe as an undivided continent. Its internationalism and its emphasis on collective property already demonstrate that it was a Marxist film, ideologically tributary to the Second International. The narrative of hope in *Somewhere in Europe* was predicated on an assumption similar to Benjamin's that the war had not only destroyed lives and property, and brought about famine, illness, and political disillusion, but that it had also created a political opening. The Allied air raids and Soviet shelling had also destroyed an unjust political order. Benjamin saw the end of World War I as bringing revolutions in Europe—among them the short-lived Hungarian Soviet Republic, in which Béla Balázs (the co-author of the film) had also been active. Returning from exile, the filmmakers of *Somewhere in Europe* thought that the unfulfilled revolutionary projects of 1919 could be completed after 1945.

4. For Jacques Derrida, the foreigner always returns to the present with a question. The foreigner's question is related to hospitality and refers to openness. How hospitable is it to the impulse of the Event, how willing to accept it, listen to its message, let it change? (2000, 9–11, 27). A similar question is posed in chapter 3 of this book by the Holocaust orphan of *Dita Saxová*.

5. The orphan unconscious is, according to Deleuze and Guattari, that which is "beyond all law"—"where the problem of Oedipus can no longer be raised" (1983, 81–82). The orphan is not integrated in a feud of the political unconscious, in a revenge narrative against the law of the previous regime.

6. Agamben argues that his concept of bare life is a self-reflexive gloss on the Hobbesian *status naturalis*. It is the unraveling of the constructed character of the *naturalis* (1998, 106).

7. "We must instead ask why Western politics first constitutes itself through an exclusion (which is simultaneously an inclusion) of bare life" (Agamben 1998, 7). "At once excluding bare life from and capturing it within the political order, the state of exception actually constituted, in its very separateness, the hidden foundation on which the entire political system rested" (9).

8. "Bare life has the peculiar privilege of being that whose exclusion founds the city of men" (Agamben 1998, 7).

9. Agamben's concepts help us understand that, when *Somewhere in Europe* depicts the antagonistic relation between orphans and the rest of the population, it presents not only a conflict between those who are inside and those who are outside the Old Order, but also the political practice of twentieth-century Europe of both excluding and including bare life and thus forcing—sometimes discursively, sometimes violently—the modern political subject to inhabit a "zone of indistinction . . . between man and beast, nature and culture" (1998, 109).

10. This twist also marks the starting point of Hardt and Negri's critique (2009, 21) of what they call the "theological" political thought of thinkers such as Agamben Their barbarian is a positive recuperation of the subject of Foucauldian biopolitics, reasserting the body, which, via its very materiality, produces resistance and cannot be totally controlled as bare life, as Muselmann (see Agamben's take on the Muselmann, from *Remnants of Auschwitz*, discussed in chapter 3 of this book) in a vision of society that is modeled by the memory of the concentration camp as "the ultimate site of control both inside and outside the social order" (Hardt and Negri 2009, 5).

11. The statement is made in his well-known essay "Vom Nutzen und Nachtheil der Historie für das Leben" ("On the Use and Disadvantage of History for Life").

12. In *Homo Sacer*, Agamben makes the distinction between *bios* and *zoē*, two concepts commonly translated as "life." The former is the life of self-improvement, the Aristotelian (political) good life; the latter is a biological category recuperated in the concept of bare life (1998, 1–2).

13. Unlike Balázs, Radványi (who later even added the aristocratic particle "von" to his name) avoided Marxist allegiances. Ideologically, Radványi proved to be something of a soldier of fortune. In the 1950s, he directed an indulgent film about the Wehrmacht, titled *Der Artzt von Stalingrad* (*The Doctor from Stalingrad*), much in line with the guilt avoidance widespread during Konrad Adenauer's Germany.

14. "There is politics because man is the living being who, in language, separates and opposes himself to his own bare life" (Agamben 1998, 8).

15. The orphans' joyful rebuilding of the fortress constitutes an idyllic primal image of non-alienated, unquantified, and free labor. They enthusiastically whistle the "Marseillaise," as their labor is collective, creative, and edifying. But the whistling and the idyllic choreography also point at Marx's interest in the aestheticization of the process of production (Lunn 1984, 18). Indeed, this can even be seen to link the film to a socialist-realist aesthetic. Labor is not only fruitful and redemptive, but also beautiful, both to perform and to watch. All the entities engaged in reconstruction team up harmoniously to the rhythm of the revolutionary song, from sawing lumber to fixing the roof, from fortifying the walls to preparing food. This cooperation occurs not in accordance with a concept or doctrine, but spontaneously, biologically—just as Kant imagined beauty to appear.

16. *Road to Life* did much more than adapt Makarenko's *Pedagogical Poem*. This was Makarenko's most widely read book, a collection of stories documenting the social rehabilitation of criminalized homeless children, a book that was translated into English with the title *Road to Life*.

17. During Stalin's Great Terror (also known as the Great Purge, 1934–1939), reeducation became a fraught concept in the Soviet discourse. Stalinism lost faith in it. The more liberal reeducation methods of the so-called environmentalists (who rejected coercion and blamed crime on social inequality) were soon replaced by more punitive approaches (Juviler 1985, 269). This change in policy is illustrated by the destiny of *Zakliuchennie* (*Convicts*), directed by Yevgeni Chervyakov, also a film about reeducation, but one released in 1936, during the Terror. Evgeny Dobrenko shows that as the Terror got under way, the Soviet state abandoned its rhetoric on "reforging of consciousness." Reeducation camps, the theme of *Convicts*, became taboo, and the film was shelved (Dobrenko 2007, 230).

18. See Juviler (1985, 262). Child vagabondage remained, "a major social disaster" long after the period of 1917–24. So did juvenile crime (264). The People's Commissariat for Enlightenment (*Narkompros*) aimed at "rescuing [the orphans] from the culture of the streets and turning them into carriers of the new culture of the coming socialist society" (266). Among the most successful of these communes was the Ulyanovsk Labor School-Commune, set up on a ruined estate along the Volga, which aimed to establish a form of participatory democracy (268).

19. The Soviet slogans advocating these policies for orphans were "No courts or prisons!" and "Behind bars is not a solution!" (Juviler 1985, 263).

20. The NEP, New Economic Policy, represented a cohabitation of socialist and capitalist economies. Facing bankruptcy, the Soviet state allowed privately owned, usually small businesses to function between 1921 and 1928.

21. Elsewhere Dobrenko adds that it is not only what he calls the "Bildungsroman-story" that makes a film like *Road to Life* and socialist realism unique. Socialist realism produces an educational narrative "in which the communist metamorphosis of individual personalities and entire collectivities is depicted" (2007, 219). "Communist" and "collectivities" are the keywords in this definition.

22. Kuksi's death confirms Agamben's thesis that "*not simple natural life, but life exposed to death (bare life) is the originary political element*" (1988, 88; italics in original). Kuksi's death shows that the originary political quality of bare life resides in its status as included exclusion: it is excluded from the polis in order to legitimize the social contract (which makes no provision for savage, barbarian, or vagrant lives). At the same time, this exclusion is included in the sense that it becomes central to the identity of the subject of the polis. Becoming a political subject, *Somewhere in Europe* reveals, is the act of distancing oneself from one's bare life, which is exactly what Kuksi's sacrifice represents.

23. An article on *Somewhere in Europe* argues that the film is primarily informed by nationalist discourse: Gábor Gergely, "*Somewhere in Europe* (1947): Locating Hungary within a Shifting Geopolitical Landscape," *Studies in Eastern European Cinema* 3, no. 2 (2012): 133–150.

24. Rebuilding film industries in Europe became one of Balázs's major concerns after 1945 (Nemeskürty 1968, 139). Besides writing scripts and producing films and stage plays, he taught at the newly reestablished Hungarian Film School, founded the Hungarian Film Research Institute, and was in charge of coordinating the subtitling of Soviet films (Zsuffa 1987, 326, 336).

25. Szőts's *Song from the Cornfields*, for example, makes extensive use of expressionist imagery.

26. Balázs must have been familiar with this critical claim from Lukács's famous essay "The Greatness and Decline of Expressionism." Here Lukács claims that expressionism (and

indeed modernism more broadly) is a form of proto-fascism. The heroes of expressionist works (as film historians Siegfried Kracauer and Lotte Eisner have also pointed out) are controlled by irrational and destructive forces. Obscure passions, harsh lighting, and flashbacks are also cinematic or narrative devices favored by American film noir, which *Somewhere in Europe* also borrows from. For example, as the camera closes in on the girl telling her story, her face is lit by the shutter-fractured light which is a staple of film noir. There is also an involuntary association with film noir in the flashback scene. As the girl takes revenge and shoots the German officer for deceiving her, her entire manner is reminiscent of the femme fatales of film noir.

27. The topic of gendered postwar melancholia will be discussed in chapter 3.

28. "In 1948, critics throughout the world spoke of a 'Hungarian neorealism'" when *Somewhere in Europe* . . . was shown at the Cannes Film Festival, and . . . they prophesized for director Géza Radványi a career like Roberto Rossellini's" (Liehm and Liehm 1977, 146).

29. As quoted in Thompson 2000, 208.

30. See also the discussion on this topic in the introduction.

2. Producing Revolutionary Consciousness in the Times of Radical Socialism

1. It is the subtitle of David Caute's seminal book, *The Dancer Defects. The Struggle for Cultural Supremacy during the Cold War* (2005).

2. This is how the *Large Soviet Encyclopedia* of 1978 identifies it, as an "artistic method of literature and art" (Porter 1988, 49).

3. The literal translation of the film's title is "Novel of a Young Marriage."

4. Even recent articles and reviews label *Story of a Young Couple* in biased and disparaging Cold War language. For example, a recent DVD review evinces the typical Cold War approach: "*Story of a Young Couple* is an especially vivid example of DEFA [the East German state-owned film studio] propaganda cinema at the point of the Cold War when Stalinism was firmly establishing its grip on the artistic ethos of the GDR" (Weiss 2011, 86). Even when more detailed, other articles on the film employ the same perspective, talking about an "exemplary embodiment of socialist realist aesthetics" (Allen 2011, 261), or the "narrative subordination of love to ideology," the "clumsy propaganda" which "makes *Story of a Young Couple* a fundamentally unromantic movie" (Urang 2006, 89). What is more interesting is that influential volumes on DEFA films edited in the GDR consider *Story of a Young Couple* a mistake, *ein Fehlgriff* (Agde 1983, 106), or they ignore it totally, as for example the influential *Film- und Fernsehkunst der DDR. Trasitionen, Beispiel, Tendenzen* (1979). A critic calls the film "*ein eklatanter Mißerfolg*" (Maetzig and Agde 1987, 449). Even Maetzig distances himself from it, regarding it as lacking creativity (Horbrügger 2007, 211).

5. Here are examples of films that stood out: *Destinies of Women* (directed by Slatan Dudow, GDR, 1952)—thematizing the temptations of West Berlin for female orphans and how the East immunizes them against such temptations; *Mitrea Cocor* (directed by Marietta Sadova and Victor Iliu, Romania, 1952)—set in a rural environment, presenting the orphan as agent of collectivization; and *Five from Barska Street* (directed by Aleksander Ford, Poland, 1954)—showing how socialist consciousness helps overcome juvenile rubble-era delinquency.

6. In the language of scholars of Soviet socialist realism, Agnes is the positive hero. Positive heroes step into a new environment politically naive and undersocialized. Here they meet educating figures. This is, according to Katerina Clark, a common trope of the Soviet socialist (socialist-realist) film of the 1930s and 1940s (1997, 29–30).

7. Deutsche Film-Aktiengesellschaft, the East German state-owned film studio.

8. The film insists on offering her exact date of birth, December 3, 1926.

9. At the party, Agnes also makes the acquaintance of her future circle of friends, which includes the slick theater and film critic Frank; the capitalist producer Dr. Plitsch; and the fallen and melancholic actress Lili, who cares more for looks and status than ideas (but has a good heart).

10. F. B. Habel (2000, 490) suggests that Moebius embodies Wolfgang Langhoff, a theater director who made a career by staging classics of German literature, some of his best performances premiering between 1949 and 1952. He was a follower of Stanislavsky who, unlike Moebius, slowly moved away from realism in favor of more Meyerholdian and Brechtian poetics.

11. *Entspannung* could also anticipate "detente," an important concept of Cold War international relations, but which will become more popular later, after the nuclear arsenals on both sides of the Atlantic have been stacked up, changing the whole understanding of a European conflagration.

12. The film makes several references to this winter and to the cold and the hunger in the Allied occupation zone. These references gesture toward the cruel American starvation policy against Germany that was in effect until the start of the Berlin Blockade. In the 1946–1947 winter, in Berlin alone two hundred people froze to death and "the population stayed at home wrapped in tattered clothes in rooms without heat, existing on a diet inadequate to sustain human life" (Bowyer Bell 1966, 253). Agnes falls seriously ill during this winter. The winter of 1947–1948 would bring similar experiences (254).

13. Burmeister's assumption is only partly valid. The departure from passive and fragile female figures takes place on the Nazi screen too. Linda Schulte-Sasse shows that, during the war, Nazi propaganda revamps its initial images of womanhood as child bearer, supporter of her husband's projects, and household manager. As more men die on the front line, women take their places in factories and offices. The women who were able to replace their men in productive activity became the models of womanhood of the late Nazi era, not very different from the ones of Soviet socialist discourse (1996, 193). This overlap shows the extent to which historical predicament conditions "propaganda" and leads to possible conflations of visions of the Soviet and the Nazi woman. Schulte-Sasse reveals that even Goebbels was aware of this uncanny overlap, as he made sure to mention that the German woman should not be mistaken for the Bolshevik one (193).

14. Later in the film, Moebius is shown becoming apologetic to Hartmann. During his trial for directing Nazi films (see note 16), Hartmann defends himself in language similar to Moebius's, arguing that his political allegiance is only for art itself. He was never interested in the politics of his films, but only in their aesthetic quality.

15. The commotion at the Westend Theater also refers to an actual event. Sean Allen shows that the scene is based on Maetzig's own experience. When his first antifascist film, *Ehe im Schatten* (*Marriage in the Shadows*), was presented in the West, at the Waterloo cinema in Hamburg, Harlan and his wife, Kristina Söderbaum (the lead actress of many of his melodramas and one of the female screen icons of the Nazi era), appeared, only be thrown out by the manager (Ascheid 2003, 263–264).

16. Harlan was the only film director of the Nazi era to be taken to court for making propaganda films. His first trial began in March 1948, but, after controversial rulings, he was acquitted under the assertion that it was impossible to demonstrate that he was the only person who had control over the content of his work. Harlan's defense used the argument that he was forced by Goebbels to direct the film, who then had control, as producer, over the final product. (Ascheid 2003, 230n8). Harlan's acquittal is one of the memorable ironic moments in the history of cinema since it almost coincides with the era in which *Cahiers du cinéma* was developing its "auteur theory," claiming that the director's vision could be discerned in

his work, even in industrial contexts such as the Hollywood studio system (and why not the German one?).

17. Maetzig himself acknowledges in a letter to the DEFA leadership that his film needs support because it has to keep up with the work at the Stalinallee (Maetzig and Agde 1987, 217). The intertwinement of art and reality was critical for him and exemplary for his time.

18. Agnes acts in a radio adaptation of Anna Seghers's novel *Das siebte Kreuz* (*The Seventh Cross*).

19. Sabine Hake documents the reactions of communist film critics of Weimar Germany. In their articles and film reviews, they repeatedly argue that a new cinema, one that is truly politically progressive, could be born only outside of a bourgeois capitalist society (1993, 191).

20. Yet in spite of the new context and Maetzig's effort to make his films popular, *Story* was a financial flop (Horbrügger 2007, 210).

21. Arendt presented her vision on this subject in her seminal *Origins of Totalitarianism*, a book that appeared in 1950. It is thus contemporary with *Story of a Young Couple* and aims to respond, from an antifascist, bourgeois humanist, and existentialist position, to some of the issues tackled in *Story of a Young Couple.*

22. "Totalitarian movements conjure up a lying world of consistency which is more adequate to the needs of the human mind than reality itself; in which, through sheer imagination, uprooted masses can feel at home and are spared the never-ending shocks which real life and real experiences deal to human beings and their expectations" (Arendt 1962, 353).

23. Two of the most articulate critics of socialist art who follow Arendt's position are Boris Groys and Evgeny Dobrenko. Referring directly to socialist art, they see its aesthetic work as an orderly and meaningful rendering of that which is posited as "the real." Socialist art contaminates the political, which functions more on aesthetic than on ethical and utilitarian principles. The world of communism wants to be beautiful, harmonious, "organized according to a unitary artistic plan (Groys 1992, 3). Dobrenko (2007, 5) also emphasizes that socialist art serves the aesthetization of politics as a derealizer of "everydayness" (a metaphysical concept echoing Arendt's "common sense"). The political function of socialist art is to transform the technologies of perceiving this "everyday," making the subject "see" socialism in reality (13), the future in the present (18), socialism as the spectacle of socialism, "a 'new reality' that bears witness to itself without needing a referent" (35). Here is Dobrenko at the peak of Arendtian discourse: "Aesthetics did not beautify reality; it *was* reality. By contrast, all reality *outside* of Socialist Realism was [nothing] but the wilderness of everyday life, waiting to be rendered for it to be read and interpreted" (4). This is also Groys's view, which reveals that, as a continuator of the Russian avant-garde, socialist art had to be concerned with the reorganizing of everyday life down to its minute details (1992, 25). Katerina Clark adopts a similar position. Socialist art "is not to any marked degree performing an aesthetic function" (1997, 27). Its function is that of the ritual and the spectacle, that is, to enable the social integration of the uprooted subject in the Great Soviet Family (29).

24. Perhaps more credit for the ideological work of the film should be given to the screenwriter Bodo Uhse. A veteran communist (since 1930), he was familiar with the cultural struggles of the interwar era. He was also an influential screenwriter and one of the most prominent journalists and fiction authors in East Germany. The reason this chapter does not trace his input is that he was critical of the film and denounced Maetzig for perverting the script.

25. In particular, the 1951 film version of Sartre's *Dirty Hands* outraged communists all over the world for presenting a bleak picture of the ruthless struggle for power of postwar communists.

26. *Story of a Young Couple* anticipates the reviews it will receive itself in the West. See *Der Spiegel* from 13 August 1952, 31–32. Ironically, it will be trashed as a heavy-handed propaganda film, just as Burmeister's film is.

27. Fuchs also theorized the aesthetization of the body, the overcoming of the difference between stage and audience, and performance and reception (Fischer-Lichte and Riley 1997, 64–65).

28. The mother is absent, emphasizing that, in the case of Dulz, parenthood is not to be understood traditionally.

29. This comment targets the stylistic heritage of Ufa, the German film company that in the postwar era was turned into DEFA, and of Hollywood. Legitimate questions about what to adopt and what to abandon from this heritage in an antifascist and anticapitalist world were posed by the GDR leadership and its film directors. Maetzig was one of them (Allen 2011, 256). What he included and what he left out is the topic of another study, which pertains to cinema's negotiation between socialist poetics and its effort to attract large audiences. *Story of a Young Couple* includes, uninspiredly, an element of cinematography and editing that was a staple of none other than Veit Harlan himself. When Agnes falls ill with pneumonia and high fever, her struggle with the disease is depicted via a series of delirium-dream sequences. Cinematographically, these visions are created through double exposure. In the same frame, blurry images of her face are collated with the content of her visions. A detailed analysis of this visual trope (and its fascistoid dimension) as employed by Harlan in his melodramas can be found in Žižek (2001, 42–48).

30. Maetzig experimented with Merin's acting in a previous film. Merin starred in Maetzig's *Council of the Gods* (*Der Rat der Götter*, 1950).

31. One can make the same comment on Maetzig's post-1989 recollections on his art, which were also voiced in a radical context, but one eager to marginalize anything that sounded communist.

32. Socialist art was supposed to be a dialectical "third way"; but its programmatic literature was haunted by contradictions. Often the denunciation of bourgeois naturalism employed language borrowed from the avant-garde, and the attack on "formalism" made use of a terminology uncannily reminiscent of realist aesthetics.

33. Sessak continued her DEFA career with similar parts. All other members of the cast, including Willy A. Kleinau, who plays the ruthless capitalist producer Plisch, started their careers after 1945. Merin was the rising star of socialist cinema, appearing in Maetzig's *The Beaverskin* (*Die Buntkarierten*, 1949) and *Council of the Gods* (1950). Among the male performers, Harry Hindemith (Burmeister) had the strongest résumé, playing in landmark productions of the era such as *Somewhere in Berlin* (1946) and *Our Daily Bread* (*Unser täglich Brot*, 1949). While Merin's career ends after *Story of a Young Couple*, Thielen's, for whom *Story of a Young Couple* was the first film, continues, especially in television films, until 1979. Among other parts, he played the lead role of Hettore Gonzaga in a 1958 screen adaptation of *Emilia Galotti*.

34. The Soviet secret police arrested Meyerhold in 1939 as World War II started, probably because of his German origin. He was killed in 1940.

35. See note 29.

36. Stanislavsky's acting technique, still hegemonic today, had its ups and downs in the Soviet Union. Ironically, it gained high currency in the land of the new enemy of Soviet communism, the United States, where it was called simply "the Method," and became the major acting style of Hollywood commercial cinema in the 1950s (for example, Marlon Brando's performance in 1954's *On the Waterfront*).

37. The fact that there is no character to embody Brecht in *Story of a Young Couple* is, as David Caute documents, caused by Brecht's problematic relationship to the GDR leadership. Although initially received with open arms by the Russian administration of Berlin (and later awarded the Stalin Prize), by the time *Story of a Young Couple* was in production, Brecht was

already a denounced author, who could still function as director only due to his international profile and the lip service he paid to the GDR regime (2005, 285–6).

38. In spite of the fact that Maetzig's first antifascist film, *Marriage in the Shadows* (*Ehe im Schatten,* 1948), was a big success on both sides of the Curtain, Maetzig still felt hesitant about his style and the political impact of his work. Sean Allen has convincingly documented that, in this period, Maetzig sought to define his directing style and questioned ideas about pathos and realism in cinema in general, and DEFA film in particular. He struggled to distance himself from the "formal traditions of Ufa's wartime melodramas" (Allen 2011, 256).

39. His declaration is quoted in a review of the film in *Neue Zeit* of 1947. See http://www .filmportal.de/node/51629/material/773726.

40. Brecht's *Mutter Courage,* Maetzig confesses, was the most influential theater experience of his life (Maetzig and Agde 1987, 36, 37).

41. The reference to Brecht is relevant because, as Peter Bürger shows, Brecht was one of the few authors who had been able to find a way out of the dead end created by the radical negation articulated by the avant-garde—a topic of high interest to the practitioners of postwar socialist art). Brecht's position is also insightful because film, unlike construction-site art, had to revolutionize its message within the technological and economic framework set by its bourgeois and capitalist aesthetics and modes of production. Bürger argues that Brecht did not reject the institution of art, as the avant-garde did, and that he used the avant-garde's attack on bourgeois art to transform the institution from inside (1984, 89). This had to be a solution for film too, which was still exhibited in theaters and had to remain the most popular medium for the workers. The pressure to overcome bourgeois naturalism came also from theoreticians of socialist acting from the Soviet Union "In my view," one such theoretician, Merab Mamardashvili, argued "this is precisely why today's actors often act badly: they naively try to perform something on stage that is a performance even in real life." This situation, Mamardashvili believed, called for a new technique that could "represent representation" (as quoted in Dobrenko 2007, 16).

42. Maetzig also admits that he learned from both Brecht and Lukács that cinema needed to be "scientific" (*wissenschaftlich*) and reflect the laws of society that determine the actions of characters. (Maetzig and Agde 1987, 193)

43. This point is made by Katerina Clark with reference to what she calls the "positive hero" of Soviet socialist literature (and film). Because positive heroes are merely a function in a ritualized spectacle, they are just a mask and have "no intrinsic self at all" (1997, 43–44).

3. The Testifying Orphan

1. The film premiered on 23 February 1968.

2. "Each Communist party is free to apply the principles of Marxism-Leninism and socialism in its own country, but it is not free to deviate from these principles if it is to remain a Communist party . . . The weakening of any of the links in the world system of socialism directly affects all the socialist countries, and they cannot look indifferently upon this" (as quoted in Judt 2005, 443).

3. Lustig leaves Czechoslovakia after the Prague Spring and returns only after 1989.

4. Zýková (2011).

5. Zýková (2011) documents that filmmakers chose Krystyna Mikołajewska for the role of Dita after seeing her in Jerzy Kawalerowicz's Oscar-nominated film *Pharaon* (Poland, 1966).

6. In "Cultural Criticism and Society," republished in *Prisms.*

7. The failure to love or, at least, to expose oneself to love suggests a loss of trust in the human. Via the medium of love, melodrama articulates a humanist discourse that transcends the social and political interpellations of the subject. No surprise then that, in the postwar era, an era in search of a new humanism, the melodramatic subplot underpins many of the early accounts of the Nazi genocide—see Kurt Maetzig's very popular *Marriage in the Shadows* (*Ehe im Schatten*, 1947) and a Czechoslovak version of it, *Romeo, Juliet and Darkness* (*Romeo, Julie a tma*, Jiří Weiss, 1959), one of the most appreciated Holocaust films of its time and also one of the earliest, since the Czechoslovak film industry approached the topic after some delay.

8. As I show later, Adorno's aesthetic theories, in particular his pronouncements against realism, straightforward storytelling, and sentimentalism, inform the film's storytelling. It is worth emphasizing here that many of Adorno's pronouncements (1992, 103) are made in the context of theorizing about leftist progressive artistic representation, in particular against socialist realism and Sartre's concept of committed art. These views on art inform *Story of a Young Couple* and *Somewhere in Europe*.

9. The use of survivors as a questioning device becomes more insightful when we remember that Dita's story is told from the perspective of 1968—that is, shortly before the Prague Spring. At this moment in the history of Eastern Europe, both political elites and society had already acknowledged the failure of radical reconstruction narratives as presented in *Story of a Young Couple*. The film goes one step further than the denunciation of Stalinism, of its "errors" and violence (which had been high in the Czechoslovakia of the Slansky trials), and aims to question the more habituated aspects of life in the modern state.

10. The post-Holocaust diegetic historian (Dita) and the post-Stalinist extradiegetic one (Moskalyk) need to be seen as "encoder(s) and decoder(s) of constellations that bear witness to the traumatic legacies of modern historical extremity" (Rothberg 2000, 11). In his 1940 essay "On the Concept of History," Walter Benjamin uses "constellation" to take distance from linear and causal notions of history. See his *Selected Writings: 1938–1940* (Cambridge, MA: Harvard University Press, 2003), 396.

11. Primo Levi describes the Muselmann as the inmate whose "body is already in decay, and nothing can save them from selections or from death by exhaustion. Their life is short, but their number is endless; they, the *Muselmänner*, the drowned, form the backbone of the camp, an anonymous mass, continually renewed and always identical, of non-men who march and labor in silence, the divine spark dead within them, already too empty to really suffer. One hesitates to call them living: one hesitates to call their death death" (1996, 90).

12. Later in the film, another suitor makes reference to the bracelet and the well-shaped body. "If you had nothing on, but this beautiful bracelet," the elderly suitor tells Dita, "I'd be able to confirm that your figure is wonderful . . . Everywhere . . . absolutely" (ellipses in original). In this context, the fetish function of the bracelet producing Dita as an object of male desire comes best to the fore, especially due to the use of the words "everywhere" and "absolutely." Moskalyk offers his viewers a lesson in Marxist commodity fetishism analysis. The fetish, "like the grain of sand in the oyster that produces the pearl, create[s] social and sexual constructions of things at intractable points that trouble the social or sexual psyche. . . . These are points where relations between people are liable to become relations between things" (Mulvey 1996, 3). The fetish hides the inconvenient truths of the human, in order to be able to serve Dita's marketing as object of desire and reduce her to being beautiful. As Dita feels insulted by the suitor's words and leaves, the suitor, frustrated at losing possession of his object of desire, concludes, "A whore is still a whore." His comment reveals his captivity in the patriarchalism of his era and in the reified human relations it produces.

13. In this context, *Urteil* becomes one of those many German words that, as Paul Celan (as well as George Steiner [1984, 207–208]) puts it, have become *gray* after Auschwitz. The

irony that invests the grayness of *Urteil* is that the word is central to the work of two authors that stand one at the beginning, the other at the end of modernity: Immanuel Kant and Franz Kafka. The first dedicated his energies to linking the idea of human to a person's *Urteilskraft* (his or her power to judge); the other was concerned with the *Kraft des Urteils*, with the infinite consequences of its pronouncement, placing *Urteil*, and the trial itself (*das Prozess*), as the basis of human barbarism. The norm and the ideal are also important in the Aryan concept of the pure race and in the racist philosophy that supported the building of ghettos and death camps.

14. In order to avoid further stereotypical feminization of the survivor, this chapter avoids discussing trauma and its effect on narrative and testimony.

15. Some of this unease was material: the starving postwar world was reluctant to return possessions or pay reparations to its persecuted Jewry. Some unease was psychosocial; it pertained to a refusal to acknowledge the horror of the war, sometimes one's complicity in it, and, at a deeper level, modern civilization's implication in this process. Czechoslovakia's president in exile, Edward Beneš, argued even before his return to Prague that war-impoverished populations would not be willing to give back to their Jews the possessions that once belonged to them. The prospect for reparations was even bleaker (Bankier 2005, viii).

16. Europe's insensitivity to the testimony of Holocaust victims is best illustrated by the lack of readership of Primo Levi's *If This Is a Man* (later translated into English as *Survival in Auschwitz*). The first edition of this classic sold a small number of copies in 1947 (Judt 2008, 45).

17. "Nor was it to show how, at a certain moment, institutions of confinement, which had existed for a long time, secreted their own theory and justifications in the discourse of psychiatrists" and other healers and agents of normalization (Foucault 2008, 34).

18. The film depicts in detail the wedding of an asylum girl and friend of Dita with such a partner. The scene is filmed with a hesitant and alienating camera in order to draw attention to its problematic nature.

19. Film critic Veronika Zýková has studied the production archive of the film and noticed that the song must have been written in the 1960s (maybe especially for the film), since its lyrics are signed by the famous Czechoslovak songwriter Pavel Kopta, who was born in 1930.

20. Reframing occurs in many other moments in the film, when Dita talks about everyday encounters, her feelings, life. In a newspaper ad, a pest control company promises to use the reliable Zyklon B for the extermination of insects. Dita's reading out loud of the ad operates the reframing, which reminds the viewer that Zyklon B was the toxic substance used in the gas chambers at Auschwitz.

21. As George Steiner (1984, 208) has shown when analyzing the poetry of Paul Celan.

22. This is a sample of language "no longer lived, but is merely spoken" (Steiner 1984, 208). By making reference to the load of death it carries, Dita renders visible the adventure of ethical use of language ("live language is the highest adventure of which the human brain is capable" [208]). Ethical use of language expresses purpose and will, and does not erase its referentiality, something that bureaucratic language aims to achieve in order to escape guilt and realization of the consequences of its decisions (Bauman 2008, 197).

23. She can also be seen as invoking her predicament as an object of *Urteil*. See note 13.

24. "Even the sound of desperation pays tribute to a heinous affirmation" (Adorno 1992, 103).

25. A similar argument, but one more focused on trauma, is articulated by Saul Friedlander and James Young. According to them, art expresses not what Friedlander calls "common memory" (a memory concerned with coherence, causation, and bringing things in order), but "deep memory" (a memory that remains inarticulable and "which continues to

exist as unresolved trauma just beyond the reach of meaning" (Young 2003, 24). This leads to the articulation of uncanny historical discourses, whose narrative skein of linear progression is disrupted, which leaves room for, even invites, alternative envisionings of the past and the questioning of mainstream drives for historical closure (25).

26. "The substantive content of a work of art can consist in the accurate and tacitly polemical representation of emerging meaninglessness, and that content can be lost when it is stated positively and hypostatized as existing" (Adorno 1991, 226).

27. Reviews in the Czechoslovak press are synthesized in an article by Veronika Zýková (2011) published on the blog *24fps*.

28. Lustig's criticism is summarized in Zýková's article.

29. Even the fact that the viewer does not hear Mikołajewska's voice on the soundtrack, but its dubbing by Blanka Bohdanová, is an astute commentary on the predicament of the survivor. It echoes the dialogue Dita has with Dr. Fitz, which suggests that, in order for a survivor to have a voice, she needs to erase her body.

30. It is true that liberalization of censorship in the late 1960s in Eastern Europe allowed more display of nudity on the screen, and many filmmakers—for example, Milos Forman in *Loves of a Blonde*—exploited the opportunity.

31. As quoted in Zýková (2011).

32. "Dita's talk is also both too theatrical and elliptical; cumulatively it becomes little more than pretentious posturing. The chic style is, finally, just too much at odds with the painful subject matter" (Liebman and Quart 1996).

33. An analysis of Dita as a post-traumatic melancholic subject (which this chapter avoids, for the ethical reasons explained above) would consider this image as the scene to which the subject who is not able to overcome trauma obsessively returns, an image of him- or herself that keeps the subject captive in the past.

34. "There can be no *one* without zero, but the zero always appears in the guise of a *one*, of a (some)thing. The name is the trope of the zero. The zero is always *called* a one, when the zero is actually nameless, 'innommable'" (Man 1996, 59).

35. See note 29.

4. Children of the Revolution

1. The film historian Günter Agde argues that Maetzig must be remembered first and foremost as an enlightener, as a filmmaker who wanted to reach the masses and educate them, and that he subordinated style and intellectual and stylistic coherence to this mission. He was more of a filmmaker columnist than a filmmaker artist (1983, 102).

2. Normalization became the name of the repression of the reforms proposed by Dubček's Action Program. In fact, Czechoslovak cinema never recovered from the politics of normalization, the blacklisting, and the emigration of its auteurs.

3. "*Camera Buff*, Kieślowski's first internationally acclaimed film, received awards at the Moscow, Chicago and Berlin film festivals. It also won the 1979 Festival of Polish Films in Gdansk. . . . The film was exceptionally well received in Poland, praised for its reflections on the nature of film-making and on the social and moral responsibilities of being an artist" (Haltof 2004, 12). Later recognition includes awards and nominations for the U.S. Academy Awards and at the Berlin, Cannes, New York, and San Sebastian film festivals.

4. The so-called Basket Three of Helsinki principles was the one that turned this conference on cooperation in Europe into one that spurred a debate on human rights that some historians believe had a direct influence on the 1989 fall of the socialist experiment. Basket Three

focused on the rights of individuals, grouped under Principles VII ("Respect for human rights and fundamental freedoms, including the freedom of thought, conscience, religion or belief") and VIII ("Equal rights and self-determination of peoples"). Sarah B. Snyder's *Human Rights Activism and the End of the Cold War: A Transnational History of the Helsinki Network* (Cambridge: Cambridge University Press, 2011) and Daniel C. Thomas's *The Helsinki Effect: International Norms, Human Rights, and the Demise of Communism* (Princeton, NJ: Princeton University Press, 2001) support the cause-and-effect argument between Helsinki and 1989. The main medium connecting the two was the network of human rights dissidents and vigilantes that developed both inside and outside Eastern Europe. Their activism gave birth to KOR, Charter 77, and the Solidarity movement, all discussed in this chapter.

5. This document is available in the Open Society Archive (OSA) Free Europe Archive under the title "Intro Helsinki" (CN 147 092100/77. Washington 7 May 1977, HU OSA 300-60-1, Box 100).

6. They were also regarded as historians, focusing like Moskalyk on earlier periods of their country's history, including Stalinism.

7. The return of the auteur in the post-socialist-realist era, and consequently of some of the values associated with auteurism, was echoed by 1956 and post-1956 political and intellectual calls for a return to Europe (imagined as the legitimate bearer of the cultural and artistic heritage of the prewar era) and for a turning away from Moscow and its radical efforts to transform the art and the society of the region (Kemp-Welch 2008, 128).

8. The collection of essays written by the two Polish poets Kornhauser and Zagajewski "became the manifesto and the theoretical formula for the generation sometimes known as the 'Young Culture' which strongly influenced filmmakers of Kieślowski's generation and the Cinema of Distrust" (Haltof 2004, 25).

9. In 1977, Agnieszka Holland published an article in which she distinguished between two types of auteurs: those who trusted the image and those who believed in reality, the stylists and the documentarists respectively. Kieślowski falls obviously in the second category (Wach 2000, 151).

10. "Cinema of distrust" is the term Haltof prefers for *kino moralnego niepokoju*, literally "cinema of moral anxiety" (2007, 29).

11. Filip is rarely presented alone in the frame. He shares his life and work with family or workmates.

12. Edward Gierek replaced Władysław Gomułka as leader of the Polish state (and the Communist Party) in 1970. His leadership is remembered as pseudo-reformist and pragmatic (Kemp-Welch 2008, 192).

13. Solidarity (in Polish "Solidarność")—its full title is the Independent Self-governing Trade Union "Solidarity"—was founded on 31 August 1980 at the Gdańsk Shipyard under the leadership of Lech Wałęsa. It grew to include almost a third of the working population of Poland and was responsible for massive protests against the regime, which led to the imposition of martial law in Poland in 1981. The Polish martial law demonstrates perhaps most eloquently the failure of socialist subject production, the party's own lack of trust in its work and its citizens.

14. I received this and other background information on the Polish film industry and resistance from the film scholar Marcin Adamczak. I express my gratitude here for his feedback.

15. In "Reflections on the Sofia Conference Meeting and Propaganda RAD Background Report/89 (Hungary)." 29 April 1977, HU OSA 300-60-1, Box 100.

16. Almost ironically, the idea of defamiliarization was central to the theorists of the socialist-realist avant-garde, which the realism of the cinema of moral distrust was opposing (see chapter 2).

17. Irka notices Filip's gesture, which confirms to her that, for the moment, Filip's gaze has diverged from perceiving life through private eyes.

18. Reproletarianization was successful. "Working-class membership in the Party increased, becoming at 46 percent the highest of the Soviet bloc" (Eley 2002, 432), but the co-opting of workers was just for show: their participation was stifled by bureaucratic measures. "Workers were 'consulted,' visibly enhancing the Party's legitimacy. But decision-making remained centralist as ever" (432).

19. Haltof talks about Filip's "suicide as a political film-maker (he 'shoots' himself with his camera)." He notices that "this meaning of the ending of *Camera Buff* had been scrupulously analyzed by Polish critics who . . . treated the ending as a sign of capitulation" (2004, 45).

20. "There were many documentaries which I didn't make. I managed to put a few of them into *Camera Buff* . . . A documentary about pavements, or about a dwarf" (Kieślowski 1998, 56).

21. One of the main points of Žižek's book on Kieślowski is to argue that, from a certain point of view, fiction films are more realistic that documentaries.

22. One of the founding goals of KOR was to offer medical help to the injured in the June 1976 protests and to workers tortured by the police (Kemp-Welch 2008, 212).

23. The producer embodies the same character and is played by the same actor as the producer of Agnieszka's documentary about Birkut in Andrzej Wajda's *Man of Marble*.

24. Candide is the eponymous character of a novel by the famous French philosopher Voltaire.

25. Wajda's Agnieszka from *Man of Marble* is also only a filmmaker in the making, half amateur, half professional.

26. Kieślowski also envisioned himself as one (Wach 2000, 20). Wach emphasizes in particular "the revolutionary power of realism" to emphasize the discrepancy between power's and resistance's diverging representations of reality (11).

5. The Family of Victims

1. Authorities and vigilante groups killed about five thousand communists and left-ists during the year that followed the defeat of the Hungarian Soviet Republic, and tens of thousands were imprisoned without a trial. Several socialists and communists had to leave Hungary and live in exile (Hill 2004, 33).

2. The Soviet Revolution, the Hungarian Soviet Revolution, and Stalin's Great Terror.

3. In the 1930s, a leftist Albert Camus expresses this position against power's mobilizing practices and reiterates it, this time targeting more clearly Stalinism, in the immediate postwar era in the *Revolted Man* (Novello 2010, 62, 138–139). The post-1975 Helsinki conference debates and Hungary's effort to implement them also inform the vision of this film. For more on this, see the discussion on the consequences of the Helsinki conference in chapter 4.

4. János's argument resonates with critiques of Stalinism formulated in the 1980s. The main one was that party bureaucrats replaced professionals in leadership positions (Rainer 2009, 240).

5. In Stalinist Hungary, "in addition to the prominent victims in the public dock, 2,000 Communist cadres were summarily executed, 150,000 imprisoned, and 350,000 expelled from the party—the victims being preponderantly wartime 'local undergrounders,' 'Westerners,' veterans of the Spanish Civil War, former Social Democrats, and senior military

personnel" (Rothschild and Mészáros 2000, 137). A socialist country that was more tolerant to its Westerners was Romania, which did not imprison its Spanish Civil War veterans.

6. Miklós Horthy was the military dictator of Hungary after the repression of the Soviet Republic in 1919, which he led (see note 1, about the White Terror). Mátyás Rákosi was the general secretary of the HCP from 1945 to 1956 and the emblematic figure of the brutal Hungarian Stalinism. He was deposed during the 1956 reformist movement and replaced by Imre Nagy.

7. Lukács's ambivalent relationship with Stalinism is detailed in chapter 1.

8. This is the thesis of the Hungarian historian and politician István Bibó, expressed in the 1946 pamphlet *The Misery of the Small Countries of Eastern Europe*. István Bibó was a minister in 1956 revolutionary cabinet of Imre Nagy. He died in 1979, but his ideas regained popularity after his death.

9. Also called *Diary for My Loves*.

10. Yet *Diary for My Children* remained Mészáros's most successful film.

11. From Marx's *The Eighteenth Brumaire of Louis Napoleon*.

12. In France András survived the Nazi bombing that killed his mother and sister, but left him in a wheelchair.

13. Here the stories of Juli, Dita Saxová, and the raped Jewish girl from *Somewhere in Europe* overlap. Memories make them resistant to the calls and mobilizations of the present. As mentioned in the previous chapters, the gendering of the practice of memory should not go unnoticed, even if it is not discussed in this book. The feminist dimension of Mészáros's films is emphasized in Catherine Portuges's *Screen Memories* (1993) and various articles on her work, such as Barbara Halpern Martineau, "The Films of Marta Mészáros or, the Importance of Being Banal," *Film Quarterly* 34, no. 1 (Autumn 1980): 21–27; Barbara Quart, "Three Central European Women Directors Revisited," *Cineaste* 19 no. 4 (1993): 58; and Constantin Parvulescu, "Betrayed Promises: Politics and Sexual Revolution in the Films of Márta Mészáros, Miloš Forman, and Dušan Makavejev," *Camera Obscura* 24, no. 71 (2009): 77–105.

14. The family story of *Diary for My Children* is not limited to the plot of the film, but also applies to its cast and crew. The Polish actor Jan Nowicki was Mészáros's husband (until 2008) and the cinematography of the film was entrusted to Mészáros's sons, Nyika Jancsó and Miklós Jancsó Jr., both born of Mészáros's previous marriage to the acclaimed Hungarian director Miklós Jancsó. Moreover, in *Little Vilma*, the actress playing the protagonist is Mészáros's granddaughter, Cleo Ladanyi.

15. Though the overlap is total in the last sequence of the film, which shows Juli and András visiting János in the high-security prison where the communist authorities keep him indefinitely incarcerated. Just like Juli's father, he is shaved.

16. Unlike Juli's father, János returns from prison. The second film of the *Diary* series shows it.

17. The odyssey of *Man of Marble*'s preproduction is insightfully documented by Paul Coates (2004).

18. But even in Yugoslavia Stalinism was rarely and only lately engaged. One of the first films to do it is Dušan Makavejev's 1971 *Mysteries of the Organism*. Another Yugoslav classic about Stalinist practices is Emir Kusturica's 1985 *When Father Was Away on Business*.

19. The Czechoslovak boldness was silenced by the Soviet tanks in 1968, and the 1970–1989 period, as Peter Hames acknowledges, was much less susceptible to the emergence of any critical voice about the Stalinist past, its purges and terror (2009, 77).

20. *Angi Vera*, which also has a young female protagonist, remains mostly a descriptive study of intensive socialist political education.

21. I am thankful to Balázs Varga for the feedback he gave me on this chapter.

22. The first film of this thematic cycle was János Herskó's *Dialogue* (1963), but there are other significant films like Ferenc Kósa's *Ten Thousand Suns* (1967), Zoltán Fábri's *Twenty Hours* (1965), István Gaál's *The Green Years* (1965), and Sándor Sára's *The Upthrown Stone* (1968). In a personal dialogue, Varga also suggests that Péter Bacsó's *Witness* (1969), which shows the 1950s differently, challenging the continuity between past and present, can also be included in this list. But Bacsó's satire was banned for ten years. Its release in 1979 was in a way a start of a new cycle of Hungarian film about the 1950s, to which Mészáros's *Diary for My Children* also belongs. This second wave includes *The Stud-Farm* (András Kovács, 1978), *Daniel Takes a Train* (Pál Sándor, 1982), and *The Day before Yesterday* (Péter Bacsó, 1981). More on this topic can be found in Petrie (1986, 29–44).

23. Literary fiction was bolder. For example, in post-1965 Romania, there was a wave of accounts focused on the persecution of party members, and their sometimes heroic resistance. It bears the name "the literature of the haunting decade" (or "obsessive decade").

24. A comparative study of these two films would reveal the overlapping mechanisms of memory dealing with political trauma and nostalgia.

25. Kádár was Hungary's post-1956 chief of state until 1987.

26. The theme of the new class division in socialism is addressed in other films by Mészáros, such as her 1973 *Riddance*.

27. In the 1950s, after Stalin's death, the leader of the Hungarian counterrevolution depicted this minority dictatorship mostly as an oligarchy, "a degeneration of power," and as Bonapartism (Rainer 2009, 232).

28. This position will of course explode early in the post-1989 years.

29. Though, as John Cunningham argues, socialist realism never truly developed in Hungary as it did in other socialist states such as the GDR and Romania (2004, 70).

Epilogue

1. Dissolution is the concept used by Charles Maier to describe the disintegration of the socialist universe in East Germany. One aspect of it is the dissolution of the communist idea and hope, which he documents convincingly in "Losing Faith," the first chapter of his book *Dissolution* (1997, 3–58).

2. In *România Liberă*, 14 June 1974, 1, 3.

3. This is the title of an article that appeared on 11 January 1977 in *România liberă* to mark the founding of the Falcons of the Fatherland.

4. *Scînteia*, 1 May 1984.

5. According to another press report, in 1980 more than fourteen thousand high school students and young adults participated in such patriotic work on these youth construction sites. See "The Plenteous Balance Sheet of the Patriotic Work of Youth in 1980" ("Bilanțul rodnic al muncii patriotice a tineretului în 1980"), *Scînteia*, 6 January 1981, 1, 5. Among them was also the infamous Danube–Black Sea Canal, which was started in the 1950s as a work camp, abandoned for more than two decades, and then reopened again under Ceaușescu's own supervision.

6. Ion Becheru, "The Education of Youth in the Spirit of Love and Respect for Work and Profession" ("Educarea tineretului în spiritul dragostei și respectului față de muncă și profesie"), *România liberă*, 18 January 1977, 3.

7. *Scînteia tineretului*, 5 October 1983.

8. *Scînteia*, 9 December 1981.

9. "The Future of the Socialist Nation" ("Viitorul însuşi al naţiunii socialiste"), *Scînteia tineretului*, 2 May 1977, 3, 5.

10. Ibid.

11. In the late 1970s, facing a baby boom, the state also set up a Center for Research in the Problems of Youth, whose surveys influenced not only propaganda but also policy decisions. To discuss its results, *Scînteia tineretului*, the mouthpiece of the Union of Communist Youth, started a weekly column, "The Dialectic of Ideas: Processes, Phenomena, Tendencies in the Thought and Life of the Young Generation." Its first article, published on 20 November 1980 and titled "Ideals of Life between Prejudice and Reality," discussed, as the title suggests, the results of a survey by the Research Center on what the young men and women of the country expected from themselves and life.

12. It was published soon after the *Scînteia tineretului* column on youth problems referred to in note 11.

13. See chapter 4 for more on the poetics and politics of the cinema of distrust.

14. "Vasile," the name of the protagonist of *Sand Dunes*, is disclosed only during the police investigation. The hero of *Contest* has no name, no past, and no story about himself, and when asked what his real name is, he replies, "I will tell you later."

15. I discuss the bargaining of the Gierek regime of 1970s Poland in chapter 4.

16. Though confession plays a central role, the disciplining practices of late socialist power diverge from the model developed by Michel Foucault in his *History of Sexuality*. Foucault argues that power seeks to create social control via a ritual of confession and guilt. Foucault uses the confessional employed by the Catholic Church as a model to understand modern political practices (1990, 17–24). The Catholic Church interpellates its subjects as sinners in order to make itself indispensable to the good life. The late socialist practice is slightly different. It does not require belief or religious zeal. It also does not seek confessions. It seeks a bargain: social silence, compromise, and a promise not to challenge its authority.

17. This game is also brilliantly theorized by Giorgio Agamben in *Homo Sacer*. See Works Cited and the discussion in chapter 1.

18. This is the conclusion of a 1984 report by the research department of Radio Free Europe, Romanian Section, by Crisula Stefanescu. Romanian SR/4 21 HU OSA 300-60-1, Box 169.

19. The title of one such article is symptomatic: "Allergy to Work Gives Birth to Monsters." The subtitle reads "It is not an incurable disease, but needs to be treated in time." *Scînteia*, 11 May 1970, 3, 5.

20. 3 August 1979, 1, 3.

21. Here talking is also unilateral, since there is no uncensored input from readers.

22. One can speculate that the politically correct socialist life goals such as "dedication to the common cause," "the struggle for the new and for more justice in the world," and especially "the continuation of the heroic deeds of their predecessors" were not actual choices of the interviewees and that they were inserted into the article to cosmeticize the results. And if they were actual choices, were they expressed honestly, or were they the outcome of the social bargain, pretending commitment to the revolutionary game?

23. *Scînteia tineretului*, 3 July 1986, 8.

24. In fact, the influence of the Western lifestyle troubled Romanian authorities so much that they declared its promotion through propaganda radio stations such as Radio Free Europe as interference in the internal affairs of a state. This stance was shared throughout the Eastern Bloc. See "Soviet Radio Says RFE, RL incompatible with Detente," 184/27, HU OSA 300-60-1, Box 100.

25. This essay had a strong influence on the Polish resistance.

26. Maier emphasizes the contradictions of the withdrawal into the realm of the private: "For Günter Gaus, the private enclaves . . . made the regime bearable and served as a safety valve. For anyone with intellectual or political pretensions, however, the allegedly benign refuge of the private sphere offered less shelter than it seemed to. It was discouraging enough that Marxist Mandarins were leery about recognizing any sort of autonomous private domain. More debilitating was the party's effort to undermine privacy with secrecy. Increasingly, secrecy—as exemplified by the pervasive presence of the state security agents, the Stasi—corrupted private relationships and undermined trust among individuals" (1997, 46).

27. His films also turn stylistically more cautious, straying away from realism, which was regarded, since the Polish cinema of distrust, as the most subversive style of late socialism. They soften their edges by becoming more "artistic." As Kieślowski put it, realism responded to the "need" of the times to tell the truth. Pița's sliding into the surreal becomes a marker of caution in the face of censorship—or maybe worse, the embracing of the experimentalism that Kieślowski scorned (see chapter 4). Moreover, it reveals not only the tight grip the Romanian Communist Party held on cultural artifacts, but also the inability of Romanian society to articulate road maps of active resistance.

Works Cited

Adorno, Theodor W. 1981. *Prisms*. New York: Spearman.
———. 1991. *Notes to Literature*. Vol. 1. New York: Columbia University Press.
———. 1992. *Notes to Literature*. Vol. 2. New York: Columbia University Press.
Agamben, Giorgio. 1998. *Homo Sacer: Sovereign Power and Bare Life*. Stanford, CA: Stanford University Press.
———. 1999. *Remnants of Auschwitz: The Witness and the Archive*. New York: Zone Books.
Agde, Günter. 1983. "Kurt Maetzig: Intervene, Enlighten, Change" ["Kurt Maetzig: Eingreifen, aufklären, verändern."] In *DEFA-Spielfilm-Regisseure und ihre Kritiker*, edited by Rolf Richter, 99–119. Berlin: Henschel.
Allen, Sean. 2011. "'Sagt, wie soll man Stalin danken?' Kurt Maetzig's *Ehe im Schatten* (1947), *Roman einer jungen Ehe* (1952) and the Cultural Politics of Post-War Germany." *German Life and Letters* 64, no. 2 (April): 255–271.
Arendt, Hannah. 1962. *The Origins of Totalitarianism*. New York: Meridian.
Ascheid, Antje. 2003. *Hitler's Heroines: Stardom & Womanhood in Nazi Cinema*. Philadelphia: Temple University Press.
Badiou, Alain. 2010. *Metapolitics*. London: Verso.
Bankier, David. 2005. Introduction to *Jews Are Coming Back*, edited by David Bankier, vii–xi. Jerusalem: Yad Vashem.
Bauman, Zygmunt. 2008. *Modernity and the Holocaust*. Malden, MA: Polity Press.
Baumel, Judith Tydor. 1999. *Double Jeopardy: Gender and the Holocaust*. New York: Routledge.
Bazin, André. 1997. *Bazin at Work: Major Essays and Reviews from the Forties and Fifties*. Edited by Bert Cardullo. New York: Routledge.
Bosteels, Bruno. 2011. *The Actuality of Communism*. New York: Verso.
Bowyer Bowls, J. 1966. *Besieged: Seven Cities under Siege*. Philadelphia: Chilton Books.
Bürger, Peter. 1984. *Theory of the Avant-Garde*. Minneapolis: University of Minnesota Press.
Butler, Judith. 1990. *Gender Trouble*. New York: Routledge.
Caute, David. 2005. *The Dancer Defects. The Struggle for Cultural Supremacy during the Cold War*. Oxford: Oxford University Press.
Cernat, Manuela. 1980. "Is the Contemporary Romanian Film a Mirror in which the Portrait of Youth Appears in a Proper Light?" ["Este filmul românesc contemporan o oglindă în care portretul tineretului apare în adevărata sa lumină?"]. *Scînteia* (16 Nov.).
Clark, Katerina. 1997. "Socialist Realism with Shores. The Conventions of the Positive Hero." In *Socialist Realism without Shores*, edited by Thomas Lahusen and Evgeny Dobrenko, 27–50. Durham, NC: Duke University Press.
———. 2000. *The Soviet Novel: History as Ritual*. Bloomington: Indiana University Press.
Coates, Paul. 2004. "Człowiek z marmuru / Man of Marble." In *The Cinema of Central Europe*, edited by Peter Hames, 173–179. London: Wallflower.

Cunningham, John. 2004. *Hungarian Cinema. From Coffeehouse to Multiplex.* London: Wallflower.

Deleuze, Gilles, and Felix Guattari. 1983. *Anti-Oedipus. Capitalism and Schizophrenia.* Minneapolis: University of Minnesota Press.

Derrida, Jacques. 1978. *Writing and Difference.* Routledge. London.

———. 2000. *Of Hospitality: Anne Dufourmantelle Invites Jacques Derrida to Respond.* Stanford, CA: Stanford University Press.

———. 2006. *Specters of Marx: The State of the Debt, the Work of Mourning, and the New International.* New York: Routledge.

Dobrenko, Evgeny. 2007. *Political Economy of Socialist Realism.* New Haven, CT: Yale University Press.

Eley, Geoff. 2002. *Forging Democracy: The History of the Left in Europe, 1850–2000.* Oxford: Oxford University Press.

Engels, Friedrich. [1884] 1993. *The Origin of the Family, Private Property and the State.* http://www.marxists.org/archive/marx/works/1884/origin-family/ (accessed 10 Sept. 2013).

Everac, Paul. 1977. "In the Name of Freedom" ["În numele libertății"]. *Scînteia* (6 April).

Falk, Barbara J. 2003. *The Dilemmas of Dissidence in East-Central Europe: Citizen Intellectuals and Philosopher Kings.* Budapest: Central European University Press.

Fischer-Lichte, Erika, and Jo Riley. 1997. *The Show and the Gaze of Theatre: A European Perspective.* Iowa City: University of Iowa Press.

Forman, Milos. 1994. *Turnaround: A Memoir.* New York: Villard.

Foucault, Michel. 1982. *Technologies of the Self.* Amherst: University of Massachusetts Press.

———. 1988. *The History of Sexuality.* Vol. 3, *The Care of the Self.* New York: Vintage Books.

———. 1990. *The History of Sexuality.* Vol. 1, *An Introduction.* New York: Vintage Books.

———. 1995. *Discipline and Punish: The Birth of the Prison.* New York: Vintage Books.

———. 2008. *The Birth of Biopolitics: Lectures at the College de France, 1978–1979.* London: Palgrave Macmillan.

Friedman, Ellen G. 2002. "Post-Patriarchal Endings: Some New American Fiction." *Modern Fiction Studies* 48 (Fall): 693–712.

Georgian, Ada, and Alexandru Mureșan. 1981. "The Factory, School of Work and Communist Life" ["Uzina, școală a muncii și vieții comuniste"]. *Scînteia* (5 March).

Ghinea, M. 1979. "The Sad Anonymity of Some Slackers" ["Tristul anonimat al unor pierde-vară"]. *Scînteia tineretului* (3 Aug.).

Groys, Boris. 1992. *The Total Art of Stalinism.* Princeton, NJ: Princeton University Press.

———. 1997. "A Style and a Half." In *Socialist Realism without Shores,* edited by Thomas Lahusen and Evgeny Dobrenko, 76–90. Durham, NC: Duke University Press.

Habel, F. B. 2000. *The Great Lexicon of the DEFA Feature Films [Das große Lexikon der DEFA-Spielfilme].* Berlin: Schwarzkopf & Schwarzkopf.

Hake, Sabine. 1993. *The Cinema's Third Machine: Writing on Film in Germany, 1907–1933.* Lincoln: University of Nebraska Press.

Haltof, Marek. 2003. *Polish National Cinema.* New York: Berghahn.

———. 2004. *The Cinema of Krzysztof Kieślowski: Variations on Destiny and Chance.* London: Wallflower.

———. 2007. *Historical Dictionary of Polish Cinema.* New York: Scarecrow Press.

Hames, Peter. 2009. *The Czech and Slovak Cinema. Theme and Tradition.* Edinburgh: Edinburgh University Press.

Hardt, Michael, and Antonio Negri. 2009. *Commonwealth.* Cambridge, MA: Belknap Press of Harvard University Press.

Havel, Vaclav. 2009. *The Power of the Powerless.* New York: Routledge.

Hegel, G. W. F. 1998. *The Phenomenology of Spirit [Phänomenologie des Geistes].* Berlin: Akademie Verlag.

Hill, Raymond. 2004. *Hungary (Nations in Transition).* New York: Facts on File.

Hobsbawm, Eric. 2011. *How to Change the World: Reflections on Marx and Marxism.* New Haven, CT: Yale University Press.

Hoover, Marjorie L. 1965. "V. E. Meyerhold: A Russian Predecessor of Avant-Garde Theater." *Comparative Literature* 17, no. 3 (Summer): 234–250.

Horbrügger, Anja. 2007. *Breakup for Continuity—Continuity for Breakup [Aufbruch zur Kontinuität—Kontinuität im Aufbruch].* Marburg, Germany: Schüren.

Iordanova, Dina. 2003. *The Cinema of the Other Europe: The Industry and Artistry of East Central European Film.* London: Wallflower.

Janicek, Karel. 2011. "Arnost Lustig, Czech-born Jewish author who survived Holocaust dies at 84." *The Canadian Press.* 26 Feb. http://search.ebscohost.com/login.aspx ?direct=true&db=n5h&AN=MYO159257564511&site=eds-live (accessed 15 Dec. 2012).

Judt, Tony. 2005. *Postwar: A History of Europe since 1945.* New York: Penguin.

———. 2008. *Reappraisals: Reflections on the Forgotten Twentieth Century.* New York: Penguin.

Juviler, Peter H. 1985. "Contradictions of Revolution: Juvenile Crime and Rehabilitation." In *Bolshevik Culture,* edited by Abbott Gleason, Peter Kenez, and Richard Stites, 261–278. Bloomington: Indiana University Press.

Kaes, Anton. 1992. "Holocaust and the End of History." In *Probing the Limits of Representation,* edited by Saul Friedlander, 206–222. Cambridge, MA: Harvard University Press.

Kemp-Welch, A. 2008. *Poland under Communism: A Cold War History.* Cambridge: Cambridge University Press.

Kerner, Aaron. 2011. *Film and the Holocaust: New Perspectives on Dramas, Documentaries, and Experimental Films.* New York: Continuum.

Kickasola, Joseph G. 2004. *The Films of Krzysztof Kieślowski: The Liminal Image.* New York: Continuum.

Kiebuzinska, Christine Olga. 1996. "Review of *Meyerhold: A Revolution in Theatre* and *Meyerhold, Eisenstein and Biomechanics: Actor Training in Revolutionary Russia.*" *Theatre Journal* 48, no. 4: 519–521.

Kieślowski, Krzysztof. 1998. *I'm So-So.* Stuttgart: State Academy of Arts.

Kollontai, Alexandra. 1992. "Communism and the Family." In *Ideas and Forces in Soviet Legal History,* edited by Zigurds I. Zile, 114–115. Oxford: Oxford University Press.

———. 2000. "From Communism and the Family." In *The Family in the U.S.S.R.: Documents and Readings,* edited by Rudolf Schlesinger, 59–69. London: Routledge.

Kristeva, Julia. 1994. *Strangers to Ourselves.* New York: Columbia University Press.

Lagrou, Pieter. 2005. "European Societies and the Remnants of Their Jewish Communities." In *Jews Are Coming Back,* edited by David Bankier, 1–25. Jerusalem: Yad Vashem.

Lahusen, Thomas. 1997. "Socialist Realism in Search of Its Shores." In *Socialist Realism without Shores*, edited by Thomas Lahusen and Evgeny Dobrenko. Durham, NC: Duke University Press.

Lang, Berel. 2000. *Holocaust Representation: Art within the Limits of History and Ethics.* Baltimore: Johns Hopkins University Press.

Lepak, Keith John. 1988. *Prelude to Solidarity.* New York: Columbia University Press.

Liebman, Stuart, and Leonard Quart. 1996. "Czech Films of the Holocaust." *Cineaste* 22, no. 1 (April). http://connection.ebscohost.com/c/articles/9604240983/czech-films-holocaust (accessed 15 Dec. 2012).

Liehm, Mira, and Antonin J. Liehm. 1977. *The Most Important Art: Film after 1945.* Berkeley: University of California Press.

Lukács, Georg. 1923. "The Marxism of Rosa Luxemburg." http://www.marxists.org/archive/lukacs/works/history/ch02.htm (accessed 10 Sept. 2013).

Lunn, Eugene. 1984. *Marxism and Modernism.* Berkeley: University of California Press.

Maetzig, Kurt, and Günter Agde. 1987. *Film Work: Dialogues, Talks, Writings [Filmarbeit. Gespräche, Reden, Schriften].* Berlin: Henschel.

Maier, Charles. 1997. *Dissolution.* Princeton, NJ: Princeton University Press.

Man, Paul de. 1996. *Aesthetic Ideology.* Minneapolis: University of Minnesota Press.

Mount, Ferdinand. 1998. *Subversive Family.* New York: The Free Press.

Mulvey, Laura. 1996. *Fetishism and Curiosity.* Bloomington: Indiana University Press.

Nemeskürty, István. 1968. *Word and Image.* Budapest: Corvina Press.

Nietzsche, Friedrich. 2005. *The Use and Abuse of History.* New York: Cosimo Classics.

Nothnagle, Alan Lloyd. 1999. *Building the East German Myth: Historical Mythology and Youth Propaganda in the German Democratic Republic, 1945–1989.* Ann Arbor: University of Michigan Press.

Novello, Samantha. 2010. *Albert Camus as Political Thinker: Nihilisms and the Politics of Contempt.* London: Palgrave Macmillan.

Petrie, Graham. 1980. *History Must Answer to Man: The Contemporary Hungarian Cinema.* New York: Taylor and Francis.

———. 1986. "The Depiction of the 1950s in Recent Hungarian Cinema." *Journal of European Studies* 16: 29–44.

Porter, Robert. 1988. "Soviet Perspectives on Socialist Realism." In *European Socialist Realism*, edited by Michael Scriven and Dennis Tate, 49–59. Oxford, UK: Berg.

Portuges, Catherine. 1993. *Screen Memories.* Bloomington: Indiana University Press.

———. 2004. "*Naplo Gyermekeimnek / Diary for My Children*." In *The Cinema of Central Europe*, edited by Peter Hames, 191–200. London: Wallflower.

Rainer, János. 2009. "Hungarian Stalinism Revisited." In *Stalinism Revisited: The Establishment of Communist Regimes in East-Central Europe*, edited by Vladimir Tismaneanu, 231–254. Budapest: Central European University Press.

Rancière, Jacques. 2004. *Politics of Aesthetics.* London: Bloomsbury.

Reekie, Duncan. 2007. *Subversion: The Definitive History of Underground Cinema.* London: Wallflower.

Robinson, David. 2004. "*Szerelem / Love*." In *The Cinema of Central Europe*, edited by Peter Hames, 173–179. London: Wallflower.

Rosenstone, Robert. 2006. *History on Film / Film on History.* London: Routledge.

Rothberg, Michael. 2000. *Traumatic Realism: The Demands of Holocaust Representation.* Minneapolis: University of Minnesota Press.

Rothschild, Joseph, and Nancy Mészáros. 2000. *Return to Diversity. Political History of East Central Europe since World War II.* New York: Oxford University Press.

Sanders, Joe Sutliff. 2008. "Spinning Sympathy: Orphan Girl Novels and the Sentimental Tradition." *Children's Literature Association Quarterly* 33, no. 1 (Spring): 41–46.

Santner, Eric L. 2006. *On Creaturely Life: Rilke, Benjamin, Sebald.* Chicago: Chicago University Press.

Satterwhite, James H. 1992. *Varieties of Marxist Humanism: Philosophical Revision in Postwar Eastern Europe.* Pittsburgh: University of Pittsburgh Press.

Schulte-Sasse, Linda. 1996. *Entertaining the Third Reich: Illusions of Wholeness in Nazi Cinema.* Durham, NC: Duke University Press.

Sîrbu, Constantin. 1981. "Political Education and Revolutionary Consciousness" ["Educţie politică şi conştiinţă revoluţionară"]. *România liberă* (14 Dec.): 3, 5.

Steiner, George. 1984. "The Hollow Miracle." *George Steiner: A Reader.* London: Penguin.

Stock, Danusia, ed. 1993. *Kieślowski on Kieślowski.* London: Faber & Faber.

Szaloky, Melinda. 2005. "Somewhere in Europe: Exile and Orphanage in Post–World War II Hungarian Cinema." In *East European Cinemas,* edited by Aniko Imre, 81–102. New York: Routledge.

Tate, Dennis. 1988. "'Breadth and Diversity': Socialist Realism in the GDR." In *European Socialist Realism,* edited by Michael Scriven and Dennis Tate, 60–78. Oxford, UK: Berg.

Taylor, Richard, Nancy Wood, Julian Graffy, and Dina Iordanova. 2000. *The BFI Companion to Eastern European and Russian Cinema.* London: British Film Institute.

Thompson, John O. 2000. "Reflections on Dead Children in the Cinema and Why There Are Not More of Them." In *Representations of Childhood Death,* edited by Gillian Avery and Kimberley Reynolds. Houndmills, UK: Palgrave Macmillan.

Tormey, Simon. 2005. "What Is 'Tyranny'? Considering the Contested Discourse of Domination in the Twenty-First Century." In *Confronting Tyranny: Ancient Lessons for Global Politics,* edited by Toivo Koivukovski and David Edward Tabachnick, 67–80. New York: Rowman and Littlefield.

Townsend, Charles E. 1995. "*Dita Saxova* by Arnošt Lustig." *Slavic Review* 54, no. 2 (Summer): 458–459.

Uchida, Hiroshi. 1988. *Marx's Grundrisse and Hegel's Logic.* New York: Routledge.

Urang, John Griffith. 2006. "Realism and Romance in the East German Cinema, 1952–1962." *Film History* 18: 88–103.

"Valahol Europaban." 1948. *Variety: Movie Reviews* (1 Jan.).

Vatulescu, Cristina. 2010. *Police Aesthetics: Literature, Film, and the Secret Police in Soviet Times.* Stanford, CA: Stanford University Press.

Wach, Margarete. 2000. *Krzysztof Kieślowski: The Cinema of Moral Unrest* [*Krzysztof Kieślowski: Kino der moralischen Unruhe*]. Cologne: KIM.

Weiss, Scott. 2011. "Review of *Story of a Young Couple* and *Eine Berliner Romanze.*" *Film & History* 41, no. 2 (Fall): 86–88.

White, Hayden. 1992. "Historical Emplotment and the Problem of Truth." In *Probing the Limits of Representation,* edited by Saul Friedlander, 37–53. Cambridge, MA: Harvard University Press.

Wiesel, Elie. 2006. *Night.* New York: Hill and Wang.

Williams, Robert C. 1977. *Artists in Revolution: Portraits of the Russian Avant-Garde, 1905–1925.* Bloomington: Indiana University Press.

Young, James E. 2003. "The Holocaust as a Vicarious Past. Art Spiegelman's *Maus* and the Afterimages of History." In *Witnessing the Disaster: Essays on Representation and the Holocaust,* edited by Michael Bernard-Donals and Richard Glejzer. Madison: University of Wisconsin Press.

Žižek, Slavoj. 2001. *The Fright of Real Tears: Krzysztof Kieślowski between Theory and Post-Theory.* London: British Film Institute.

———. 2006. "Jacques Lacan's Four Discourses." http://www.lacan.com/zizfour.htm (accessed 10 Sept. 2013).

Zsuffa, Joseph. 1987. *Béla Balász: The Man and the Artist.* Berkeley: University of California Press.

Zýková, Veronika. 2011. "Dita Saxová—the Girl Who Arrived Too Soon." ["Dita Saxová—dívka, která dospěla příliš rychle"]. *25fps* (25 Dec.). http://25fps.cz/2011/dita-saxova/ (accessed 27 Nov. 2012).

Index

acting, 16, 52, 53, 58, 59, 63–67, 85–87
adaptation, 4, 18, 51, 73
adoption, 4–5, 59, 118, 122, 139, 142, 157, 159n7
Adorno, Theodor, 72, 74, 81–82, 85
aesthetics, 32, 77, 78, 95, 165n23, 166n32; of film, 39, 41, 45, 163n4
affirmation, 56, 57, 63, 64, 70, 169n24
Agamben, Giorgio, 5, 25–26, 32, 76–78, 88–90
Albania, 71
alienation: aesthetic, 67; effect, 87; political, 9, 13, 16, 109–110, 117, 153, 155, 158; social, 3, 141, 142. *See also* defamiliarization (*Verfremdung*); estrangement
All My Good Countrymen, 133
amateur, 98; actor, 40; film festival, 96, 115; filmmaker, 97, 109–112, 114–116
Angi Vera, 134, 135
anticommunist discourse, 133, 136, 139, 153, 157
antifascism, 20, 51, 52
Antonioni, Michelangelo, 87
Arendt, Hannah, 5, 57, 64, 136
Aristarco, Guido, 38
art, 11, 45, 64, 84–85, 92, 99, 114; autonomous, 50, 51–63; bourgeois, 55, 67, 93; institution of, 46, 94, 100; Marxist, 37; militant, 50, 95, 99; revolutionized, 65; role of, 11, 32, 46, 51, 65; socialist, 45–46, 52, 55, 64, 66, 67, 100; socialist-realist, 93–94
Auschwitz, 18, 19, 72–74, 76, 78, 85, 88. *See also* camp
auteur, 92–94, 100, 110–111, 113–114, 116, 127
avant-garde, 45, 47, 55–57, 64, 66, 93, 112; political, 33, 34; Soviet, 37

Babylon theater, 59
Badiou, Alain, 9
Balázs, Béla, 30–39; *Somewhere in Europe*, 6, 19, 43, 48, 72, 79, 90, 119, 130
bare life, 5, 25–26, 32, 38, 75, 78
Bartók, Béla, 31
Bazin, André, 39, 41–42
beauty, 73–74; aesthetic, 46, 84, 87; female, 69, 72, 76–78, 80, 81
Becher, Johannes, 52
Belgrade, 13

Benjamin, Walter, 55, 75
Berlin, 3, 17, 48, 49–51, 50, 54, 55; East, 53, 59; West, 12, 58
Berlin Blockade (Airlift), 48, 58
Beyond the Hills, 156, 157
biomechanics, 48, 66–67
biopolitics, 26
bios, 27, 32, 38, 161n12
Bosch, Hieronymus, 83, 84
Bosteels, Bruno, 10
bourgeois drama, 51, 53
bourgeoisie, 53
Brecht, Bertolt, 55, 56, 67–68
Brezhnev Doctrine, 71, 93
Brezhnev era, 96, 98, 99, 106, 111
Bride in the Train, The, 141
Brynych, Zbynek, 73
Bucharest, 17
Budapest, 17, 71, 118, 119, 126, 137
Budapest Sunday Circle, 30, 31
Bugajski, Ryszard, 134
Bulgaria, 1, 44, 71, 134
Bürger, Peter, 46
Butler, Judith, 10

camera, 18, 24, 89, 96, 97, 102–103, 110–115; angles, 23; distortion, 40; 8mm, 96, 102; focus, 43; movement, 28; self-scrutiny, 106. *See also* cinematography
Camera Buff, 7, 8, 9, 12, 13, 92–115, 142, 143
Camouflage, 93, 98, 99, 100, 101, 113, 145
camp, 35; body, 75, 80–81, 84, 87; concentration and death, 20, 23, 24, 73, 75, 77–79, 86, 122; experience and memories of, 7, 70, 75, 76, 79, 90, 161n10; reeducation, 34. *See also* Auschwitz
capitalism, 1, 2, 54, 79, 101, 136, 155, 158; and the camp, 78; global, 156; and socialism, 44
Capri, Aldo, 76
catharsis, 11, 36, 52, 90
Caute, David, 45
Ceaușescu, Nicolae, 138, 139, 146, 150
censorship, 10, 11, 100, 109, 135, 155, 157; abolition of, 72, 98; conflict with, 134; self-, 113–114; Stalinist, 39

Chaplin, Charlie, 4
Charter 77, 143, 155
Cheka, 33, 34
childhood, 41, 129, 130
China, 10
Christianity, 15
church, 15; Catholic, 98; Orthodox, 157
Chytilová, Věra, 72, 94
cinema: art-house, 3, 11, 85, 92; auteur-driven, 92; commercial, 37, 38, 40, 94; Czechoslovak, 87; of (moral) distrust, 95, 98, 100, 110, 141, 143, 145, 153; Eastern European, 11, 16, 39, 44–45; Hungarian, 38–40, 43, 134, 136; institution of, 115; national, 3; Polish, 93, 95, 134, 136, 142; political, 37, 64, 93; Romanian, 140, 154; and society, 11, 38; socialist, 63, 64; Soviet, 32, 38, 126; Stalinist, 45. *See also* film
cinematography, 85, 86, 87, 135
Clark, Katerina, 35–36
class: consciousness, 44, 102, 105; enemy, 35, 120, 124, 139; hegemonic, 145; privilege, 4; struggle, 13, 44, 142. *See also* working class
Cold War, 14, 35, 45, 46, 47, 49, 51, 57, 121, 124, 135
collectivization, 44
Comintern, 31, 123
Communism, 1–2, 7–10, 30, 36, 71, 74, 118, 125; and the church, 15; compromises, 43, 72, 154; Eastern European, 13, 72; European (Euro-communism), 11, 38; illegalist, 111; Polish, 102; proto-, 31; Soviet-style, 31, 32, 34, 35, 44, 68, 126, 135; state, 34
Communist Party, 2, 6, 10, 11, 32, 54, 58, 101, 150; Hungarian (HCP), 31, 118, 120, 123, 128; German, 50, 53; gerontocracy, 72; Polish, 106; reproletarianization, 105; Romanian, 8, 140
Communist Student Union, 139
confession, 145, 147, 148, 149
Contest, 142–143, 155, 156
co-productions, 11
corporeality, 61, 63
cultural socialism, 51, 55, 56, 64
culture, 5, 52, 81, 99, 115; bourgeois, 53; guiding (*Leitkultur*), 153; modernist, 56; political, 10, 16, 44; popular, 3, 56, 140
culture industry, 55
Cunningham, John, 39, 174n29
Czechoslovakia, 1, 14, 74, 93, 101, 153; 1968, 71, 73, 77, 86, 133; anti-Semitism, 79; orphans, 3

Daneliuc, Mircea, 134, 141
Danube, 17
Debussy, Claude, 129

DEFA, 67, 92
defamiliarization (*Verfremdung*), 65, 67–68. *See also* alienation
Deleuze, Gilles, 17
Derrida, Jacques, 6, 27, 35
dialectical materialism, 6, 46, 58, 69, 95, 97
Diamonds of the Night, 73
Diary for My Children, 8, 12, 13, 43, 93, 118–137, 158
Diary for My Father and Mother, 126
Diary for My Loved Ones, 126
dictatorship of the proletariat, 31, 37, 71, 97
Dirty Hands, 58
dissident, 95, 101
distribution, 11, 55
Dita Saxová, 7, 12, 13, 70–91, 92, 118, 122, 129, 137
division of labor, 30, 32, 60
Djulgerov, Georgi, 156
Dobrenko, Evgeny, 34, 35, 45
Doctor from Stalingrad, The, 92
domestication, 105, 106, 109, 110, 117
Dudow, Slatan, 55
Dzerzhinsky, Felix, 34

Eastern Europe, 1–6, 9–16, 19, 43–45, 71–72; authorship, 92; Brezhnev era, 96; development, 30, 68; exiles, 118; history of, 39; immediate postwar, 31, 35, 41, 127; political consciousness, 98; reformism, 97; resistance, 105, 153; Stalinist, 48, 70, 125, 134; transformation of, 26
Eisenstein, Sergei, 37
Ekk, Nikolai, 31–34, 38, 157
Eley, Geoff, 55
Emilia Galotti, 51
Engels, Friedrich, 5
entertainment, 3, 52, 56, 64, 99, 105; Nazi, 58, 65
escapism, 52, 111
Esposito, Roberto, 5
estrangement, 6, 7, 86, 88. *See also* defamiliarization (*Verfremdung*)
Europe, 1, 13, 27, 34, 41, 79, 81, 138, 157; Central, 17, 46, 125; fascist, 23; postwar, 6, 12, 24, 33, 74; return to, 94; Western, 102, 124
Event, 23–26, 27, 34, 41, 74
Everac, Paul, 152, 153
exclusion, 5, 25, 149, 151, 161n7

Falcons of the Fatherland, 139
fascism, 9, 12, 15, 27, 39, 64, 124; Nazism, 53
Faust, 53
Filip the Kind, 141, 143

film: antifascist, 53, 58; art-house, 38, 112; bourgeois, 45; commercial (entertainment), 3, 39, 40, 56; documentary, 108, 111; Eastern European, 3, 5, 31, 155; experimental, 111, 112; feature, 3, 55; festivals, 96, 107, 112, 115; high-budget, 46; Holocaust, 73; Hungarian, 31, 39; mainstream, 45, 47; Nazi (fascist), 56, 58; oppositional, 11; patriotic, 3; Polish, 96, 101, 134, 141, 143; political, 5, 11, 12, 43, 68, 99; popular, 37; propaganda, 3, 69, 54; post-1989, 158; reconstruction (rubble), 14, 20, 25, 27, 39, 47, 50, 156; Romanian, 141, 143; silent, 32; socialist, 11, 45, 68; socialist-realist (Stalinist), 6, 41, 137; Soviet, 34; talking film, 32; youth, 141. *See also* cinema
Film, 103
film club, 98, 99, 103, 108
film industry, 31, 38, 42, 141
financing (of film), 59
Firemen's Ball, 72
Fišer, Luboš, 89
flashbacks, 40–41, 48, 89, 128
forgetting, 26–27, 40, 53, 80, 81, 84, 127, 128; creative, 37; rituals of, 82, 85
formalism, 58, 86, 111; Russian, 46
Forman, Milos, 72, 94
Foucault, Michel, 5, 25, 80
Fox Hunt, 191
free market, 101
Fuchs, Georg, 61, 66
Full Steam Ahead, 136

gender, 41, 135
German expressionism, 41–42
German Reichstag, 17
Germany, 31; Federal Republic of, 49, 54; German Democratic Republic, 1, 45, 48, 49, 50, 51, 55, 65, 67, 71, 101, 134; Nazi, 50
Germany Year Zero, 41, 42
Gierek era, 99, 100, 106; administration, 96; regime, 8, 105, 109, 114, 117
glasnost, 13, 97, 101
Goma, Paul, 154
Good Bye, Lenin!, 134
good life, 27. See also *bios*
Gorbachev, Mikhail, 13, 97
Great Depression, 4
Great Terror, 33, 46, 118, 119, 123, 124, 130, 131, 162n17
Grosz, George, 55
grotesque, 84–85
Groys, Boris, 5, 46, 56

Guattari, Felix, 17
Gypsies, 144

Haltof, Marek, 109
Hames, Peter, 87
Hardt, Michael, 13
Harlan, Veit, 62
Hauser, Arnold, 31
Havel, Vaclav, 9, 72, 95, 99, 110, 148, 153–155
Heartfield, John, 55
Hegelianism, 31
hegemony, 155
Hellberg, Martin, 51, 65
Helsinki Treaty, 13, 93, 101, 152
heroism, 42, 79
Hitler, Adolf, 23, 40, 50
Hobsbawm, Eric, 136
Holland, Agnieszka, 95, 143
Hollywood, 4, 11, 40, 56
Holocaust, 82, 84–88, 90; context, 75, 77; orphan, 70, 79, 91; victim, 72. *See also* survivors
homelessness, 33, 37, 43, 57
Honesty and Glory, 137
House between the Fields, The, 141
human rights, 141, 152, 171n4
humanism, 22, 72, 76; bourgeois, 56; sentimental, 37; socialist, 139, 141
humor, 26
Hungarian film academy, 39
Hungary, 1, 40, 43, 70, 71, 119, 135; 1970s, 93, 101; economy, 44; exiles, 118, 134; political situation, 31; Stalinist, 121, 123, 130, 133
Hurbinek, 88–90

identity, 17, 26, 37, 120, 139, 152; class, 30; family, 122, 129, 136; memories and, 137; political, 28, 30; work and, 140
ideology, 45, 48, 102, 105, 108, 136, 154; of form, 42; of professionalism, 115; of success, 100, 142, 145, 146, 155
immunization (political), 5, 57
imperialism, 53
institutionalization, 72, 79
intellectuals, 9, 39, 48, 72, 100, 113, 122, 155; leftist (Marxist) 30, 51, 101, 124, 152
intelligentsia, 47
International, The, 16; Second, 119, 160n3; Third, 121. *See also* Comintern
International, The, 31
Interrogation, 134
intimacy, 75, 132
Iordanova, Dina, 96, 136

Iron Curtain, 47, 156
irony, 67, 76–85, 90, 112
Israel, 74
Italian neorealism, 38–41

Jakubisko, Juraj, 72
Jewish people, 3, 74, 78, 79, 80, 81, 86, 130
Jew Süss, 54
Joke, The, 133
Judt, Tony, 3, 24, 53, 71
Jurga, Andrzej, 98, 101, 106, 108, 109, 115, 116

Kabale und Liebe, 51
Kadár, Ján, 72
Kádár era, 134, 135
Kaes, Anton, 85
Kafka, Franz, 83, 148
Kant, Immanuel, 18
Katowice film school, 98
Khrushchev, Nikita, 123, 135
Kid, The, 4
Kieślowski, Krzysztof, 7, 92–116, 143
King of Thieves, 156
kitsch, 57, 58, 67
Kodály, Zoltán, 31
Kołakowski, Leszek, 102, 105, 106, 109
Kollontai, Alexandra, 1, 3, 69
KOR, 98, 101–103, 105, 111, 117, 141; independent
   thinking, 106, 155; and revisionism, 109, 110
Korda, Alexander, 38
Korean War, 49
Kornhauser, Julian, 94, 115, 171n8
Kristeva, Julia, 6, 87
Kultura, 103
Kundera, Milan, 72
Kuron, Jacek, 98, 103, 108
Kyrgyzstan, 118, 126

Lady Zee, 156
Lahusen, Thomas, 45, 46
Lamprecht, Gerhardt, 20
Large Soviet Encyclopedia, 46
Larks on a String, 72, 133
Last Laugh, The, 40
Latin America, 74
Lenin, Vladimir, 19, 31, 34
Leninism. See Marxism-Leninism
Lesznai, Anna, 31
Levi, Primo, 18–19, 21, 24, 76, 78, 88–89
Liebknecht, Karl, 50
Liehm, Antonin and Mira, 39, 136
life in truth, 9, 147, 153, 154
Little Orphan Annie, 4

Love, 134–135
Lukács, Georg, 12, 31, 40, 124, 162n26
Lustig, Arnošt, 73, 86
Luxemburg, Rosa, 12, 31, 36, 102

Maetzig, Kurt, 56–67, 92
Makarenko, Anton, 33
Makavejev, Dušan, 94
Makk, Karoly, 134
Man, Paul de, 90
Man of Iron, 155
Man of Marble, 62, 112, 113, 142; resistance
   through cinema, 93, 101; Stalinism, 68, 124,
   133–135
Mannheim, Karl, 31
marriage, 68, 73, 74, 79, 90, 105; market, 80–81
Marriage in the Shadows, 67
Marshall Plan, 48
martial law in Poland, 14
Marx, Karl, 19, 32, 100, 122, 127, 158
Marxism, 9, 10, 30–31, 36, 37, 52, 102, 117; col-
   lectivist, 71; revisionist, 109
Marxism-Leninism, 7, 12, 35, 36, 52, 71, 97, 139
melancholia, 14, 70, 73, 81
melodrama, 39, 75, 137; fascist, 53, 56, 58
memory, 3, 8, 27, 40, 84, 126, 130; Cold War, 124;
   collective, 17, 79, 80; community of, 127–129;
   concentration camp, 70, 72, 75; of orphans,
   15, 26, 120, 121; of war, 52
Menzel, Jiří, 72, 80, 133
Mészáros, Marta, 8, 93, 118–137, 158
Meyerhold, Vsevolod, 66–68
Michnik, Adam, 103
Microphone Test, 141
migration, 24, 28, 74, 157
Mikołajewska, Krystyna, 73, 85–87
Minna von Barnhelm, 51
modernity, 5, 6, 7, 13, 16, 69, 77, 110, 127
monumentalism (in acting), 63, 64, 68
Moscow, 1, 30, 71, 123, 126, 137
Moscow Art Theater, 66
Moskalyk, Antonín, 7, 70–91, 92, 137
Mother of Kings, 134
Mount, Ferdinand, 129
Mungiu, Cristian, 156
Murderers Are among Us, The, 20
Murnau, Friedrich Wilhelm, 40
Muselmann, 76, 77, 84, 88, 89
musical, 4

Nagy Imre, 135
Nathan der Weise, 52
national cinema, 3

nationalism, 79, 138
nationalization, 44
Nazi genocide, 82, 85. *See also* Holocaust
Nazism. *See* fascism
Negri, Antonio, 13
Němec, Jan, 72, 73
Nemeskürty, István, 39
NEP (New Economic Policy), 33
new man, 1, 3, 8, 33, 69, 136, 152; new human, 7, 139, 158
New Order, 27, 32, 40, 61, 62, 64–65, 119; building of, 16, 20, 41, 47, 56, 108, 156; integration, 91; legitimacy, 38; subject, 7, 53, 69, 96, 137; orphans and, 15, 28
New Testament, The, 15
New Wave, 92, 93; Czechoslovak, 72, 73, 85, 87, 93, 94, 133
newsreels, 20, 115
Nietzsche, Friedrich, 26
Night and Hope, 73
nomads, 21, 22, 24, 25, 27–30
North Korea, 10
Nosferatu, 40
nostalgia, 129, 157
Nowicki, Jan, 130

occupation: of Germany, 47, 49, 54; Soviet, 1, 58, 135
OGPU Labor Commune, 33
Old Order, 21, 23, 25–27, 34, 38, 39, 43, 51, 55, 57, 90
Opening Middlefield Player, 141
orphanage, 4, 73, 77, 80, 96, 97, 114, 119, 121

Paisan, 20
People Factory, 33
People from the Mountains, 128, 130
performance, 10, 98; artistic, 50–52, 54–55, 58, 59, 61–64, 67; and imitation, 48; interiority, 66; of Mikołajewska, 86–87; work and, 68
personality cult, 46
persuasion, 2, 37, 47–48, 61, 65, 147, 148; gentle, 16, 123
Petrie, Graham, 39
Piscator, Erwin, 55
Piţa, Dan, 8, 9, 141–156
Plato, 1, 5, 15, 97
Pogrebinskii, M. S., 33
Poland, 1, 71, 93, 96, 105, 139, 153; 1970s, 8, 97, 98, 101, 108, 116; authorship, 92; economy, 44; elites, 100; opposition, 103, 117, 141, 148; orphans, 3; pogroms, 79
Politika, 103

Portuges, Catherine, 125
post-socialism, 156–157
poverty, 20, 21, 30
Power of the Powerless, The, 9, 99, 148, 153
Prague, 17, 73, 83
Prague Spring, 71, 72, 133
Prayer for Katerina Horowitzowa, 73
private sphere, 5, 9, 152, 153
proletariat, 44, 53, 57, 63, 94, 109. *See also* working class
Proletkult, 51, 55
propaganda, 2, 45, 46, 101, 129, 138, 142; anticommunist, 135, 139, 157; capitalist, 47, 49, 57, 59, 64; pro-Soviet, 69
prostitution, 75
public sphere, 8, 9, 11, 93, 96, 101
Pudovkin, Vsevolod, 37
punks, 152
purges, 34, 44, 119, 128, 134

race, 15
Radek, Karl, 37
Radio Free Europe, 139, 153
Radványi, Géza, 6, 27–43, 48, 72, 79, 90, 92, 119, 130
Rainer, János, 134
Rákosi, Mátyás, 123; era, 137, 138
realism, 58, 65, 86, 94, 95, 98, 110, 114, 117; biomechanics and, 66; bourgeois, 94; commitment to, 112, 143; oppositional, 110; psychological, 87; in socialist film, 63, 94, 141. *See also* Bazin, André
reception, 55, 56, 59, 64
Red Army, 19, 31, 45, 18
refugees, 19
religion, 21, 52, 116
repetition, 8, 15, 128, 130, 135, 158
revolution, 6, 13, 15, 37, 44, 65, 138, 139, 158; Bolshevik (October or Soviet), 1, 34, 66, 81; communist, 11, 99; and consciousness, 32; 1956, 13, 14, 70, 71; Budapest 1919, 124
Road to Life, 31–38, 157
road to socialism, 71, 126
Robinson, David, 134
Romania, 1, 2, 93, 141, 145, 152, 153, 154; and 1968, 71; 1980s, 138, 146, 155; economy, 44; opposition, 101; Stalinist, 14, 134
Rome, Open City, 20
Rosenstone, Robert, 37
Rosi, Francesco, 18
Rossellini, Roberto, 21, 40, 41, 42
Rothberg, Michael, 75
Rousseau, Jean-Jacques, 148

rubble woman (*Trümmerfrau*), 68
Russian Question, The, 58

Sand Dunes, 8, 14, 142–156
Santner, Eric, 26
Sartre, Jean-Paul, 58
Schmitt, Carl, 25
secret police, 33, 34, 35, 103
Selektion, 78, 81, 83
self-government, 98, 99, 105, 106, 155
self-reflexivity, 68, 85, 114
Sequences, 134
Sica, Vittorio De, 40
Simonov, Konstantin, 58
Singing Makes Life Beautiful, 136
Snapshot around the Family Table, 141
social bargain, 105, 148, 150, 151, 152, 154, 155
social Darwinism, 78, 155, 156
socialism, 1–16, 47–49, 55, 61, 69, 96, 97, 101,
    149–150; achievements, 94; antifascism, 53;
    Candide of, 114, 116, 117; critique of, 11, 13, 74,
    101; cultural struggle, 113; Eastern European,
    10, 14, 70, 71, 110, 134, 158; experience of, 1,
    103; failure of, 142–144; fate of, 72; late, 138,
    140, 141, 146, 154, 155, 156, 158; non-Stalinist,
    31; optimism, 91; post-1968, 113; post-
    totalitarian, 148; radical, 67; revisionist, 110;
    Romanian, 152; scientific, 100; Soviet-style,
    35, 36, 70, 71; state, 95, 102, 108, 116, 117, 142,
    153; subject of, 61, 93, 97, 102, 106, 116, 117, 142,
    150; with a human face, 71; workers in, 109
socialist realism, 37, 43, 44–47, 56, 58, 92, 93–
    95, 99
socialization, 15, 79, 98, 156
Solidarity (Solidarnosc), 96, 97, 112, 134, 136,
    141, 143, 155
Somewhere in Berlin, 20
Somewhere in Europe, 6, 12, 19–43, 48, 92, 130,
    155; Bildung, 7; immediate postwar era, 47;
    orphans, 90, 117; reconstruction, 79, 119;
    socialism, 74, 116
Song from the Cornfields, 39
sovereignty, 22, 25, 28, 37, 38, 149
Soviet montage (Soviet avant-garde cinema),
    23, 40, 37
Soviet Union, 10, 13, 33–35, 38, 43, 45, 46, 133;
    hegemony of, 70, 125; control, 2, 12, 16, 44,
    71; exile, 118, 122; opposition, 153; reformism,
    13, 101
Stakhanovism, 108, 138
Stalin, Josef, 58, 123; Alley (Stalinallee), 50,
    54–55, 60, 61–63, 62, 67, 68; death of, 70, 126;

era, 48, 133, 136, 138; genius leader, 12, 31, 46;
    ideologue, 19
Stalinism, 10, 122–126, 134–139; doctrine, 31, 125,
    153, 155; historical period, 10, 12, 13, 118, 224;
    political order, 43, 46, 71, 146; Stalinization of
    Eastern Europe, 31, 33, 47, 125
Stanislavsky, Konstantin, 66
Staudte, Wolfgang, 20
Story of a Young Couple, 6, 12, 45–69, 74, 137, 155
studios, 44, 46
Stuhr, Jerzy, 96
style, 43, 72, 110, 133; cinematic, 11, 16, 42, 92,
    103; corporeal, 48, 61, 63; directing, 62, 65;
    visual, 24, 41. *See also* acting
subject production, 2–3, 6–10, 51, 114, 155;
    deradicalization of, 71; Eastern European, 16,
    138; materialist, 5, 31; imitation and, 48; im-
    manentist, 43; socialist, 70, 76, 150, 156–158;
    Soviet-style, 68
sublime, 18
suicide, 73, 84, 90, 106
survivors, 24, 73–74, 132; Holocaust, 7, 13, 18, 20,
    79–90; of socialism, 154; of Stalinism, 123; of
    World War II, 6
Szőts, István, 39, 128

Tate, Dennis, 45
Taylor, Elisabeth, 74
television, 92, 103, 106, 107, 111, 115
Terezin (Theresienstadt), 73
testimony, 91, 127, 128, 130, 145; of death camp
    survivors, 7, 79–85, 87–90; film making
    as, 102
thaw, 126
theater, 11, 47, 51, 52, 53, 55, 61; antinaturalist,
    66; bourgeois theater, 50, 59; classical, 65;
    epic, 67–68; movie, 19, 123, 128, 137
theatricality, 74–76
Tito-Stalin split, 44, 48, 133
Tiupa, Valery, 56
Toller, Ernst, 55
totalitarianism, 5, 9, 12, 64, 136
Transport from Paradise, 73
trauma, 3, 15, 74; resistance and, 7, 8
Two-Step, 142, 143

Uchida, Hiroshi, 30
Ufa, 67
Union of Communist Youth, 139, 151
United States, 12, 18, 74, 134
Urania Theater, 59
utopia, 13, 55, 61, 119

Vatulescu, Cristina, 34, 35
violence, 37–38, 85, 124, 133, 143, 156, 158; and language, 82; physical, 80, 123; political, 123, 129, 138; representation of, 84; of socialism, 35; of war, 6

Wajda, Andrzej, 95, 112, 133, 155. See also *Man of Marble*
Warsaw, 17; boy, 18–20; ghetto, 17; Pact, 71
Weimar era, 45, 47, 51, 53, 55, 56
Western influence, 142, 151–153
Western liberal democracy, 5, 71
White Terror, 119
Whooping Cough, 134
Wiesel, Elie, 75, 78, 80, 88
Woman Alone, A, 143
Women without Names, 92
workers, 56–57, 105–106, 108–109, 137; art, 61, 93; brigades, 54; clubs, 99; community of, 2; condition of, 117; councils, 135; female, 15;

independent, 102; Polish, 116; protests, 96; Stakhanovite, 68–69, 155; young, 139
working class, 46, 102; Communist Party and, 106; condition of, 108, 109, 117; ethics, 139; German, 53. *See also* proletariat
World War I, 21, 33
World War II, 1, 3, 6, 17, 33, 117

Yugoslavia, 3, 133

Zagajewski, Adam, 94, 115
Zanussi, Krzysztof, 93, 95, 98–101, 106, 107, 143, 145
Zaorski, Janusz, 134
Zebrowski, Edek, 95
Zhdanov Doctrine, 44, 47, 53
Žižek, Slavoj, 10, 13, 94, 102, 106
zoē, 32, 38. *See also* bare life
Zsuffa, Joseph, 37
Zuckmayer, Carl, 58

CONSTANTIN PARVULESCU holds a tenured Senior Lecturer position at West University of Timisoara, Romania. He specializes in Eastern European studies, and in the relationship between film, media, history, and politics. He founded the Center for Eastern European Film and Media Studies at West University of Timisoara. He is the co-editor of *A Companion to the Historical Film,* and his work has been published in influential journals of history, political science, and film and cultural studies.